Entertainment, Journalism, and Advocacy

Entertainment, Journalism, and Advocacy

Competing Motivations in the True Crime Podcast Ecosystem

Lindsey A. Sherrill

LEXINGTON BOOKS
Lanham • Boulder • New York • London

Published by Lexington Books
An imprint of The Rowman & Littlefield Publishing Group, Inc.
4501 Forbes Boulevard, Suite 200, Lanham, Maryland 20706
www.rowman.com

86-90 Paul Street, London EC2A 4NE, United Kingdom

British Library Cataloguing in Publication Information Available

Library of Congress Cataloging-in-Publication Data

Names: Sherrill, Lindsey A., 1985- author.
Title: Entertainment, journalism, and advocacy : competing motivations in the
  true crime podcast ecosystem / Lindsey A. Sherrill.
Description: Lanham : Lexington Books, 2023 | Includes bibliographical references
  and index. | Summary: "This book explores the exponential growth of true crime
  podcasting and its effects on the growth of criminal justice reform advocacy in the
  United States. Sherrill argues that true crime podcasts exist as hybrid organizations
  with multiple goals, including entertainment, criminal justice reform advocacy, and
  journalistic inquiry"— Provided by publisher.
Identifiers: LCCN 2022056405 (print) | LCCN 2022056406 (ebook) |
  ISBN 9781666906011 (cloth) | ISBN 9781666906028 (epub)
Subjects: LCSH: Podcasts—Social aspects—United States. |
  True crime stories—Social aspects—United States. | Criminal justice,
  Administration of—United States. | Investigative reporting—United States.
Classification: LCC PN1992.928.S47 S54 2023 (print) | LCC PN1992.928.S47 (ebook) |
  DDC 791.46/7—dc23/eng/20230123
LC record available at https://lccn.loc.gov/2022056405
LC ebook record available at https://lccn.loc.gov/2022056406

♾️™ The paper used in this publication meets the minimum requirements of American National Standard for Information Sciences—Permanence of Paper for Printed Library Materials, ANSI/NISO Z39.48-1992.

For Hae.
You wrote in your diary, "Remember me forever."
We do.

And for Cynthia Shackelford—mentor, teacher, friend—who literally tracked me down when I tried to give up journalism; who had the greatest laugh to ever grace this earth; who showed me who I wanted to be when I grew up.
Thank you.

Contents

Acknowledgments

First of all, thank you to Brian Webber for sticking by me over these crazy last few years. You always believe in me, even when I don't believe in myself. I adore you.

Thank you to my late grandmother, Dean Graham. From teaching me to read to introducing me to murder mysteries to convincing me to apply to our beloved alma mater, I am the woman I am today because of you. I miss you every single day.

Thank you to Caroline Cody for reminding me that I DO have a life outside of my work. Here's to another 20 years!

I would also like to thank all of the faculty members, colleagues, and friends who have helped me along the way with this project, from dissertating to final manuscript. Thank you to my committee chair and advisor, Dr. Wilson Lowrey, for being the first person to not say, "That's not a thing" when I pitched this crazy idea. You never once told me to think or dream smaller (even when maybe I should have!), and I'm grateful for all of the support in this research and beyond. I would also like to thank all of the members of my dissertation committee, Dr. Matthew Barnidge, Dr. Suzanne Horsley, Dr. Miriam Sweeney, and Dr. Matthew Weber, for their feedback and support. Also thank you to Dr. Ryan Broussard for always being willing to be a "peer"—whether that meant coding or debriefing or commiserating. I owe you many king cakes.

A special thank you to Erin Hendricks, my dear fairy "podmother." I never would have guessed that a Reddit post would lead me to your incredible database, or that we'd become internet friends through our shared passions (and traumas). Thanks for being willing to answer questions and for always knowing the best new content to feed my podcast habit.

Thank you to Dr. Andy Billings for your advice on the publication process. Your experience and insights were invaluable!

Thank you to my University of North Alabama students and colleagues who have put up with me during the writing of this book—I know I've been even more scattered than usual. To Kevin Scott, my TED Talk coach—thank you for helping me dig down into the best parts of my research. My conversations with you helped form the final chapter of this book, and I appreciate your thoughtful feedback.

Finally, thank you to all the brilliant and generous podcasters who were willing to speak with me. You are all busy people doing important work, and I am honored that you made time for me.

Chapter 1

Adnan, Melinda, and Me

On March 24, 2003, Melinda Wall McGhee went missing from my hometown.

At the time, I was working for a local paper. I didn't cover crime stories (I was the football and hurricanes girl), but I was fascinated with her case. I've remained fascinated for almost 20 years, despite never hearing another piece of evidence. Every few months I'll search her name, but there is never a break in the case. Occasionally, someone will attempt to tie her to a serial killer, like the Baton Rouge co-ed killer Derrick Todd Lee or Jeremy Bryan Jones (Staff Reports, Oct. 4, 2004), or the abductions of other women in Mississippi and Oklahoma. But it never pans out. Melinda is still missing, and I can't stop thinking about her.

I was not a *Serial* podcast early adopter. The craze had been ongoing for around six months when I finally listened. I remembered a *This American Life* episode from October 2014 in which Sarah Koenig teased the podcast about Adnan's case, but I found nothing particularly memorable or compelling in the story at the time. When I finally download the podcast, I was hooked. The style reminded me of the radio dramas I had loved as a kid, like dramatized Nancy Drew or Hardy Boys books, as well as the true crime narratives I'd long consumed as a guilty pleasure.

I say "guilty," because the true crime of my youth was splashy and salacious. I remember watching *Unsolved Mysteries* and *Rescue 911* as a child far too young for those narratives. While I don't have an actual memory of hearing about Ted Bundy's execution in 1989, something of him must have crept into my kindergartener brain, because I clearly remember having nightmares of Bundy crawling in through my window. My grandmother began passing on her Mary Higgins Clark murder mysteries to me while I was still in elementary school. My mother didn't approve, so I would read them tucked inside my textbooks when I should have been studying. Contraband books or not, fictionalized crimes felt far less guilty.

Then, of course, came JonBenét. I have endless hours of footage from the early days after her murder etched into my brain. The Christmas she died, my entire family had the flu, and I remember sitting up late with my dad, watching the coverage, both of us too sick and weak to turn it off or move to our beds. When I see grainy pictures of the little dolled up JonBenét or the Ramsey parents, alternatively combative and tearful, I feel those memories like a fever dream—hazy, blurred, colorful, and so, so sad.

The day the O. J. Simpson verdict was read on live television, I watched it with my mother and grandparents. In one of those strange quirks of memory, I remember we were slicing a Viennetta ice cream cake, the height of '90s sophistication. I didn't know anything about criminal justice and even less about race or domestic violence at that time, but I do remember feeling there was something off about the reactions of all the people around me. That's probably the first time I started to look at true crime stories and think, "There's a lot more going on here."

The first time I remember being truly captured by a criminal justice narrative was reading *To Kill a Mockingbird* (Lee, [1960] 1999). I have a clear memory of my uncle gifting the book to me, and I still have that copy, a beautiful hardcover 40th-anniversary edition. Not only did the book open my eyes to the realities of Civil Rights era racial and sexual politics' intersection with the law, it was also one of the first crime narratives to capture me with its use of locality (Punnett, 2018)—I grew up not far from Monroeville, and I knew the pine hills and Alabama voices of the characters like I knew my own palms. Something about that sense of connection made the crime and injustice at the center of the story resonate deeply.

I had been immersed in the Laci Peterson case in the months before I learned about Melinda. I remember staying late at the newspaper office, avoiding my actual work by devouring every bit of the drama as it unfolded—the pretty pregnant woman missing on Christmas Eve; the strange, bleached-blonde highlighted husband; Amber, the mistress trying to help while being slut-shamed on nightly news. I lost all interest in that when Melinda disappeared.

Melinda Wall McGhee disappeared from her home in Atmore, AL, a small town on the Florida line, sometime between 8:30 a.m. and 4 p.m. on March 24, 2003. Her husband, Troy, came home from work to find blood and signs of struggle and reported her missing. Her car, keys, phone, and purse were all still at their home at the end of a dead-end road (Staff, March 24, 2021). I vividly remember talking about the lurid details of this case with friends, as well as in the newsroom. It was rare in our town that we had this type of crime, and it was both terrifying and thrilling to be near the coverage of the case. I've gone back to old articles, the National Missing and Unidentified

Persons System (NamUS), the Doe Network, Websleuths, and the Charley Project, but there haven't been updates in a long time. In 2009 and 2010, two areas were searched—a gravel pit and a rural area behind a church—but no evidence was recovered (Staff, February 1, 2009). Reading these accounts, I'm often surprised not to see details I clearly remember learning about the case. I wonder now if those "details" weren't actually bits gathered from newsroom sources but rather memories of the many, many whispered rumors swirling. Over the years, I would search her case occasionally but began to tell myself I'd probably never know.

Then, a decade later, *Serial* grabbed me in a way nothing had in a long time. I vacillated with Koenig between certainty of Adnan's innocence and certainty that he was lying. I usually listened during my runs and still associate certain parts of the case with shady streets and warm, floral-scented spring evenings.

Before *Serial*, I had never really listened to podcasts (in fact, I think my only previous experience was downloading a missed episode of *Fresh Air* to catch an interview with Matthew Weiner to get my *Mad Men* fix between seasons). By the time I joined the *Serial* craze, *Undisclosed* had begun, so I rushed headlong into their episodes, desperately needing more, more, more about the story. A few months later I binged all 34 of the original *Serial Dynasty* episodes. As I began writing my dissertation, I listened to *Crime Writers On . . .*'s early episodes, and I caught the *Serial* bug all over again.

As I listened to these productions about Adnan and Hae for the first time, I started to notice a community forming. There were other podcasts and podcasters connected to these podcasts, and the producers and listeners seemed to all have common ground. These new podcasts weren't just about true crime for entertainment's sake (though there are many of those that I certainly enjoy); they were focused on a bigger mission. They all pointed—some directly, some by implication—to the need for criminal justice reform in the United States. As I was noticing this phenomenon, I was also returning to graduate school. I began doing some initial research, mainly Google Scholar searches for "podcasting," "*Serial*," and "new media and criminal justice." Nothing. I started pitching my ideas about what I had noticed to professors and colleagues. I received blank stares or outright disbelief that what I thought I saw was "a thing."

Fast forward a few months. South by Southwest 2017 hosts panels on podcast communities. The Broadcast Education Association convention features special panels on podcasting. Suddenly, people stop questioning my proposal as "a thing." Obviously, they say, it's "a thing."

I tell these stories because they underscore how close this research is to my heart. This movement, of criminal justice reform through podcasting, was my obsession long before it became a research goal. I have to admit to having re-listened to *Undisclosed* all the way through three times, and *Serial* four—no, five—times. As I approached this stream of research, I was very aware of the biases I carried. I watched this phenomenon grow and believe myself to be so intimately acquainted with that growth that it takes conscious effort to back up my own anecdotal evidence with sources and citations. I have been invested in these podcasts, as well as their associated social media communities, for several years now, and I am hard pressed to remember the last day that I didn't listen to at least some part of an episode.

In conducting the research for this book, I realized that I had to be constantly aware of my own emotional connection to this work. My initial concern with interviewing, that I would be star-struck or "fan-girling" over my subjects, wasn't as much of a problem as I expected—my issue was reminding myself that I am not the expert. While I may be more invested than the average podcast fan, I am still a fan, and my parasocial relationships with these producers are not evidence. It was a challenge not to turn the interviews into free-wheeling celebrations of a shared passion, especially when interviewees gushed about the podcasts that inspired them or described incidents of seeing their work affect real-world change in the criminal justice system. When one participant described how he must fight the impetus to "fall in love with his interviewees," I felt that, deeply. I know collective identity is real in this population because I felt it every time one of my interview participants excitedly told me about their true crime fandom or their desire to solve a case—or about the first time they listened to *Serial*.

In order to combat these biases, I set parameters for myself: Number one, pretending I knew nothing. This was hard, especially when I wanted to ask for more details about things that had no relevance to my study, or I had to act as if I did not know the identity of a podcaster participants were describing but trying not to name. Second, sticking closely to the interview questions and prompts so as not to lead participants was a challenge. I chose to stay away from questions about content and instead focus on relationships and resources as conceptualized by the theoretical framework. Third, I allowed myself the "fan" moment only at the end of the interview, after all data was collected and the recorder was off. It would have been dishonest not to tell Rabia Chaudry that the title of my dissertation came from her bestselling *Adnan's Story*, I reasoned, or not to tell Amber Hunt that her soothing voice had gotten me through a tumultuous summer. As another safeguard against my own biases, I included podcasters whose podcasts I have never heard and know next to nothing about. Hearing the same kind of responses from them helped reassure me that the validity of the other findings was sound.

From a theory-application standpoint, I made a conscious decision not to look back at literature or review my research questions before my first reading of the transcripts. For the first round of analysis I looked at notes I had taken during the interviews and read with an eye for emerging patterns and words or phrases that "stuck out." After this inductive reading, I went back to the literature and code sheet and re-analyzed the transcripts through a theoretical lens. The same themes still stood out, but the patterns began to make sense, and unexpected findings were obvious in the first-round notes that didn't quite "fit."

One of those "hard-to-fit" findings was how participants described competition and relationships. Going into the interviews, they were all a big family in my mind, but I was prepared to be surprised. Maybe my subjects weren't a part of this close, goal-oriented supportive community I imagined—maybe they all hated each other, and I'd romanticized this whole phenomenon. What I found was a mix of responses that, in hindsight, make the "family" analogy spot-on. Many of these podcasters are connected, some loosely, some inextricably. They support and encourage, but they also fight and backstab and compete. I was, perhaps more than anything, surprised by how small the population felt when people talked about their connections. Everyone, it seems, really does know everyone else.

While I've tried to separate myself as much as possible from the analysis, I know that I am still too close. Participants described ethical struggles around finding entertainment in the suffering of others versus the desire to keep someone's memory alive. I've definitely felt that even to the point that I've sometimes continued listening to something I didn't enjoy because I felt like a forgotten victim deserved my attention—it sometimes feels like the least I can do. If anything, this research has increased my sense of collective identity as both a fan and a constituent. It feels appropriate that the first day of the semester in which I began writing my dissertation was the 20th anniversary of Hae Min Lee's disappearance. The day I completed preliminary results was the day Adnan was denied a new trial by Maryland's Supreme Court. And now, several years later as I write these words and continue this work, DNA from Hae Min Lee's murder has finally been tested and the Baltimore state's attorney has recommended a new trial, giving her a chance at justice and Adnan a chance at proving his actual innocence (Levenson, Sept. 14, 2022).

The discovery of how far my collective identity with this population goes was perhaps the most surprising moment. When two participants described podcasters as having a "narcissism" that allows them to believe they can make a difference or solve something where investigators have failed, and that people will actually want to hear their voices, I agreed. Yep, I said, you're right. That's something most people don't think. I don't.

But as I've continued this work, an idea keeps popping up in the back of my mind. Radio journalist Sarah Delia told me, "Everyone wants to make a radio show," pointing to a childhood playing with cassette recorders. I knew what she meant—I'd been that kid on my bedroom floor playing deejay.

Before I started working at the newspaper in my teens, I'd tried to get a job at the local radio station. Whatever that personality trait might be—narcissism or a desire to speak truth for justice—it's definitely in me somewhere too. Maybe—someday—I'll start digging into case files too, carrying a recorder "just in case." I have the beginnings of a relationship network now. I have the journalistic skills to investigate and write. And I can't stop thinking about Melinda.

Meanwhile, I'll be listening to *Serial*. Again.

Chapter 2

True Crime, Podcasting, and the *Serial* Effect

This is a Global-Tel link prepaid call from Adnan Syed, an inmate at a Maryland Correctional facility . . .

If, like me and millions of others, you caught the *Serial* bug, reading that sentence likely triggered the familiar theme music in your mind. The automated phone operator introducing Adnan calling from prison was our first introduction to *Serial*'s world. And then, Sarah Koenig's instantly recognizable voice prompted us to start thinking about crime and evidence in a new way with one question: "Could you remember what you did on an ordinary Friday in 1999?" (Koenig et al., 2014).

"Suddenly the podcast was sexy," Rabia Chaudry (2016, p. 263) wrote, describing the "astronomical" success of *Serial* and the tsunami of podcasts and related media that arose in its wake. Her statement, one line in an exhaustive book about the case that inspired *Serial*, echoes the way we often speak of cultural phenomena, as overnight sensations, sudden bursts of inspiration, or some kind of serendipitous crossing of the right stars. But such simplistic descriptors ignore the real forces that converge, often in the background or below the surface, and discounts both the ecological factors and strategic actions that transform specific media from artifacts to cultural conversation, and, in some cases, cornerstones of a social movement. The development of podcasting from a little-known, limited-use technology to a widely utilized platform with a huge and often mobilized fan base is a prime example of the way media organizations evolve and interact with each other and society. How does a media product—be it investigative journalism, entertainment, or some hybrid of the two—grow beyond simple popularity and become the impetus for a social movement? It is clear that the podcasts that grew after *Serial*—both directly and indirectly related—have had effects that ripple far beyond their growing fanbases.

In late 2014, *Serial*, from the producers of *This American Life* (Chicago Public Media, 1995), began streaming and almost immediately became a cultural sensation. The podcast, which explored the investigation of the murder of Hae Min Lee in Baltimore in 1999 and the subsequent trial and conviction of Adnan Syed, expanded on the format of the *This American Life* radio show—a calm, rational narrator, crisp editing and production, and compelling narrative told through a diverse range of voices. But *Serial* was different. As weeks went by and the 12 episodes were released—serially, as implied by the title—a cultural phenomenon was created. The cultural fascination with the podcast was unusual for any single piece of media, but especially so for a podcast, a format that had languished at the audio industry fringes for over a decade, home mainly to public radio rebroadcasts, comedians, and distance-learning (Berry, 2015; Hammersley, 2004; MacDougall, 2011; McClung & Johnson, 2010; Meserko, 2015). When first released, each *Serial* episode averaged 1.2 million downloads (Merry, 2014). The show remained in the iTunes Top 100 for over three full years and continued to chart intermittently despite not releasing a full episode between March 2016 and September 2018 (iTunes Chart, 2017, 2019; Koenig et al., 2014). In November 2014, the *Serial* podcast became the quickest podcast at the time to reach 5 million downloads (Roberts, 2014).

Much has been written about the reasons for *Serial*'s success in the popular, trade, and academic press. Some authors speculate that something about narrator/producer Sarah Koenig's style drew listeners, while others point to the "inside journalism" format that allowed listeners to feel a part of the investigation and understand a process usually not seen outside of newsrooms (Columbia Journalism Review, 2016). *Serial*'s popularity was also due in part to the fact that it was not just an engaging narrative, but that it was based on a real story. *The Washington Post* addressed this a few weeks into the *Serial* phenomenon:

> As a pop culture obsession, *Serial* is an outlier, not because it's a podcast, but because it's a true story. And that raises a host of questions, including: How are we supposed to talk about this? Fans use the language of popular television; they talk of bingeing and addiction and fear of spoilers. Yet Hae Min Lee is not Laura Palmer [of fictional series *Twin Peaks*]. She was an actual teenager. (Merry, 2014, para. 16)

The true story element of *Serial* wasn't just part of the draw to the podcast—it was likely *the* draw. Adnan and Hae's story has been credited not only with spurring interest in podcast listening in general but also with drawing interest to other true crime narratives, a phenomenon that became known as the "*Serial* effect" (e.g., Boling & Hull, 2018; Cecil, 2020; Goldberg,

2018; O'Connell, 2015; Quirk, 2016; Vogt, 2016). As *Serial* took over the pop culture conversation in late 2014 and early 2015, true crime fans, many who, like me, may have been closeted in their obsession for years, had an outlet. It was suddenly not only acceptable to love true crime—it was cool.

True crime obsession has surely existed in some form as long as humans have been storytelling—think of ancient stories of mythical murders and vengeance, or crowds gathered to be entertained by the spectacle of public gallows. Long before Truman Capote's groundbreaking based-on-a-true-story *In Cold Blood* (1966) introduced millions to long-form crime entertainment, true crime had existed as a small but mighty sub-genre of journalism and literature (Browder, 2010; Burger, 2016; Punnett, 2018). While Capote's book still contained elements of journalistic norms in the fact-finding and presentation of true crime events, this "new journalism" (Plimpton, Jan. 16, 1966, para. 13) allowed storytellers to be more literary in their treatments of crime narratives. This meant that authors were able to focus on parts of the story journalists may not have, such as the psyche and emotions of criminals or the writers' own affective relationships to the stories (Browder, 2010). Capote himself, in an interview with the *New York Times*, pointed to the importance of descriptive, emotion-rich narrative storytelling in crafting true crime: "To be a good creative reporter, you have to be a very good fiction writer" (Plimpton, Jan. 16, 1966, para. 14).

In the twenty-first century, true crime media has only continued to skyrocket in popularity. In 2015, *The Guardian* called true crime a "publishing super-brand" and noted the *Serial* podcast and HBO's *The Jinx: The Life and Deaths of Robert Durst* as the biggest cultural phenomena of that year (Lawson, December 12, 2015). In February 2018, Michelle McNamara's *I'll be Gone in the Dark* (2018), a posthumously published true crime and personal memoir about her obsession with the unsolved Golden State Killer case, debuted as the *New York Times* number one bestseller. The book inspired a three-episode podcast, and McNamara was cited as having been instrumental in solving the 30-plus-years cold case when a suspect was arrested in April 2018 (48 Hours, 2018).

True crime podcasts are one of the fastest-growing mediums in the genre. While there are multiple true crime podcasts that predated *Serial*, such as *Generation Why* (2012), and *True Murder* (2010), these podcasts did not gain the cultural significance of *Serial*. *Serial's* huge fanbase, when they had exhausted available information about Syed and Lee, sought similar true crime narratives. The succeeding podcasts, like *Undisclosed* and *Suspect Convictions*, addressed some of the criticism of the true crime genre, such as how people of color, the poor, LGBTQIA+ individuals, and other marginalized members of society were often portrayed as the criminals in true crime but seldom as the victims. Others specifically sought to give voice to populations like prisoners, refugees, or people with mental illnesses (McHugh, August 31, 2017). These podcasts turned true crime tropes around, challenging formulaic depictions of the police as always the heroes, the guilty as always punished, and that victims and perpetrators are neatly delineated (Browder, 2010). This new breed of true crime introduced the idea that everyday people—listeners and fans with no connections or training in the law or social justice—could affect real change. This contrasted with the twentieth-century model of true crime:

> While true crime may be a form of documentary, it is a dystopian version. Whereas the traditional documentary is generally designed to raise people's consciousness about terrible conditions in order to effect change, true crime presents a picture of problems that are insoluble, because they are rooted within the individual psyche and often have no apparent roots in social conditions. We are in the realm of the psychopath or, more frequently, of the sociopath, whose evil has no visible cause: legislation cannot remove the source of the problem. (Browder, 2010, p. 126)

In the immediate wake of the *"Serial* effect," a community of true crime podcasters who rejected this old formulation of true crime first began to emerge. Many of the post-*Serial* productions were fan discussion podcasts that lasted only through the initial 12 *Serial* episodes or which evolved to cover other topics (i.e., *Slate's Spoiler Special* and *Crime Writers On . . .*), but others came with specific goals. These podcasts and podcasters focused not only on true crime, like *Serial*, but also specifically on wrongful convictions, cold cases, and miscarriages of justice. *Undisclosed* (Chaudry et al., 2015), which debuted just a few months after *Serial* ended, gained a following based on the popularity of Adnan and Hae's story. The three lawyer-hosts of *Undisclosed*, one a family friend of Adnan Syed, reexamined each part of the story *Serial* had revealed, uncovering new evidence, and presenting a compelling case that Syed was in fact, as hinted by Koenig, innocent of the crime. Around the same time, *Serial Dynasty* (now *Truth & Justice*; New Beginning, Inc., 2015) debuted, covering both *Serial* and *Undisclosed* and encouraging fan crowd-sourcing to find new evidence. This trio of podcasts—one by radio professionals, one by lawyers, and one by a fan—were early iterations of the phenomenon that drew my interest, the development of the true crime podcast population and its relationship to a growing social movement for criminal justice reform. In order to better understand this particular podcast population, let us first explore the growth of podcasting as a media form.

PODCAST EVOLUTION AND RESEARCH

The term "podcasting" was coined in 2004 by journalist Ben Hammersley to describe web-based audio distribution (Hammersley, February 11, 2004).

He noted special features of the medium, including interactivity with internet listeners, portability of MP3 devices (this was well before the iPhone and widespread "app" usage), and the emotional intimacy of the audio format. Hammersley quoted National Public Radio journalist Christopher Lydon, who described the new technology as "a different kind of radio" and "something that newspapers can only dream about" (Hammersley, February 11, 2004, paras. 6, 8). Initial buzz around this emerging technology was so loud that 2005 was declared "the year of the podcast" (Bowers, December 30, 2005). Despite the praise of podcasting's possibilities, the medium remained underused throughout the following decade, even leading some writers to declare, "Podcasting is dead" (Iskold, August 28, 2007). Bottomley (2015) notes the role that evolving technology played in podcast dissemination during those years, moving from radio to RSS (Really Simple Syndication) feeds, then RSS to iPod, and blossoming with the Apple iTunes upgrade of 2014 which made podcasts easily searchable and a part of every iPhone's default interface. In 2006, Edison Research found that only 22% of Americans even knew what a podcast was. By 2018, that number was up to 64%, with 17% of respondents having listened to a podcast in the last week (Edison Research, 2018).

Podcasting's popularity has only continued to grow, as we can see quantitatively by the most recent Edison's *The Infinite Dial* report statistics: As of 2021, over 193 million Americans had consumed some form of digital audio media in the past month, including 86% of consumers under age 34 and 46% of consumers over age 55 (Edison Research, 2021). Of those listeners, 176 million reported being weekly listeners, averaging over 16 hours of streamed audio content per week. Seventy-eight percent—over 222 million—Americans reported being familiar with podcasts by 2022, with 116 million consumers reporting that they had listened to a podcast within the last month. Weekly podcasts consumers listened to, on average, eight podcasts per week, with 19% of those saying they consumed 11 or more podcasts weekly (Edison, 2021).

Podcasting's growth to "cognitive legitimacy" (Aldrich & Fiol, 1994), or mass familiarity, can be seen throughout pop culture as well. In late 2021 and early 2022, stories from tech media to mainstream news covered controversies surrounding Joe Rogan, one of the biggest names in podcasting (e.g., Patterson, December 10, 2021; Romano, Feb. 23, 2022; Rosman et al., 2022). Hulu's *Only Murders in the Building* (starring comedy legends Steve Martin and Martin Short), a comedic look at a trio of misfit neighbors who start their own true crime podcast, became one of the biggest hits of 2021. Even Carrie Bradshaw, the iconic *Sex and the City* columnist, got her own podcast in the 2021 reboot of the show, *And Just Like That. Law & Order: SVU*, the longest-running scripted live action series in television history (Shaw, March

2, 2020), tapped into the podcast zeitgeist in its 500th episode, featuring a cold case solved by a journalist-turned-true crime podcaster who turns out to be a predator himself (Wolf et al., 2021).

Early academic research on podcasting primarily focused on the educational uses of the medium and that trend continued into the 2010s (e.g., Cosimini et al., 2017; Drew, 2017; Evans, 2008; Skiba, 2006). Other research emerged, particularly within critical-cultural and performance studies, focused on specific podcast genres[1] such as comedy (e.g., Meserko, 2015; Piper, 2015). Building on the post-*Serial* zeitgeist and the ten-year anniversary of the "year of the podcast," the *Journal of Radio & Audio Media* devoted a symposium and its November 2015 issue to podcast media, representing a shift in the way communication researchers discussed podcasts (Bottomely, 2015; Johnson, 2015). In the issue, Berry revisited his earlier discussion of the possibilities of podcast technology and dubbed the post-*Serial* era "the golden age of podcasting" (Berry, 2006, 2015). Other authors addressed podcasts as storytelling and extensions of broadcast radio programs, software advancements, competition between digital and traditional audio formats, and podcast fan communities (Cwynar, 2015; Florini, 2015; Morris & Patterson, 2015; Pluskota, 2015; Salvati, 2015). Most of these articles are exploratory or commentary rather than empirical research, aimed at building a case for future research and addressing possible reasons for the seemingly sudden boom in podcast popularity.

Other researchers have delved deeply into particular podcast phenomena. While the research in this book does not focus on the media effects of true crime podcasts, some overview of this literature seems important for understanding how listeners become personally involved with podcasts to the point that they are willing to engage in collective action with podcast-associated social movements. McClung and Johnson (2010) used a survey of listeners active in podcast-related social media groups to determine listening motivations. They found that listeners used podcasts for entertainment and mood management; the ability to "time-shift," that is, to listen at their preferred time rather than a scheduled time like a traditional radio broadcast; to build their digital libraries; to support programs or sponsors associated with podcasts; and for the social aspects of fan communities. Florini (2015) also described the social aspects of podcast listening, exploring communities built around podcasts by and for Black people. These communities, she notes, often overlapped, with fans of one podcast likely to interact with fans of other, similar podcasts. Hancock and McMurtry (2017) used case studies and qualitative content analysis of fan forums to study the development of fan groups and identification within the genre of the horror podcast. More recent research has looked at podcast listening motivations beyond the true crime genre (e.g., Chan-Olmstead & Wang, 2022; Perks et al., 2019), ideological signaling in news podcast descriptions (Funk & Speakman, 2022), and how producers weathered the COVID-19 pandemic podcasting market (Broussard et al., 2022). Boling and Hull (2018) examined uses and gratifications in true crime podcasts specifically, noting particular differences in listening motivations by gender, and finding that social interaction was an especially important motivation for female listeners.

There are other effects for podcast listeners that may be compared to earlier research on audio media. Berry (2006) contrasted podcasts with broadcast radio, writing that radio is the equivalent of going to a newsstand and searching for a desired publication, while podcasting is the equivalent of having subscriptions of your favorite publications delivered to your door on a regular, predictable basis. Swanson (2011) echoed the importance of choice and convenience to podcast listeners. "Podcast listeners are empowered listeners. They have complete freedom to review, select, download, and listen to programming on a myriad of subjects any time they wish" (Swanson, 2011, p. 183.)

MacDougal (2011) described podcasts as an extension of "secondary orality," focusing on the medium not as new technology but as part of the ancient tradition of narrative storytelling. His phenomenological view positions podcasts as unique for both their on-demand character and their ability to be consumed as listeners go about their daily routines. This creates both distance from immediate surroundings (i.e., listening through headphones while riding the subway is simultaneously a public and a solitary act) and increased perception of social presence with the podcasts' hosts. "The podcast," he wrote, "and particularly, the podcast listened to on the move, may be part of an evolution in parasocial phenomena and a fundamentally new form of mediated interpersonal communication" (MacDougal, 2011, p. 716). Dimmick, Feaster, and Hoplamazian (2011) also wrote about this factor of digital media, noting that interstitial uses ("no-where places" and "no-when-times," Caronia (2005) called them) serve as functional alternatives to other interactions. While Dimmick and colleagues (2011) largely described interstitial or on-the-go usage as replacing other traditional media interactions, MacDougal wrote that this media use may replace or supplement interpersonal interactions, specifically tying parasocial interaction to podcast listening. If parasocial interaction becomes a listening component for individual fans of a media product, then affective, emotional components are activated, and a connection, even a "friendship" with hosts, may be felt. These social motivations for podcast listeners are interesting for communication scholars, as they represent an evolution to digitally mediated interaction with hosts and other listeners rather than the "functional alternative" to interpersonal interaction that earlier audio media may have served (Perse & Courtright, 1993; Rubin & Stepp, 2000).[2]

Other media effects found for podcasts include transportation, or the feeling of being "in the story" (Brown, 2015; Florini, 2015), and identification with podcast hosts and subjects (Piper, 2015). It is interesting to note that popular press explanations for podcasts' ability to mobilize listeners mention many of the same effects. Simpson (October 14, 2017) and McHugh (August 31, 2017) both described podcasts as powerful based on the emotional intimacy of audio narrative, the portability and convenience of podcast technology, and the ability to engage with podcast hosts and other listeners via social media and email. Research on fan community around earlier media products found that the combination of these factors—emotional connection, shared involvement with a media product, and so on—related to creating a psychological sense of community and strengthening the bonds between fans (Obst et al., 2002). Today, with the prevalence and ease of social media, fans are able to have immediate and intimate exchanges with a fan community. Other scholars have noted that the freely accessible, easily shareable, and on-demand nature of podcasts, especially highly produced, imaginatively engaging podcasts like *Serial*, makes them an important new frontier for public scholarship and a catalyst for mainstream discussions that might otherwise be dismissed.

> Unlike traditional forms of reporting that privilege a few dominant voices, audio media can foreground the voices and perspectives of nearly all individuals in the story. In *Serial*, Koenig incorporates the actual voices of the people involved in the story whenever possible . . . *Serial's* representation of multiple voices and viewpoints decenters any single authoritative truth in such a way that pushes listeners to question the very notion of authoritative voice. (Doane et al., 2017, p. 120)

TRUE CRIME PODCASTS AND REAL-WORLD IMPACTS

Academic literature specifically related to true crime podcasting is still limited but is expanding rapidly. In 2016, when I first began pitching my ideas on the topic to professors and colleagues, I could find very little literature to support my claims. Since then, researchers have published on various facets of true crime podcasting, including portrayals of domestic violence (e.g., Boling, 2020; Slakoff, 2021); the meaning of "justice" in true crime (e.g., Boling, 2019; Paquet, 2021); and industry growth (e.g., Sherrill, 2020). Meanwhile, popular press has been effusive in crediting these podcasts with affecting public knowledge about the criminal justice system. Siobhan McHugh, a professor at Australia's University of Wollongong, has written extensively about podcasts, calling them a "powerful socio-political force" (August 31, 2017, para. 1), and citing podcasts from the United States, Australia, and Sweden with explicitly social and political change goals (primarily related to criminal justice, but also to issues like LGBTQIA+ rights and climate change). Susan Simpson, a lawyer and host of multiple podcasts, wrote:

> While podcasting is a relatively new area of expansion for the [true crime] genre, it's had a transformative effect. Through podcasts, true crime fans can hear new content, but take a step further. Podcasts allow fans to become actively involved themselves, by connecting with the hosts, other listeners, and a growing network of criminal justice reform advocates. True crime podcasts are often at their best when they're covering stories that are still in need of answers, or where justice may not have been done—that's when the public awareness and engagement that podcasts can inspire have the best chance of making a real-world impact on the cases being covered . . . Do we want to grab the attention of listeners and entertain them for a few episodes, or can more be achieved? . . . We don't explore criminal mysteries for the sake of it. (October 14, 2017, paras, 4, 8, 10)

Evidence of these real-world impacts is easy to find. News media in Baltimore, MD, discussed the impact of podcasts in nearly every article about the 2018 State's Attorney race. Candidate Thiru Vignarajah was described as "the *Serial* prosecutor" and forced to defend his position in multiple interviews (e.g., Associated Press, September 15, 2017; Manas, May 11, 2018; Woods, March 31, 2018). The incumbent, Marilyn Mosby, was also tied to *Undisclosed*'s coverage of her role in the trial of Baltimore police officers for the killing of Freddie Gray in 2015 (Chaudry et al., 2015). Ironically, she was back in podcast news and the *Undisclosed* orbit in March of 2022, this time as the Baltimore City State's Attorney to recommend forensic testing in the Hae Min Lee case (CBS Baltimore, March 10, 2022). By the time they announced an end to the podcast in March 2022, the *Undisclosed* team had played a direct role in ten exonerations, two stays of execution, one commutation, and another dozen petitions for relief or appeals (Chaudry et al., 2015; Wheeler, Sept, 13, 2019).

The *Breakdown* podcast, a production of the *Atlanta Journal-Constitution* newspaper (AJC, 2015), focused on miscarriages of justice in Georgia, has been noted for its effects on cases in that state as well. The *Southern Political Report* cites *Breakdown's* coverage of the Justin Chapman case as an important factor in raising local awareness of the importance of holding judges, prosecutors, and defense attorneys accountable (Wolf, November 23, 2016). Judge Mary Staley specifically noted *Breakdown* in her statement on the need for a change of venue in the 2016 Justin Ross Harris case, noting that the podcast had contributed to "pervasive" media attention in the Atlanta area (Season two, episode six, AJC, 2015). Another Georgia-based true crime podcast, *Up and Vanished*, was praised by *Huffington Post* for the "undeniable" role that the podcast played in an arrest finally being made in the 12-year-old disappearance and murder of Tara Grinstead (Capewell, February 24, 2017, para. 12; Tenderfoot TV, 2022). In perhaps one of the most stunning achievements at the time by a podcast and its listeners, in 2018, Edward Ates, a man serving life in prison for murder, was granted parole based on new evidence discovered by *Truth & Justice*'s host and fans. Ates's attorney from the Texas Innocence Project issued a public statement crediting the podcast: "This good thing has happened to a good man and his precious family because of you. You are the difference makers" (Clayton, April 2, 2018, para. 2). In 2019, evidence discovered over the course of investigation by the *In the Dark* podcast led all the way to the U.S. Supreme Court and a ruling in favor of Curtis Flowers, a Black defendant in Mississippi who had been retried six times for the same crime (*Inside Radio* June 21, 2019; Slotkin, Sept. 5, 2020).

Understanding the unique position of these post-*Serial*, ideologically motivated true crime podcasts requires taking a multifaceted approach. Within the true crime podcast genre, there are various types of podcasts in various styles, ranging from comedic to somber to gory to strictly journalistic, and these types are supported by varying audiences and audience interests. From the perspective of organizational ecology, explored in the next chapter, the true crime podcast population exists in a niche, that is, a supportive space conducive to the evolution of similar organizations and other entities with similar resource requirements. Within this niche, true crime podcasts seem to exist in sub-niches, with boundaries that may not always be clearly delineated from entertainment, journalism, or strictly activism oriented-media. For example, podcasts like those cited by Simpson (October 14, 2017) may have different characteristics than those that are less explicitly goal-oriented. The sub-niches are interesting from the perspective of social movement theory (SMT) as well. Looking at this population through the lenses of organizational ecology and SMTs (Carroll & Hackett, 2006; Hannan & Freeman, 1977, 1989; McCarthy & Zald, 1977; McAdam, 1999; Melucci, 1985) can help us to understand how these media products have evolved, relate to one another, create sustainable streams of resources, and what the landscape of the media ecosystem they occupy looks like.

Even those true crime podcasts that appear to be solely entertainment-oriented (e.g., *My Favorite Murder*, Hardstark & Kilgariff, 2016) display characteristics of what social movement scholars call "democratic media activism" (Carroll & Hackett, 2006). That is, podcasts are media forms that allow for non-elite access to modes of production, resources, and dissemination of information. Carroll and Hackett describe democratic media activism as not democratization *through* media but rather *of* the media; it is less about a subversive message than it is about subverting the traditional power structures of corporate media (though subversive messaging may be a goal for some producers). In one of the earliest analyses of podcasting's possible effects on the future of media, Berry (2006) called it "disruptive technology" that would force "the radio business to reconsider some established practices and preconceptions about audiences, consumption, production, and distribution" (p. 144). Berry continued,

> What Podcasting offers is a classic "horizontal" media form: producers are consumers and consumers become producers and engage in conversations with each other. At a grassroots level there is no sense of a hierarchical approach, with podcasters supporting each other, promoting the work of others and explaining how they do what they do. (Berry, 2006, p. 146)

This kind of media is especially relevant to study in the digital age, as new platforms and technologies constantly and easily emerge, allowing producers and consumers to explore new ways of interacting, sharing information, and creating sustainable models of production. In layman's terms, the existence of accessible broadcast technology to virtually anyone with a computer or cellphone has fundamentally changed how audio information is produced and consumed. These new true crime podcasts offer an example of media products existing simultaneously as business ventures and social movement actors. Many podcasts acquire sponsors and advertisers, solicit patronage, and operate in tandem with other for- and nonprofit media outlets. At the same time, some producers see themselves as "reform advocates" making "real-world change" (Simpson, October 14, 2017, para. 4). Observing the ways in which this dual-identity is negotiated, monetized, and leveraged throughout the life cycle of these media products can help us better understand how social movements evolve in our increasingly digitized world.

In addition to their portability, affordability, and shareability, these podcasts provide a platform for voiceless victims and subvert traditional media tropes (Doane et al., 2017; McHugh, August 31, 2017). Greer (2017) uses *My Favorite Murder* as an example of podcasts taking the murdered victim—an object to be viewed voyeuristically or as only a piece of evidence in traditional true crime—and making them a real, flesh-and-blood personality through the power of aural evocation. Other scholars, particularly in feminist media studies, point toward the ability of these podcasts to empower producers and listeners by creating a platform for marginalized voices, such as women, people of color, the incarcerated, and those whose vocal style might be excluded from mainstream broadcasts (Doane et al., 2017; Tiffe & Hoffman, 2017).

While there are plenty of true crime podcasts that do not have motives beyond entertainment, those that do operate in many ways as "social movement organizations (SMOs)" (McCarthy & Zald, 2002), mobilizing fans, securing resources, and spreading issue awareness. The study of social movements' emergence and development has a long history, spanning the fields of sociology, communication, organizational studies, and psychology for over a hundred years (e.g., Buechler, 1993; Breton & Breton, 1969; LeBon, [1895] 1947; McAdam, 2017). This scholarship runs the gamut from a focus on resource mobilization to group identity, political and social processes, and the organizational structures of movements. Yet past research on organizational identity and evolution, social movement mobilization, and collective action is fragmented, and as such, it provides different, sometimes conflicting and sometimes overlapping, explanations for how the transformation from individual and collective awareness to action occurs. Fans of media products spend time critiquing and dissecting the issues discussed in that media. This parsing of issues can lead to what social movement scholar Doug McAdam (2017) called "issue ownership." That is, when communities feel a connection to a particular issue, they are more likely to take action or attempt to organize in some way to affect real-world change. Cecil (2020) specifically saw this collective issue of ownership in her ethnographic exploration of true crime fandoms: "Modern true crime allows people to bond over violence, victimization, and justice" (p. 140). McAdam's (2017) and Obst and colleagues' (2002) research on fans, communities, and mobilization suggests that the formation of community and identity between fans and hosts of a media product may partially explain how some of these true crime podcasts have evolved from entertainment into movement organizations.

The media ecosystem that contextualizes the "*Serial* effect" offers a prime case for analysis of both these theoretical and practical questions. First, podcasts are an emerging and still under-studied media technology. Despite the age of the medium, podcast research has been scarce, and the communication field still has much to understand about how producers mobilize resources for sustainability, growth, and social action, and the particular media effects of podcasts on listeners and fans. The explosion of the true crime podcast population has occurred very quickly and has had real-world impacts, as noted earlier. The ability of this medium to gain a large audience and invigorate massive fan communities both on- and off-line makes it a media phenomenon worth studying. Second, the interviews and population research in this manuscript help to expand the theory around hybrid organizations, like goal-oriented podcasts. Academics in organizational ecology and SMTs have noted parallel concepts and "symmetrical gaps" (Greve et al., 2006; McCarthy & Zald, 2001; Van Zomeren et al., 2008) between these theories and have suggested that combined applications of parallel concepts from these theories may fill the gaps in our knowledge of collective action and organization.

My interest in studying the true crime podcast phenomenon was, in part, to help bridge these gaps by considering multiple conceptual approaches in tandem. In doing so, I began to better understand the communicative processes that unite the organizations within this population around collective identity and common causes, and how those organizations and the stakeholders within them negotiate and redefine organizational forms and boundaries as that identity evolves. In the coming chapters, I'll also examine some of the environmental and organizational forces—competitive and collaborative relationships between organizations, sustainability of organizational resources, renegotiation of messaging and goals—that allow these entities to exist as both successful media products and movement agents.

Specifically, this book focused on the development of collective action and identity around social movements in relation to the concepts of ecology of organizations. That is, how do the structural mechanisms explained by organizational ecology—the creation and growth of populations as aggregates of entities with similar forms, the evolution of organizational legitimacy, the acquisition of resources—interact with the theoretical components of SMTs, such as group identity, organization of collective action, and development of effective messaging?

In the following chapters, I'll walk you through my exploration, from the evolution of ecological and movement theories to the challenges of mapping a population as dynamic as true crime podcasts. I'll also share what I learned from interviewing the podcasters themselves, including Rabia Chaudry, the woman who brought Adnan's story to Sarah Koenig, and thus, the world. These interviews allow me to let you into the processes behind the stories that we hear, including how the producers see their organizations situated within evolving and emerging niches and sub-niches of the true crime genre and their relationships to social movement goals. What I won't discuss are the media effects of podcasts on individual listeners (though I do recommend Dawn K. Cecil's excellent book *Fear, Justice & Modern True Crime* for more on that topic; Cecil, 2020). Instead, I'll focus on the producers and organizations within the population; the mechanisms by which the population has emerged, sought resources, sustained itself, and developed; and podcasters' relationships to collective action for collective goals at the organizational level. By sharing these insights, it is my hope that we—the true crime obsessives—can better understand how to harness our interest in true crime to make real-world changes.

NOTES

1. The term "genre" is used here as an accepted conventional rather than theoretical term. Genre theory is deeply complex and "the attempt to define particular genres in terms of necessary and sufficient textual properties is sometimes seen as theoretically attractive but it poses many difficulties. . . . Genres can therefore be seen as

'fuzzy' categories which cannot be defined by necessary and sufficient conditions" (Chandler, 1997, p. 3). The categorization of particular genres is used as a kind of shorthand to make communication about texts or media artifacts more efficient. Noting that genre depends on intertextuality (Wales, 1989), that is, its relationship to other texts, media descriptions, and constantly evolving social categorizations, this chapter will use "genre" as the generally accepted broad categorization by producers and consumers. The "true crime genre" is described as such by podcast trade media, social media fan groups, and the producers themselves. While the boundaries of genre are permeable and constantly shifting (Chandler, 1997), the term as it is used colloquially seems sufficient for this examination.

2. In the traditional conceptualization of parasocial relationships, the relationship is "imagined" in that it is one-sided, and no longer considered "parasocial" if reciprocal interaction occurs. However, newer research expands this definition to include limited two-way fan interaction: "Media consumers now have new ways of interacting with media personae through Facebook, Twitter, weblogs, fan sites, and other interactive media, making the dyadic one-dimensional description of PSI incomplete. Audience involvement is not merely a lone psychological enterprise; it involves interaction with others, including discussing favorite personae, reading their tweets, sending them text messages, watching them through media with friends, and personally attending their events with others" (Brown, 2015, p. 263).

Chapter 3

Understanding Organizational Growth and Social Movements

Joey Watkins, Afrikka Hardy, Curtis Flowers, Arpana Jinaga, Elizabeth Andes, Kelly Cochran, John Meehan, Tara Grinstead, Hae Min Lee, Jeannette and Dannette Millbrook, Temujin Kensu, Mitrice Richardson, Sheryl Sheppard, Sebastian Pasqual.

If you recognize any of these names, there's a strong chance you heard them on a true crime podcast. These individuals—some perpetrators, some missing persons, some victims of crimes, some victims of the criminal justice system—don't have the instant name recognition of John Wayne Gacy or Jeffrey Dahmer or JonBenét Ramsey. And yet their stories have helped to change how we understand crime and justice as millions have listened and grappled with issues like systemic racism, misogyny, and classism in how we talk about crime.

As the podcast landscape has grown over the past two decades, hundreds of these true crime podcasts have begun but ultimately ended production, while a few dozen others have reached enormous levels of mainstream success. Podcasts, whether produced by an amateur in their noise-proofed closet or funded by a multi-million-dollar studio, require resources and an audience to thrive. In some cases, that audience may listen for reasons beyond entertainment. If an audience begins to take issue ownership of a cause, their podcast fanship may extend beyond simply listening to communicating with other fans and advocating on behalf of a cause. High-profile examples of this include *Serial*'s Adnan Syed case, but there are many examples of lesser-known podcasts having real-world effects (e.g., Cecil, 2020). In each of these cases, podcast producers must find ways to maintain their organizations, while also building collective identity. In order to understand this process, I examined podcasts related to criminal justice reform advocacy through the lenses of organizational ecology theory and social movement theories (SMTs). In this chapter, I'll delve into the history and development of these theories and how they can help us understand why and how true crime podcasts have become so successful.

ORGANIZATIONAL ECOLOGY

Organizational ecology is an approach to understanding organizations that emerged from sociology and management studies in the mid-twentieth century. Like ecological studies in biology, organizational ecology focuses on how individual entities—here, organizations—are affected by and evolve to fit their environments, which conditions lead to diversity of organizational forms and how organizations are founded, grow, and fail. It also focuses on the political, social, and economic forces that act on organizations (Hannan & Freeman, 1977, 1989).

Early ecological scholarship reaches back to the 1960s and 1970s, when researchers first presented components of the theory, such as the *liability of newness* (Stinchcombe, 1965), *isomorphism* (Hannan & Freeman, 1977; Hawley, 1968), and a focus on populations within communities (Trist, 1977). Hannan and Freeman (1977) theorized a coherent set of assumptions and sub-theories (sometimes called "theory fragments") that set the foundation for organizational ecology as we know it today. Their work has been followed by hundreds of empirical and analytic publications expanding the theory (e.g., Carroll, 1984; Carroll et al., 2002; Dimmick, 2003; Lowrey, 2012; Polos et al., 2002; Weber et al., 2016).

Organizational ecology takes a distinctly different view of organizations than older, more familiar "adaptive" management perspectives ("adaptive" in organizational studies literature refers to internal strategic management shifts rather than external, environmental adaptation; Aldrich & Pfeffer, 1976; Hannan & Freeman, 1977, 1989). While organizational ecology recognizes the importance of management and internal structure, it argues that the older adaptive paradigm did not account enough for the environments in which organizations exist. Organizations, ecologists argue, do not exist in a vacuum, where only internal decisions and structure or even economic competition affects them. Instead, ecology takes account of factors beyond competitive relationships within an industry, such as how organizations are affected by sociopolitical and cultural factors. These factors may be as limited as a change in regulation that opens a niche for more organizations or as large as the invention of entire new technologies. In one such ecological study, Greve et al. (2006) examined the development of the micro-radio industry as a response to regulatory changes that allowed small stations to take advantages of bandwidth openings and resources unused by larger, corporatized radio. Their analysis provides an example of a population emerging in response to a sociopolitical change. The invention of the internet and the subsequent spread of digital platforms is an example of a large-scale, cultural, social, and economic change that spawned entirely new organizational forms and industries. Organizational ecology accounts for these environmental possibilities and considers both internal, organizational (endogenous) forces and external, environmental (exogenous) forces as an explanation for why organizations form, change, succeed, or fail, and the availability of exploitable resources.

Levels of analysis are especially important to organizational ecology. These levels include the organization level, population level, and community level. Organizations belong to populations, and related populations form the community level. Baum and Shipilov (2006) explain this relationship: "The outcomes for organizations in any one population are fundamentally intertwined with those of organizations in other populations that belong to the same community system" (p. 55). In the aforementioned example from Greve and colleagues (2006), changes to regulations on large radio stations affected the population of micro-stations as they both were part of a larger broadcast radio community.

In addition to levels, there are three main assumptions of organizational ecology:

1) Populations are defined by some "unitary shared characteristic" (Hannan & Freeman, 1989, p. 45) of member organizations. These characteristics may include dependence on particular resources, similar goals, hierarchical structures, core technologies, or market strategies and can encourage homogeneity of forms and practices among organizations within the population.
2) Populations can be defined by boundaries of what are *not* acceptable actions, as well as by common forms and identity.
3) Populations and the organizations within them are subject to inertia so that even if radical changes occur, they are often (though not always) the product of slow, long-term processes. (Hannan & Freeman, 1989)

These assumptions are derived in part from three main concepts of organizational ecology: niches, inertia, and density dependence. These "theory fragments" are interrelated and include features such as resource dependence, isomorphism, liabilities of age, organizational form, boundaries, constraints, and legitimacy (Carroll, 1984; Deephouse & Suchman, 2008; Hannan & Freeman, 1977; Singh & Lumsden, 1990).

Niches

I mentioned niches in the previous chapter to illustrate how the true crime genre fits within the larger podcast industry. *Niche* within organizational ecology theory is broadly defined as the relationship between population and environment, specifically, the role of the population in the community (Dimmick, 2003; Hannan & Freeman, 1989). Populations are aggregates of organizations situated within niches, and the concept that organizations will be selected into niches where they can best survive is called *fitness* (Hannan & Freeman, 1977).

For example, the beer brewing industry is a population made of individual producers within the larger alcoholic beverage producer community (Carroll & Swaminathan, 1992). The micro-brewers in Carroll and Swaminathan's analysis operated differently from the large-scale brewers and exploited resources (i.e., modes of production, ingredients, consumer markets) not used by their larger counterparts. This is also an example of levels of specialization within niches (explained in more detail next). Niches are not empty spaces—instead the "niche" is a concept used to explain common characteristics of organizations using common resources and to define relationships between organizations with similar target markets, missions, or goals (Dimmick, 2003).

What niche a population fits can be determined by several factors. Products produced, market strategies, and resource needs affect niche placement. For some industries, geographic space may be a determinant. For example, the niche of local television news or terrestrial radio stations is constrained by geographic boundaries. This population might consist of several such stations and be a part of a larger population of local media forms, including newspapers or magazines.

In earlier research, communication scholars thought of population niches as largely determined by technological domain (e.g., newspapers; Carroll & Hannan, 1989); however, media digitalization has complicated this taxonomy. Dimmick (2003) focused on the particular nature of the ecology of media industries (both traditional and digital) from a communication perspective. While geography may still be a constraint for some media (such as the previous example), the internet has changed how other kinds of media interact and how their niches are determined. Dimmick tied ecological research to the Uses and Gratifications approach from communication and media effects traditions (Katz et al., 1973), coining the term *niche gratifications*. In this perspective, media niches are defined based on the particular gratifications obtained by their consumers. Gratifications are resources, as they represent the needs and selection choices of their consumers. In economic terms, gratifications equal the utility of a particular media—gratifications represent the benefits consumers gain from using the media—and these affect how the media producer or organization will advertise, the content choices they may make, and who their competitors will be. Time is considered a limited resource for media, as consumption is constrained by being in the correct place at the appropriate time (e.g., being at home to catch a live television broadcast) or by possible volume of media intake (e.g., a consumer cannot utilize more than 24 hours of content in a day) (Dimmick, 2003; Dimmick et al., 2011). Mobile-use media, like podcasts or e-books, also provide different gratifications and competitive relationships. An "information on the go" (Dimmick et al., 2011) medium like a podcast may serve as a functional alternative to broadcast radio, thus situating it in an overlapping niche of competition with both other podcasts and radio for the time and attention of consumers. Media niches may also be determined by genre, as particular genres serve different user gratifications (Barton, 2009; Lowrey, 2012).

While members of populations may be dissimilar in many ways, niche membership is defined by varying more from organizations outside of the population than from one another (Dimmick, 2003). Organizations within the same population share characteristics, such as common resource dependence, collective identity, core technologies, market strategies, or similar organizational forms. These "clusters of features," as well as socially defined boundaries, determine the organizational forms within a population (Hannan & Freeman, 1989; Polos et al., 2002; Weber, [1922] 1947). Network relationships may also help clarify organizational forms and define population boundaries, as knowledge and resources are shared or competed for among population members, thus tying organizations within that population to one another (Dimaggio, 1986).

Hannan and Freeman caution that "Populations of organizations . . . are not immutable objects in nature but are abstractions useful for theoretical purposes" (1977, p. 934). Polos and colleagues (2002) explain that an organization's form is a cultural product and is not merely determined by niche qualities. Form may be defined by how those outside the organization (i.e., consumers, competitors, opinion leaders) perceive it: "What do social agents recognize when they 'see' a form, or more precisely, how do they identify form boundaries?" (Polos et al., 2002, p. 86). In this case, "form boundaries" may be conceptualized as socially constructed ideas, where there is strongly shared agreement about similarities and differences among organizations and populations.

Organizational form may also be defined through organizational identity. Like form, identity may shift throughout the life cycle of organization based on exogenous and endogenous pressures and constraints. Identities are defined by satisfying constraints, such as fitting inside socially recognized boundaries or having relational ties with other similar organizations (Tilly,

1986). Polos and colleagues (2002) call these "social codes" and note that these may be implicit or explicit. It is important to note that these social codes are not always clear, and organizations risk angering constituents or losing legitimacy (see below) if they violate expectations based on their perceived form or identity:

> Organizational identity defines a certain range of acceptable or unacceptable behavior (taken-for-granted norms) and . . . problems with change processes, including resistance from change recipients, arise when change processes lead to culturally unacceptable behavior and practices (Jacobs et al., 2008, p. 246).

The connections between these factors—organizational members, internal architecture, and relationships with the environment—are important to consider, as changes to one part of an organization may not always cause the organization to shift to another population or niche. For example, a major change in management structure or internal policy may have little or no effect on the perceived form and identity of the organization for external stakeholders (Polos et al., 2002). The socially constructed nature of organizational form and identity is especially important for communication scholars, as it is primarily a *communicative* process of negotiation and renegotiation between organizations and stakeholders (Hsu & Hannan, 2005; Weber, 2017). Stated more simply, successful organizations learn what kinds of organizational goals are desirable and acceptable through feedback from and conversations with internal and external stakeholders.

Structural Inertia

Structural inertia refers to the tendency of larger and older organizations to become more rigid in their processes over time, and thus less able to react quickly to environmental disruption. As organizations grow and develop more defined internal structures (e.g., management, organizational culture and norms, subunits, internal politics), they become less able to adapt to the environment. Inertia may also affect organizations and populations through external constraints, like barriers to industry entry or exit, information availability, or market forces (Aldrich & Pfeffer, 1976; Hannan & Freeman, 1977). While inertia can serve a functional role in the organization, such as routinizing procedures and internal structures for efficiency, it can also be a liability if organizations cannot quickly react to environmental challenges. An example of this is the failures of traditional newspaper organizations who were unable to shift to online readership and advertising models in the rise of the digital age (Weber, 2017). While structures that develop as organizations becoming more "institutionalized" or formally structured may increase the perceived legitimacy and resources of the organization, institutionalization also makes adaptation more difficult. This inertia is not a problem (and may actually be a strength) in stable environments—inappropriate change can be disastrous—but it becomes a liability in unstable environments, leading to what is known as the *liability of ageing* (Singh & Lumsden, 1990). Conversely, while younger, smaller organizations may be able to adapt more quickly to unstable environments, they do not possess the excess resources or legitimacy to bounce back from disruption, illustrating the *liability of newness* (Baum & Shipilov, 2006; Carroll, 1984; Stinchcombe, 1965). This lack of resource slack often explains early "mortalities," also known as *failings*, in a population.

A less discussed phenomenon in ecology literature is the *liability of adolescence* (Baum, 2000). This phenomenon is observed in populations where plentiful resources allow new organizations to start off strong and multiply quickly. After this initial period, the market becomes saturated and resources may become scarce, leading many of the original organizations to fail. Those that survive the adolescence period—by remobilizing or restructuring—emerge stronger and are less likely to fail over the long term.

Density Dependence

Density dependence focuses on foundings and failures in populations and how other organizations are affected by those industry entrances and exits (Baum, 2000). Density refers simply to the number of organizations within a population at a given time. Like other components of ecology theory, density dependence is based on concepts from biology. For example, the animal population within a pond may increase, or become denser, until a point of equilibrium is reached, at which the maximum amount of resources is being utilized by the maximum number of individuals. If density of the population increases beyond this point, some individuals will die (or try to find a new pond) as the available resources cannot adequately support the expanding population. The same principles apply to populations of organizations. Growth rates are density dependent in that populations may expand or contract based on the ability of new and existing organizations to acquire and use resources. The density of a population will be correlated with resource availability as newer or smaller organizations compete with more established organizations. The niches in which populations are located have *carrying capacities*, that is, a maximum number of organizations that can be supported by the resources available. Population density within niches evolves through processes of variation, selection, retention, and competition. Variation is the human behavioral component, as leaders attempt to make strategic adjustments to the organization in response to the environment. These attempts to change organizations may lead to a diversity of forms within populations or result in *isomorphism* as organizations attempt to mimic more successful forms. Organizations are "selected out" of a population if they are not able to adapt, either by failing or by moving to another niche with a better "fit." Organizations will be retained in a population until an environmental disruption causes an organization to fail, often due to liabilities of aging. Newer populations will be more heterogenous, while more established populations will tend toward homogeneity as isomorphic mimicry and selection lead to retention of the most optimal forms (Aldrich & Pfeffer, 1976; Baum, 2000; Carroll, 1984; Dimmick, 2003; Hannan & Freeman, 1977; Lowrey, 2012; Stinchcombe, 1965).

Legitimacy (discussed in more detail next) and density are also related. As population density increases, organizations within that population are more likely to be considered legitimate, as the growth of common forms, increasingly recognizable to both the public and other populations, is noticed (Weber et al., 2016). This relationship between density and legitimacy may occur through various processes. An organizational form may receive attention from institutions (e.g., competitors, regulators, media), and thus be perceived as legitimate. The legitimation of a particular organizational form will in turn signal to nascent organizations that a population is a "safe bet," thus increasing their willingness to join the population and increasing the density of that population. Alternatively, increasing the density of a population may signal to important outsiders (e.g., institutions, other populations, new organizations) that a population is legitimate. The processes of legitimation and density growth may happen in either order or in tandem (Audia et al., 2006; Weber et al., 2016).

Finally, competition between organizations and populations will affect density. Competition is dependence on the same or similar resources, and different levels of competition will result in different relationships (Dimmick, 2003). These relationships may be symbiotic (organizations depend on one another), commensualistic (organizations complement each other), neutral (no effect on each other), or fully or partially competitive (overlap of all or some resource needs) (Baum, 2000). Too much overlap in resource needs may cause one or all of the overlapping organizations to fail. "To avoid the detrimental effects of intense competition, there must be some critical difference in the niche of populations—some difference that lowers overlap—that allows them to coexist" (Dimmick, 2003, p. 38). Some populations may also exhibit *relational density* or formal relationships between population members and key actors that decrease rates of mortality (Amburgey & Rao, 1996).

Density considerations are also different for digital or emerging media populations. Barriers to entry are low, and niches may be more *elastic* for these organizations (Lowrey, 2012). Niche elasticity means that the carrying capacity of the niche is less strictly fixed so that the maximum number of possible entities supported may depend on factors beyond traditional resources. Digital media is less constrained by geographic space (unlike traditional media, like a radio transmission) and less physical capital is involved (e.g., there is no printing press and delivery driver for online news). While there may be a limit to the number of television or radio stations a single community can support, possible audiences for digital media are virtually unlimited, as theoretically, anyone in the world with internet access is a possible audience. These low barriers to entry also allow for easier access by media start-ups, many of whom organize and maintain themselves based on interests or passions beyond financial gains, though they may evolve over time in order to secure legitimacy or more resources (Lowrey, 2011). As noted earlier, constraints to time and attention as well as utility to the audience become important considerations for how these media compete and survive.

Resource Partitioning and Speciation

Within niches, organizations may exist as *generalists*—that is, organizations that use more resources, have a broader range of capabilities, and are more able to handle environmental change—or as *specialists*. Specialists have a more limited focus and use resources more efficiently but are more likely to be unable to recover from environmental changes (Baum, 2000; Hannan & Freeman, 1977, 1989). Niches may have central and peripheral organizations with different resource dependencies. This division of resources is called *resource partitioning* (Carroll, 1985; Carroll et al., 2002; Greve et al., 2006). Large, generalist organizations focus on the center of the market and tend to compete with one another, using similar resources and targeting the same customers. As generalists compete for the center of markets and resources, specialists emerge in order to exploit resources and customers on the periphery of the market (Mezias & Mezias, 2000). The larger, more central organizations will use more resources, thrive in less stable environments due to resource slack, and be more generalist. Peripheral organizations will depend on the remaining resources of the niche, have more susceptibility to environmental changes, and be specialists. While specialists may be more likely to fail due to environmental changes, they have the advantage of efficiency since they do not carry slack resources. Generalist organizations are more stable and able to survive disruptions but are more prone to inertia, and so may not be able to pivot quickly when needed. *Niche width* also determines resource partitioning. Niche width is the available resource space conducive to population growth. Specialists tend to be small, but, depending on the availability of the specific resources they require, may thrive in the margins, and grow into large organizations. Generalists, on the other hand, though usually larger organizations, may sometimes remain small because they require a more diverse range of resources than is available in their niche (Carroll, 1985). The emergence of generalists and specialists is also affected by the mortalities of each organizational form. As generalists increasingly compete with one another, their mortalities may increase, which frees resources and allows for the emergence of more specialist organizations (Mezias & Mezias, 2000).

New, specialized organizations may also emerge through the process of *speciation* (Weber, 2017). These organizations may be on the periphery of the niche or may become part of a separate population of related organizations. Speciation, in contrast to other organizational change processes, can happen very quickly, as new organizations or populations "branch out" from the existing population following disruptions such as major competitive threats or technological innovation. At the time of speciation, the emerging organizations will have full access to resources revealed by the disruption until the density of the new population increases.

Weber (2017) describes three conditions that must exist in order for speciation to occur. The first is a stable population. In a stable population, current organizations have taken-for-granted forms, similar resource dependencies, and are likely to ignore environmental changes. The second condition is inertia. The longer a population is stable, the stronger inertia becomes, as organizations routinize processes becoming larger, less nimble structures. The third condition is routinization of communication. Knowledge, information, and resources are shared through set channels, making these organizations less likely to consider outside information and less able to adapt when instability occurs (Weber, 2017).

Speciation occurs in five stages: (1) a disruption impacts a population; (2) the population fragments; (3) new organizational forms emerge; (4) new forms grow; (5) the new population stabilizes, and competition occurs between new and old forms (Weber, 2017). As the emerging population evolves, actors in the new forms are likely to communicate with others within the new population. While these intra-population channels of communication may be a factor in inertia in older populations, they allow emerging populations to learn from one another and to gain legitimacy from their relationships. This kind of communication is seen especially in online organizations (Weber, 2017; Weber et al., 2016).

Legitimacy

Organizational legitimacy is strongly related to all of the aforementioned concepts of organizational ecology, as it addresses "the normative and cognitive forces that constrain, construct, and empower organizational actors" (Suchman, 1995, p. 571). Legitimacy may be conceptualized as both a resource for organizations and as part of defining form and identity. Isomorphism in populations may help confer legitimacy to members when they mimic organizations that are already seen as successful, and growing density increases the perceived legitimacy of emerging populations (Deephouse & Suchman, 2008; Hannan & Freeman, 1977; Weber et al., 2016).

The concept of legitimacy can be traced to Max Weber's early sociological work ([1922] 1946). Suchman (1995) defines legitimacy as "a generalized perception of assumption that the actions of an entity are desirable, proper, or appropriate within some socially constructed system of norms, values, beliefs, and definitions" (p. 574). Legitimacy is negotiated and conferred by *legitimacy agents* (e.g., government regulators, accreditors), *legitimacy mediators* (e.g., media or other social actors that publicly assess legitimacy of organizations or forms), or *legitimacy guidelines* (e.g., imbedded community or societal norms that may be constantly renegotiated) (Deephouse & Suchman, 2008). As with form and identity, legitimacy can be a product of communicative processes, as stakeholders negotiate and redefine what is "appropriate" (Weber et al., 2016).

Legitimacy of organizations is often discussed in terms of cognitive and sociopolitical legitimacy. Aldrich and Fiol (1994) explain:

> Cognitive legitimation refers to the spread of knowledge about a new venture. . . . Sociopolitical legitimation refers to the process by which key stakeholders, the general public, key opinion leaders, or government officials accept a venture as appropriate and right, given existing norms and laws (p. 648).

Cognitive legitimacy is "taken-for-grantedness," that is, the point where an organizational form is widely understood, no longer requires explanation and is viewed as an appropriate way of accomplishing goals. Lowrey's (2012) research assessed the cognitive legitimacy of blogs as organizational forms. At a certain point, after blogs became popular, news and popular media stopped defining them when they were mentioned, thus signaling that the general public was aware of what a "blog" or a "web log" was and that substantial cognitive legitimacy had been reached. Mere mentions by media of an organizational form also serve as both a source of legitimacy and an indicator of legitimacy. While increased public discussion about a form (in the case above, a new media format) may signal "this is becoming important and worth writing about," a decrease in mentions may also indicate that the form (or technology) has become so ubiquitous that it is no longer unusual or newsworthy (Deephouse & Suchman, 2008).

Sociopolitical legitimacy may be conferred by honors or awards, but it may also come from a general societal acceptance that an organizational form is behaving in a way that fits societal rules:

Legitimation is largely a question of "satisficing" to an acceptable level, and the absence of "problems" is more important than the presence of positive achievements. Legitimacy is also fundamentally non-rival; it is rarely a zero-sum game within any given population; indeed, positive feedback loops and a "logic of confidence" tend to produce win-win ceremonies of mutual affirmation among legitimate actors. Further, legitimacy is homogenizing, producing herd-like conformity along whichever dimensions the prevailing rational myths establish as legitimacy defining. Further, precisely because legitimacy is non-rival and homogenizing, it paints with a broad brush and tends to attach to all entities that share a given form. (Deephouse & Suchman, 2008, p. 61)

This "broad brush" allows organizations and organizational leaders to "co-opt" legitimacy through establishing relationships with other, already legitimized actors. Organizations may also co-opt legitimacy through projecting an image of shared values and exchanging resources with other population members or with adjacent populations (Downing & Pfeffer, 1975; Weber et al., 2016). Gaining legitimacy is vital to organizational success and survival. While the mobilization of resources may be a source of legitimacy for organizations (Lowrey, 2012), a lack of legitimacy may block organizational access to resources. Hirsch and Andrews (1984) discuss the ways that failing to meet the expectations of stakeholders can threaten legitimacy. They point to two important ways organizations' legitimacy may be threatened: organizations may lose legitimacy by failing to meet their goals, or they may lose support if their core values and goals are deemed unacceptable, and out of accord with larger sociopolitical institutions. In either case, a loss of legitimacy will make an organization more likely to fail.

Carroll and Swaminathan (2002) found that in some cases, identity may be a constraint on legitimacy of organizations and may affect both generalists and specialists. In their qualitative study of the brewing industry, they found four possible explanations for the role of identity as a constraint in some industries. These explanations include:

1) Specialists, regardless of actual product quality, may be perceived as producing higher quality products than generalists.
2) Consumers may identify with specialists as a rebellion against mass-production or homogenization.
3) Identifying with specialist brands may be a form of consumer self-expression.
4) A level of status may be conferred to specialists as they are perceived as "experts." (Carroll & Swaminathan, 2000)

These explanations also suggest that, in contrast to other assumptions from organizational ecology, legitimacy in the case of identity-based organizations is more affected by identity congruence—meeting the "normative" expectations of consumers—than by density of the population. Perhaps most relevant to the true crime podcast population is Carroll and Swaminathan's assertion that this identity-based legitimacy and targeted marketing may be especially applicable to media organizations. They write, "The sustained appeal of specialist organizations appears to emanate from their identity" (Carroll & Swaminathan, 2000, p. 752). My earlier (Sherrill, 2020) content analysis of mentions of true crime podcasts in online newspapers illustrates how public perceptions of legitimacy for that population have evolved. As true crime podcasts' population density grew around the initial release of *Serial*, so did mentions in the media. This signaled growing population legitimacy as more journalists and consumers began to recognize true crime podcasts as legitimate organizational forms.

Strengths and Weakness of an
Organizational Ecology Approach

Organizational ecology offers advantages over other paradigms of organizational studies as it considers a variety of variables and levels of analysis, including environmental pressures, economic factors, social legitimacy, internal politics and behavior, and management strategy. This perspective is also well suited to empirical and analytic approaches and a variety of methodologies, from computational modeling and statistical analysis to in-depth interviews and ethnography (e.g., Carroll & Swaminathan, 1992; Monge et al., 2011; Raff, 2000). Hannan and Freeman (1989) note that ecological approaches are to be differentiated not only from adaptationist approaches (like strategic management) but also from social Darwinism and gradualist approaches: "survival of the fittest" is not an appropriate conceptualization of organizational ecology, as "fit" is dependent on multiple exogenous factors and will change with environmental disruptions. Unlike gradualist perspectives, ecological perspectives recognize that evolution may occur through sudden, drastic disruptions rather than only slow, methodical processes (Hannan & Freeman, 1989). Ecological paradigms are also contrasted with determinist perspectives of organizational studies (Burrell & Morgan, 1979), which focus on the power of management and individual organizations to control their operations while ignoring or undervaluing environmental forces.

There are, however, weaknesses in this theory, particularly in the measurement and definitions of such amorphous concepts as boundaries, forms, and identity (Carroll, 1984; Hannan & Freeman, 1989; Diani, 2013). As these concepts are constantly evolving through communication and social interaction, they are difficult to operationalize and quantify. Measurement weakness also lies in the idea of aggregations versus relationships. Populations are often conceptualized as aggregates of organizations with the same characteristics, but they may also be considered networks of relationships (Dimaggio, 1986). Carroll (1984) cautions that researchers must be aware of this duality and be careful not to use nominal variables to account for continuous processes. Baum (2000) and Amburgey and Rao (2014) also caution that demography of populations is often conducted inappropriately, leading to biased determinations of density and mortality. They argue that organizations that fail are often unaccounted for in the literature, as it is difficult to find information on organizations that no longer exist. Larger, more stable organizations are then overly represented in studies, thus leading to incorrect conclusions about entire populations (Hannan & Freeman, 1989).

SOCIAL MOVEMENT THEORIES

In addition to existing as media organizations with maintenance orientations, many true crime podcasts are or have acted as catalysts for, or at the very least mobilizers of, social movements. As Doane and colleagues (2017) write, podcasts like *Serial* and its successors present new voices, new spheres for debate, and may motivate listeners to act through both entertainment and strategic discourse. Because of this dual nature, SMTs can help us to understand the members of this population that exist to do more than entertain.

Shared across SMT approaches is the idea of collective identity and action, based on Smelser's (1962) model of collective behavior. Melucci (1995) defined collective behavior as "an interactive and shared definition produced by several individuals (or groups at a more complex level) and concerned with the orientations of action and the field of opportunities and constraints in which the action takes place" (p. 44). This "field of opportunities and constraints" suggests an ecological system.

While organizational ecology offers tools and explanations to understand the structural components at work in this system and the processes by which the system is maintained, SMT explains the mobilizing mechanisms that allow actors within this system to come together and to attain goals. Undergirding this collective behavior is a collective identity, a social process, which may be created dynamically as a result of action or serve as a unifying force to spur action (Cohen, 1985). Within the true crime podcast population, each organization or population may have differing specific goals or methods but many seem to share a commitment to justice and a moral imperative to spread information and encourage advocacy. This is evident in the popular press descriptions of these podcasts (i.e., Simpson, October 14, 2017; McHugh, August 31, 2017; Wheeler, Sept. 13, 2019), as well as in the way the podcasters I interviewed describe their work.

SMTs, like organizational ecology, are concerned with meso-level phenomena; that is, they focus on organizations and collectives rather than macro, societal level issues or micro, individual-level phenomena. SMT approaches, developed for over a century from psychology, sociology, and ethnic and revolutionary studies research, offer a set of tools to better understand the uses of organizational communication, mass media phenomena, media ecology, and the utilization of new and alternative mediums in the creation and mobilization of social movements. Communication within movements, between ideologically associated groups, and between movements and society is central to SMT. SMT paradigms include Resource Mobilization, Classical/New Social Movements/Identity approaches, and the Political Process Model (PPM) (Cohen, 1985; McAdam, 1999; McCarthy & Zald, 1977; 2002; Melucci, 1985; Tilly, 1978). Some scholars have tied the resource mobilization and political process paradigms of SMT to organizational ecology through explicit comparison of levels of analysis and core concepts such as legitimacy and collective action (e.g., Amburgey & Rao, 1996; Greve et al., 2006; Hannan & Freeman, 1989; McCarthy & Zald, 1977, 2002), and these paradigms offer concepts for better understanding how podcasts can be used to mobilize collective action. The concepts of these approaches offer a *systemic* rather than competing view of social movement development (Carroll & Hackett, 2006; Melucci, 1985), allowing this study to account for both structural and ideological explanations for podcast organization and population development.

SMT approaches have varied widely in focus and application, often concentrating on particular phenomena associated with specific kinds of collective action. Because this collective action appears in diverse patterns depending on the historical period, sociopolitical systems, and involved actors, scholars have arrived at a variety of conclusions about the nature of movements. Traugott (1978) credits the focus on different exogenous and endogenous factors for producing "a field of study loosely joining phenomena so diverse as to defy explanation by any single theoretical framework" (p. 42). However, McAdam (1999) points to three uniting factors across all paradigms of SMT. The first factor is political processes. Political processes describe the environmental constraints and opportunities of the system in which a movement exists. The second factor is mobilizing structures, encompassing the organizations and networks that facilitate resource acquisition. The final factor is framing processes, or the social construction of "shared meanings and cultural understandings . . . including a shared collective identity" (McAdam, 1999, p. ix). This framing process is continuous and "require[s] participants to reject institutionalized routines and taken for granted assumptions about the world and to fashion new world views and lines of interaction" (McAdam, 1999, p. xxi). Movement framing may be strategic by organizations and

leaders in order to legitimate and motivate members and represents a trans-
formative process of mobilizing existing coalitions to action.

McAdam and others note that the minimum requirement for movement
existence is *group efficacy*, that is, a shared sense of aggrievement about a
problem and an optimism about the possibility of collective solutions (Bandura, 1995; Klandermans, 1984; McAdam, 1999). Members of social movements are defined as collective actors whose interests are routinely accounted
for in the decision-making process (Gamson, 1990). When podcasters think
about the gratifications sought by their audience, they are also considering the
interests of potential collective actors.

Classical/New Social Movement Theories/Identity Approach

Both "new" and "theory" are misnomers, as this SMT paradigm is more
accurately a school of approaches rooted in older research by Tourainne,
Castells, Marx, Melucci, and Habermas (Buechler, 1995). These classical
approaches are older and have more literature but are less formally developed
than either resource mobilization or political process approaches. Rather
than having structured tenants, scholarship in this paradigm often takes a
more critical/cultural approach and defines movements by collective awareness and identity rather than actual strategic goals. The classical approach
focuses almost entirely on the formation and maintenance of group identities.
Classical scholars have focused on specific movements using critical and
analytic methods, particularly historical analysis. This approach posits that
social movements today are not formed based on an identity of class struggle
(e.g., nineteenth- and early twentieth-century revolts) but rather on voluntary associations. Voluntary movement associations are seen to be largely
ideational and created by collective awareness and desire for change. These
movements may frame symbolic victories as successful action in that their
goal may be simply bringing societal attention to a problem. Many authors in
this paradigm see movements as symbolic challenges to political and cultural
norms rather than strategic, goal-oriented organizations (e.g., Melucci, 1985,
1995; Eder, 1985). Habermas's (1987) writing on the public sphere helped
to solidify these ideas somewhat but still fell more on the side of symbolism.
Others (e.g., Buechler, 1993, 1995; Melucci, 1985, 1995) saw something fundamentally different about twentieth-century movements like the Civil Rights
or women's movements that required more identity-focused paradigms. The
classical paradigm also posits group identity or organization as a sufficient
outcome of collective action, rather than as only one factor that contributes
to desired, tangible outcomes (Cohen, 1985; Diani, 2013).

While Resource Mobilization Theory (RMT) and PPM approaches often
place less emphasis on symbolic, nonrational action, the classical approach

embraces it. "The central process [of new social movements] is the social construction of a collective identity that is symbolically meaningful to participants and logically precedes any meaningful calculation of the costs and benefits of joining in collective action" (Buechler, 1993, p. 228). Classical approaches focus on the power of social interaction to create large-scale change. Melucci (1985) wrote that movement actors "fight for symbolic and cultural stakes, for a different meaning and orientation of social action. They try to change people's lives, they believe you can change your life today while fighting for more general changes in society" (p. 798).

Classical approaches place a strong emphasis on the individual and are more psychologically than politically focused. This approach can be traced to mass society or "mass-man" theorizing which viewed movements as non-structured systems arising from individual anxiety, alienation, or fear (LeBon, [1895] 1947; McAdam, 1999; Zimbardo, 1969). In this view, individuals who join movements are seen as somehow different from individuals in "normal" society—they are marginalized or even somehow pathological. Collective behavior in classical movements occurs because of a strain or disruption to the system status quo, often the result of extreme inequity between groups.

Criticism of the classical approach points out that the role of the environment and sociopolitical structure is seldom incorporated in these analyses. This approach has been criticized for making overreaching conclusions and focusing too much on symbolic analysis rather than empirical evidence (Cohen, 1985). However, more recent scholars from this paradigm, like Buechler (1994, 1995) and Melucci (1985, 1995), attest that movements today operate in a post-classist environment. They situate this approach as a contrast to earlier Marxist views of collective action as being primarily driven by material factors such as economic inequality. This new social movements' view of the classical approach largely disregards the effects of material resources and motivators on movements as well as the role of the environment writ large. This is a problem for the paradigm, as collective identity will not necessarily be sufficient to result in tangible collective action. Cohen (1995) uses the example of the U.S. Civil Rights movement to illustrate this weakness. If identity and shared awareness of injustice had been enough to create a large-scale movement, Black Americans had ample cause long before the 1950s. Action, however, resulted from the confluence of identity, awareness, resources (in the form of changing political climates and increasing mass media saturation), and substantive support from important political leaders. These researchers have found other evidence to contradict the idea that individual emotion or collective identity is enough on their own to facilitate movement (even symbolic) action (e.g., Cameron, 1974; Freeman, 1973; Shorter & Tilly, 1974). These scholars argue that movements do not emerge from individuals coming together because of a cause; instead, they arise through individuals connecting over a cause through already established networks of interactions. Some kind of formal organization is required to create action from individual discontent (McAdam, 1999).

Resource Mobilization Theory (RMT)

In response to the criticisms of the prevailing classical theory, scholars began to focus on the resource mobilization perspective of movement action. This perspective views movements as strategic responses to political systems and sought to correct the disregard for environmental and organizational factors in the classical perspective. Unlike earlier European social movement models predicated on late nineteenth- and early twentieth-century movements, the RMT approach was born out of mid-twentieth-century movements that did not fit previous paradigms (Buechler, 1993; Canel, 1997; Jenkins, 1983). This approach sees social movements as being composed of rational actors who work in strategic ways. These movements are less reliant on charismatic leadership than those in earlier research and depend more on "rational actions oriented towards clearly defined, fixed goals with centralized organizational control over resources and clearly demarcated outcomes that can be evaluated in terms of tangible goals" (Jenkins, 1983, p. 529). This paradigm assumes that the availability of resources for mobilization is the driving factor behind moving collective awareness of an issue toward collective action. Beyond availability, organizations must have the legitimacy and strategic knowledge to secure and utilize the resources available. This paradigm sees the best strategy for movements to mobilize resources as structuring themselves into an organizational form, also called a *politicized* identity (Diani, 2013; Huddy, 2002; Van Zomeren et al., 2008). There are four main assumptions that undergird the ability of movements to organize into effective collective action in this perspective. These assumptions are (1) widespread knowledge of how to join or form a movement; (2) norms (or at least ideals) of free speech and assembly; (3) mass media that is friendly to covering movements; and (4) recognition that legislative and electoral action is not enough to make the changes the movement desires (e.g., legalization of an issue like LGBTQIA+ rights does not necessarily signal social acceptance). Also, while McCarthy and Zald (1979, 2002) do not use the same terminology, these four assumptions also require perceptions of group efficacy (McAdam, 1999). Resources in RMT may be physical, monetary, or symbolic. McCarthy and Zald (1977, 2002) and Oberschall (1973) described possible resources as legitimacy, skills, money, facilities, labor, rights or access to material goods and services, authority, moral commitment, trust, knowledge, and industry standards.

McCarthy and Zald's (1977, 2002) RMT shares several fundamental concepts with organizational ecology, though it is important to note that these shared concepts do not represent a formal, unified framework for analysis of organizational structure, form, and competition as organizational ecology does. As discussed later in this chapter, use of organization ecology concepts in studies framed by a social movement context has been extremely rare. Paralleling the ideas of organization, population, and community, RMT focuses on environmental support and constraints on social movement organizations (SMO), social movement industries (SMI), and social movement sectors (SMS). RMT also includes similar concepts to niche and resource partitioning theory, suggesting that SMI are made of specialists and generalists and that niches have limited carrying capacities. While the terminology used is not identical to that of organizational ecology, McCarthy and Zald (2002) address the idea that SMS have pools of resources that are divided among SMI and SMOs, utilized based on the specializations of those entities (e.g., local versus national chapters, resource-gathering versus information-spreading organizations) and shared based on competition and negotiation. These SMOs may have competitive or commensualistic relationships. Density has been discussed, along with the effects of foundings, legitimacy, liabilities of newness and aging, and mortalities SMO. Legitimacy is important to RMT, as industries and organizations require sociopolitical and cognitive buy-in to grow and thrive. Also similar to organizational ecology, some RMT research has focused on the role of professionalization and institutionalization in the legitimacy of SMO and industries. Boundaries between types of entities are well defined in RMT, and RMT focuses on the societal conditions necessary for movements to mobilize. Carroll and Hackett (2006) approached these boundaries from the perspective of alternative media, suggesting that nontraditional media forms, such as independent or "alternative" local newspapers and now, podcasts, use democratic media action to sidestep the requirements of traditional media, thus redefining the movement's boundaries. Also interesting to media-based SMO is McCarthy and Zald's (2002) discussion of *technologies of mobilization*, or specific types of communication utilized within social movement sectors.

Some criticisms of this approach are that while RMT assumes that formal organization is necessary for resource mobilization, it does not fully address other ways in which efficacy and group identity form, nor does it account for the persuasive power of leaders' communication. McAdam (1999) calls discontent and group efficacy "psychological resources" and argues that while inequality may always be present in a society, changing *perceptions* of resource availability drive movements: "Resources do not dictate their use, people do" (p. 21). RMT also fails to account for indirect or symbolic action within movements, such as an individual donating money to or spreading information about a cause that does not directly affect them. Some researchers (Jenkins & Perrow, 1977; McAdam, 1999) have pointed out that resources must often be mobilized by actors who are working to benefit some other stakeholders: "In the case of deprived groups, the aggrieved population is usually incapable of generating a social movement on its own" (McAdam, 1999, p. 29). This is especially relevant for the discussion of the true crime podcasts that advocate for criminal justice reform, as their membership is made of organizations and individuals often advocating on behalf of incarcerated populations or deceased victims. RMT also cannot explain how individual motivation leads to collective action and maintenance of organizational connections (Buechler, 1993; Canel, 1997; Melucci, 1995), as can be seen in the framing process factor of new SMTs. RMT assumes collective identity and shared motivation but does not fully conceptualize this process, starting instead from an assumption that there are existing structural movement components. Finally, despite its acknowledgment of the importance of the environment to social movement growth, RMT research tends to ignore the subtleties of the political opportunities that allow movements to mobilize and achieve success (McCarthy & Zald, 2002).

The Political Process Model (PPM)

The PPM specifically seeks to add the component of political opportunity to the resource mobilization approach. More recent movement research by Morris (2000) further expands the RMT and classical paradigms to examine the causality and success of movements. Morris's work builds upon the earlier PPM (McAdam, 1999; McAdam et al., 1996; Oberschall, 1973; Rule & Tilly, 1975; Tilly, 1978), by examining the informal networks and preexisting structures that may be utilized as resources. Most recently, McAdam (2017) revisited previous RMT research and stressed the necessity of what he calls "mobilizing emotions" (p. 194), such as anger at injustice or fear of threat, to create collective action.

The PPM views movements as more political than psychological, developing through continuous, dynamic processes of interaction with their sociopolitical environments. While it accounts for mobilizing emotions, PPM views movement actions as primarily rational processes by stakeholders to advance collective interests. While the organization of these movements may be noninstitutionalized, PPM still requires sufficient structure to leverage resources or exert political pressure. "The political process model is based on the assumption that movements only emerge over a long period of time in response to broad social, economic, and political processes that afford insurgents a certain structural potential for collective action" (McAdam, 1999, p. 60). Like RMT, PPM is an ecological perspective of movements, focusing on endogenous and exogenous factors of organization, collective efficacy, and alignment with the environment. It sees movements as economic actors, taking rational steps to decrease power disparities so that the cost to the environment of suppressing a movement becomes greater than the cost of the movement to sustain itself. PPM also acknowledges the different kind of actors that may enact social change, such as *elite contention* by established political actors. McCarthy and Zald (1977) use the example of the Sierra Club as a movement organization that is part of a century-old, politicized environmental movement with elite actors. At the other end of the movement spectrum is *popular contention*, in which newly mobilized, self-identified political actors may have some reliance on non- or newly institutionalized structures or forms (McAdam et al., 2003).

McAdam (1999) criticizes the application of the PPM in movement scholarship rather than its concepts. One such application is the operationalization of threats and opportunities. While Tilly's (1978) foundational PPM scholarship explored the interactions of perceived threats to a group and the environmental or political opportunities for action, later scholars focused on one or the other as movement motivations. McAdam theorizes that both threats and opportunities may be considered mobilizing factors and that these concepts may interact and coexist in the same movement. Likewise, the ignoring of nuanced variation in network relationships between movements (both as partners and challengers) has also been a problem in PPM application. Relationships act as both environmental constraints and opportunities and are vital for the growth of resources and legitimacy. Melucci (1985), though writing from the classical perspective, also theorized that the identity and legitimacy of organizational forms are increased through communicative action, such as "submerged networks" of connected individuals between organizations, further strengthening McAdam's (1999) assertion that relational networks must be considered in social movement models. Other opportunities that are often ignored include political changes beyond the local reach of movements. For example, the Arab Spring movement of the late 2000s received international attention, serving as an example of movement mobilization in the Twitter age far beyond the countries it affected. McAdam called these *symbolic political opportunities*; that is, attention to other successful movement forms (through media coverage or political rhetoric) increases the salience of collective action far beyond the reach of related social movement organizations (McAdam, 1999).

THEORETICAL SYNTHESIS

True crime podcasts represent an interesting media phenomenon both from the perspective of practical and theoretical implications. As a rapidly growing cultural phenomenon, their popularity suggests continued interest from both outside and within academic contexts. Many of these podcasts are hybrids, existing as media organizations with relations to entertainment, journalism, and pop culture, and, simultaneously, as movement organizations, with ties to social and political change advocacy. Because of these podcasts' dual orientations, they must first focus on *maintenance*, or the basic organizational and structural processes needed to support a media operation. This means acquiring resources, targeting audiences, and dealing with competition. They also operate from a *movement* orientation, balancing goals, identity, and collective awareness with audience members around social issues like the epidemic of missing persons, police misconduct, wrongful convictions, and other criminal justice reform topics. Based on their hybrid orientation, this population is a prime subject for exploration of the dual nature of many emerging digital platforms and for utilizing the synthesized application of organizational ecology and SMTs.

Using combined approaches of organizational ecology and SMTs to explain meso-level phenomena is logical when the sum of the literature is considered. Hannan and Freeman quote Tilly (1978), the father of the political process model, on the first page of *Organizational Ecology* (1989) and go into great detail about the application of ecology to the study of movements. They write,

> Even relatively amorphous social movements have a higher likelihood of success if they can utilize existing organization . . . organizations are more than passive actors: most societal change begins with actions from organizations. Indeed, organizations are constructed as tools for specific kinds of collective action. (Hannan & Freeman, 1989, p. 3)

Hannan and Freeman explain that while organizations have all the hallmarks of collective action—efficacy, resources, collective identity—formal organizations bring competencies to movements. These competencies include reliability and stability, internal accountability and consistency, efficiency in resource mobilization, and routinization. They caution, however, that with these core competencies comes inertia, potentially making SMO less able to adapt to their environment.

Organizational ecology scholars Amburgey and Rao (1996) and Carroll (1984) also cite SMTs and draw parallels. Amburgey and Rao (1996) write:

> In a related vein, albeit with a different vocabulary, social movement theorists have suggested that the relationship between moderate and radical social movement organizations and the interplay between organizations championing a movement and organizations promoting a countermovement influence the fates of issues. Ecological models of niche width can be used to model how diffuse competition between moderate and radical movement organizations influences the rates at which they attract new members. . . . Density-dependent models of evolution may shed light on the coevolution of movements and

counter-movements, and on how organizational dynamics underlie the rise and fall of issues. (p. 1281)

Within the social movements literature, scholars have also suggested ecological frameworks be incorporated. McCarthy and Zald (2002) specifically cite ecology as a lens to extend resource mobilization perspectives, and McAdam (2017) also noted the usefulness of ecological perspectives in social movement research. The approaches have multiple overlapping or similar concepts—levels, density, legitimacy, inertia, boundaries, resources—and also what both Greve et al. (2006) and Van Zomeren et al. (2008) call "symmetrical gaps." Interestingly, while scholars often suggest that these theory approaches work well together, there has been very little research actually following those suggestions. McCarthy and Zald's (2002) review of resource mobilization research specifically addresses this, noting that they find it unusual that more overlapping research does not exist, particularly on the effects of population density on movement legitimacy.

Synthesis in Past Research

There are a few scholars who have, at least partially, combined ecological and social movement approaches (e.g., Diani, 2013; Carroll & Hackett, 2006; Greve et al., 2006; Minkoff, 1999), though many of these works are theoretical analyses rather than empirical applications. Empirical studies have focused only on select concepts from both theories, such as density and legitimacy. Greve et al. (2006) identified particular weaknesses in ecology and SMTs and used a combined approach (along with the "production of cultural" perspective, which is beyond the scope of this book's exploration) to explore reasons for the emergence of media organizations. Organizational ecology, they argued, focuses only on the distribution of resources and the latent possibilities in the social space—such as resource partitioning theory and its explanation for why small specialists are able to emerge and grow—while ignoring the motivations of individual organizations and individuals that, beyond environmental disruption and resource partitioning, may lead to "entrepreneurial attempts" and speciation processes in populations. From an SMT perspective, Greve's et al. (2006) study sought to uncover how population density and diversity of organizational forms affect SMI. Their findings shed light on the unique ways that media organizations, particularly those related to social movements, interact. While older ecological research focused on competition from emerging new entities that derive from resource partitioning, Greve et al. (2006) identified *community resources* (Carroll, 1985), or sharing between organizations, that altered perceptions of niche width and elasticity. They also found increased population density led to an increase in organizations and individuals with specialized knowledge about the SMI. Rather than leading to increased competition, this density of knowledgeable actors became a community resource and increased perceived legitimacy of the organizational form. Within the population, increases in diversity of forms led to greater audience attention and movement membership. While diversity of organizational forms had been found to be a negative factor in terms of the growth of certain organization populations in earlier research (Ingram & Rao, 2004), it became a positive "symbolic output" (Hannan, 1988) for media organizations within the SMI. Part of this "symbolic output" came from the identity of the micro-radio stations examined. In this case, diversity of form was a goal rather than a weakness. That is, these stations considered their identity to be predicated on heterogeneity in opposition to dominant, commercial radio. Because they were goal (or movement) oriented rather than only financially oriented, the diversity of forms that proved negative in earlier research (Ingram & Rao, 2004), became a strength within the movement orientation. Greve and colleagues (2006) caution, however, that a point was eventually reached where too much density and diversity within a population drove the audience away by overwhelming them with choices.

Sandell (2001) researched organizational growth in Sweden using a synthesis of the theories and showed that resource availability alone cannot explain the growth of movement organizations. In the case of the movement organizations analyzed, density of the population was more indicative of interest in (and thus, membership growth of) social movements. In other words, many very small organizations within a SMI/population are a more significant indicator of movement success than a few large, stable organizations. This is relevant to the true crime podcast population, as it suggests that the explosion of true crime podcasts may not be indictive of an oversaturation of the market, but rather of a deeply invested, collectively identified audience. Additionally, both Koopmans (2004) and Carroll and Hackett (2006) illustrated the merit of a combined theoretical approach, especially in cases of democratic media activism, such as citizen journalism or emerging, democratic media platforms.

Analytic scholarship has also shed light on the ways these theories may be co-utilized. Van Zomeren and colleagues (2008) conducted a meta-analysis of 182 studies of collective action. While their findings deal largely with psychological, individual-level phenomena in movement participants, they do suggest an important rationale for using dual ecological and SMT approaches to understand movement organizations. This rationale is that for any collective action, there is an interaction between the agency and motivations of organization or movement leaders and environmental factors. Cost-benefit considerations are thus important to sociopolitical opportunities and collective identity if successful action is to occur. In order for scholars to fully account for the emergence and development of social movement phenomena, multiple theoretical positions must be considered. Diani's (2013) proposal offers another relevant synthesis for consideration. While not adopting organization ecology directly, he does suggest that social movements may themselves be conceptualized within the social space in what he calls organizational "fields." He proposes the study of movements through examining networks, boundaries, resources, collaborations, joint membership in movement organizations, collective identity formation, and organizational change (or inertia). Identity in this combined perspective is examined both at the movement level (the community/field) and the organization level (population members; Diani, 2013).

Symmetrical Gaps

Within both theories there are gaps that ignore or underexplain parts of organizational and environmental phenomena that seem glaringly absent when studying dual-oriented, emerging media populations. Organizational ecology literature is weak on the concept of identity. While it recognizes that identity is important to definitions of organizational form and the "boundary work" involved in differentiating "legitimate" forms, it is unclear on the hows and whys of identity formation, and it does not explore the full consequences of identity formation. As Gioia et al. (2000) and Polos et al. (2002) discuss, organizations can change their structure and form and yet retain their identity. The consequences of this change are not fully accounted for by organizational ecology. Identity may be of more importance for certain kinds of organizations and industries, thus changing how legitimacy is determined for those populations, the reasons for population growth, and the impact of population growth (Carroll & Swaminathan, 2000).

SMTs, especially the classical approach, have been criticized for focusing on identity to the point of ignoring more concrete, instrumental factors, such as resources, initial mobilization, and strategy (Cohen, 1985; Diani, 2013). Within SMTs, RMT does address mobilization and strategy, but it ignores the social construction and renegotiation of boundaries and de-emphasizes the impact of identity formation. These gaps in the theory appear to be complementary—ecology offers ways to understand how organizations and populations compete and evolve for survival, while SMT further explains social processes and consequences of boundary creation, identity, and identification with organizations and the larger causes behind them.

CONCEPTS FOR EXPLORATION

As I considered all of this prior literature, as well as the questions that kept coming up in popular and trade press discussions about true crime podcasts, I set out to explore this phenomenon and to act on the suggestions of prior theorists. By focusing on relationships, collaboration, and shared resources (e.g., Diani, 2013), I wanted to understand how goal-oriented podcasters build identity and networks while attracting listeners and mobilizing resources. Did these producers see their audiences as a resource in ways beyond targeted advertising and publicity as I suspected? If so, this is in line with Dimmick's (2003) concept of niche gratifications, which drive audiences to choose media products, as well as Gamson's (1990) conceptualization of movement members as actors whose interests are vital for movement success. The audience, if they buy into the presented goals, has the potential to become a part of the movement organization and to participate in the social construction of form, boundaries, and identity. The PPM helps to explain how collective awareness of issues interacts with environmental opportunities to mobilize movements.

Focusing on the ecological concept of boundaries in connection to form, it seemed possible that fan communities helped direct the central movement organizations (here, podcasts), in the direction that they believe is most congruent with the movement's identity. Scholars have discussed this bi-directional boundary work, writing that audiences/constituents/consumers define an organization at least as much as the organization defines itself (Gioia et al., 2000; Polos et al., 2002). This is reminiscent of Albert and Whetten's (1985) seminal definition of organizational identity as being composed of "how we see ourselves" and "how we are seen." As mentioned ealier, McAdam (2017) wrote that communities are quick to point out when leaders or organizations go against movement goals as understood by the community or to suggest new directions or issues. Fan communities also grow around a particular product (or, constituents grow around a movement) based on the specific gratifications they receive (Dimmick, 2003). For those media products that have specifically articulated goals beyond entertainment, were podcasters aware of audiences having certain expectations that act as boundaries to the organization?

Other ecological work on institutionalization of organizations and populations may help explain how fan communities become active rather than passive. Lowrey (2017) wrote about institutionalization in the case of fact-checking websites. These sites began as offshoots of legacy outlets, often as supplements to other media products. Over time the population of these sites, through mimicry and development of shared norms, became "a thing"; that is, they gained cognitive legitimacy. With cognitive legitimacy came agreed-upon, taken-for-granted norms and expectations of the population, which foster institutionalization. In the case of the fact-checking sites, members of the population took on institutional characteristics of traditional journalism and developed recognizable norms. McCarthy and Zald (2002) note the understudied importance of professionalization and institutionalization in movement organizations and industries, and McAdam (2017) and Cohen (1985) both write that social movements may sometimes follow this path to institutionalization. It seems likely that movement-oriented media products, like some true crime podcasts, may follow a similar tract.

As new organizations appear, the population becomes denser. In the case of podcasts, fan communities often overlap (what SMT calls voluntary, non-exclusionary membership and ecology calls commensualistic relationships) and share information (Florini, 2015). Both SMT and organizational ecology have the advantage of examining the mobilization of fandoms and social movement populations from an environmental perspective. Rather than focusing solely on media and psychological effects (like parasocial interaction or psychological sense of community), they also include the sociological concept of the environment. This allows sociopolitical pressures and opportunities to be evaluated, such as the role of cultural legitimacy and cultural norms. These concepts—particularly when approached from both perspectives—allow us to better understand how individual effects, community identity, and societal level forces work together to create coherent and effective action.

I've centered my dual application of organizational ecology and social movements theory on a specific genre of true crime podcasts around several major themes. First, what does the ecosystem, comprised of all types of true crime podcasts, look like today, nearly a decade post-*Serial*? This includes both foundings and failures of true crime podcasts, as well as how the density of the population has shifted over time.

Second, how do creators involved in one niche of this vast population think about their podcasts as organizations with maintenance and resource requirements? The size and variety of forms in this population open the door for exploration of multiple ecological processes. The heterogeneity of the podcasts in the genre, both in style and substance, suggests that resource partitioning or speciation processes may be at play in the true crime podcast niche (Carroll, 1985; Weber, 2017). While there are indications that some podcasts in the niche exhibit isomorphism, even publicly stating their intentional mimicry of *Serial* (e.g., AJC, 2015), it is not clear how others emerged or how their forms were determined. Knowledge of density, mortalities, and resource mobilization for this population is also lacking. How have density and legitimacy developed and interacted in this population? How are resources partitioned and are populations showing signs of nearing the carrying capacities of their niches? While other studies have examined small segments of this population (e.g., Boling & Hull, 2018; Doane et al., 2017; Greer, 2017), no community or population-level analysis has been conducted, leaving scholars to speculate about the breadth of the phenomenon.

Next, I wanted to understand podcasters' connections to social movements for criminal justice reform, and how they see true crime podcasts fitting into that movement. I also wanted to understand the tension between ecological and movement perspectives in the day-to-day operations of the podcasters—if they consider their podcast to be a hybrid organization, how do they balance organizational maintenance and advocacy? As demonstrated in the previous chapter, it's clear that at least some members of the true crime podcast population exist both as media products and SMO. These podcasts, like those described by Simpson (October 14, 2017) and McHugh (August 31, 2017) represent democratic media action (Carroll & Hackett, 2006; Greve et al., 2006), where the media products offer counternarratives to mainstream media, discuss case theories for more than the sake of entertainment, or act in terms of strategic objectives (i.e., "finding the real killer"). This suggests that producers may be addressing particular audience gratifications. Considering the gratification users are seeking is an example of a democratic participatory process in the creation of organizational boundaries, which invites questions about the communicative processes that define organizational form, identities, and boundaries within this population (Hsu & Hannan, 2002; Jacobs et al., 2008; Polos et al., 2002; Weber, 2017)

Finally, I wanted to know what I was missing—what other factors might be a part of true crime podcasters' decision-making processes that I, as an outsider, might never have considered? In the following chapters, I focus on each of these themes—the true crime podcast ecosystem, ecological and social movement perspectives of podcast creators, navigating the dichotomy of hybrid organizations, and emerging factors—and examine how both structural, organizational forces and the evolution of collective identity and action are at work in the true crime podcast population.

Chapter 4

Understanding the True Crime Podcast Ecosystem

Everyone and their mom has a podcast.

—Sarah Delia

I have seldom been as nervous in my life as the day I interviewed Rabia Chaudry.

There I was, in my graduate school apartment, perched on my bed with my laptop, my phone, and my notes. I'd closed my dog in the other room and checked my battery levels and recording apps a dozen times. She wasn't my first podcaster interview—that was Colin Miller, also of *Undisclosed*, who, because he was first and foremost in my mind a professor, seemed like the people I worked with every day. But Rabia! Rabia was the fierce advocate I'd first heard introduced in episode one of *Serial*. I always picture her as Sarah Koenig described—surrounded by files, boxes, and stacks of paper, diligently examining each scrap to find the one that would help her client. Colin Miller had vouched for me and given me her contact information, but I still remember the thrill I got when I saw her name in my inbox and her simple message: "Sorry for the delay in getting back to you. When would you like to talk?"

For fans of advocacy-based true crime podcasts, Rabia is a bit of a star. You can buy prayer candles with her image as "Saint Rabia" online, and her name comes up often in podcast social media fan groups. Her book, *Adnan's Story: The Search for Truth and Justice After Serial* (2016), made the *New York Times* bestseller list and won multiple nonfiction book awards. But long before her rise to podcast fame, Chaudry was actively fighting for controversial causes. She worked as an immigration lawyer, courted controversy as a participant in the Muslim Leadership Initiative, and served as a fellow with the New America Foundation and Truman National Security Project (Chaudry, June 24, 2014 & Nov. 21, 2016). She's continued to write about discrimination, particularly against Muslim women, and, in 2017, started another podcast, *The 45th*, with fellow *Undisclosed* host, Susan Simpson, to follow the Trump administration's rhetoric and actions from the perspective of law and policy. All of this is to say, Chaudry is known for being a fearless advocate for what she believes. Frankly, she's kind of a badass.

Chaudry's long history fighting Islamophobia and discrimination played a huge role in her starting the *Undisclosed* podcast. In a June 2020 interview, Chaudry told a journalist that *Serial*'s failure to fully explore the role xenophobia and religious bias played in Syed's case drove her to tell the story in a more nuanced way: "When you have an entire community outraged and you dismiss it, that's deeply problematic" (Williams, June 30, 2020). I felt a little of that outrage from Rabia when I pressed her about criticisms from some listeners about the ethics of her advocacy for Adnan as a long-time family friend. "Somebody has to do that," she told me. "There's not a single wrongful conviction that gets overturned or exoneration that happens without someone. It could be a family member, it could be somebody that read about the case. There has to be one person on the outside who was advocating."

When I began looking for true crime podcasters to interview, I knew I wanted to talk to those who, like Rabia, were unapologetic advocates for their cases. I was also interested in those who covered true crime for other reasons—as journalists, as teachers, or even as fans. The true crime podcast ecosystem is vast, and the podcasts within it range from the serious to the morbid to the comedic to the disturbingly graphic. While there are many popular podcasts that tell crime stories in compelling and informative ways, I was interested mostly in those that tell stories to encourage audiences to act in some way—to advocate, to donate, to help, or to learn more about the criminal justice system. Starting with Colin Miller of *Undisclosed* was an obvious choice.

Podcasters involved with the early *Serial* off-shoots such as *Undisclosed* have received major attention in trade, academic, and popular press. Colin Miller, one part of that show's trio of hosts, is a professor and associate dean at the University of South Carolina. Miller had also been interviewed by an acquaintance, Kelli Boling, whom I had met along with Ian Punett[1] at an academic conference presentation about true crime media. At Boling's suggestion, I mentioned that connection when I contacted Miller for the first time, then used his recommendations to approach other podcasters. This personal connection, along with both of us teaching at southeastern universities at the time, made Miller easier for me to reach than a subject like Sarah Koenig of *Serial* who was likely overwhelmed with press and publicity. I also attempted to recruit participants from different kinds of true crime podcasts,

podcasts with different lengths of production (i.e., both older and very new podcasts), and hosts and producers from different backgrounds (i.e., journalists, lawyers, hobby-podcasters, academics, men, and women). Varying these conditions would provide a "heterogeneous domain," or a more accurate picture of the ecosystem through which to apply theory, and might also allow for unexpected findings. After my initial interview with Miller, I recruited other participants through snowball sampling—that is, they were selected and contacted on the basis of recommendations or introductions from earlier interviewees.

But I'm getting ahead of myself. Before delving into interviews, it was important first to understand the vast ecosystem of true crime podcasts. The podcast industry has incredibly low barriers to entry; essentially, anyone with the capability to record and post audio to the web can produce a podcast. As of April 2018, Apple Podcasts reported over 525,000 active podcasts of multiple genres and over 50 billion episode downloads (Locker, 2018). By 2021, that number had grown to over 2 million podcasts (Winn, December 12, 2021). That statistic does not account for inactive but still accessible podcasts, inactive and inaccessible podcasts, and those housed on other platforms. This makes the task of identifying all of the podcasts in a single genre monumentally challenging, as there is no single database or filter that can possibly "catch" every new entrant to the podcasting market. Before interviewing any podcasters in my niche of interest—those with focuses in criminal justice reform or advocacy—I first wanted to understand just how big the whole population of true crime podcasts had become, as well as to see if the pop-culture narrative that *Serial* had been the real beginning of true crime podcast popularity would hold up under scrutiny.

POPULATION ANALYSIS OF THE TRUE CRIME PODCAST ECOSYSTEM

Population analysis is one of the most widely used methodologies in organizational ecology research (Monge et al., 2011). It has also been used, though far less often, in exploration of social movement industries (SMIs) and sectors (SMSs) (McCarthy & Zald, 2002). Population analysis is useful for discovering the density of populations, as well as evidence of cognitive legitimacy and resource competition. The first parameter I set for my initial exploration was how to treat different podcasts produced by the same organization. At the time, autumn of 2018, podcast networks and mega-producers like Exactly Right, Parcast, and Wondery were in their nascent stages, and the majority of the true crime podcasts I discovered were independent creative projects or stand-alone offerings from traditional media organizations. In order to simplify the analysis, I elected to treat podcasts as single organizations regardless of their producers, similarly to how Lowrey (2012) analyzed health blogs in the early stages of that population's growth. Another way to think of these organizations is as "pre-organizations" (Lowrey, 2012) or "organizations-in-creation" (Katz & Gartner, 1988). That is, new podcasts, whether affiliated with an existing organization or produced by content creators with no intent of ever formally organizing, share characteristics with other types of companies—they compete for resources and audience, negotiate their place in the industry, and exchange knowledge with other producers and organizations. Another rationalization for my choice to treat podcasts as individual pre-organizations is that a major characteristic of the true crime podcast population, its diversity of styles, topics, and formats, matches the findings of other researchers showing that populations inclusive of pre-organizations are more likely to exhibit a range of organizational forms (Katz & Gartner, 1988).

I defined podcasts in my demography as web-based audio productions (Hammersley, 2004), regardless of length or method of distribution (e.g., iTunes, Spotify, creator websites). While some podcasts, such as *Reveal* (The Center for Investigative Reporting, 2013), may also be aired on public radio, the web-based nature of the format puts them in the podcast category regardless of additional avenues of distribution. The term "podcast" may also refer to the entire series of a production, such as all the seasons of *Serial*, or may refer to a single episode (Bottomley, 2015). "Podcast" in this demography refers to the entire production, regardless of the number of episodes.

There were other complications to consider. Beyond the difficulty of finding new podcasts and determining the exact numbers of existing podcasts, genre categories are limited, and often do not include a "true crime" category, instead separating podcasts into larger genres. For example, until July 2019, iTunes, now Apple Podcasts, did not include a True Crime category (Magellan AI, July 30, 2019). This meant that a popular podcast like *My Favorite Murder* would be listed as "comedy" by both Apple podcasts and TopPodcast .com, while other true crime podcasts might be listed as "News & Politics," "Society & Culture," "History" or "Government," or even "Religion and Spirituality." Even after the True Crime category update, when I conducted my updated population demography in 2022, I found nearly seven dozen podcasts that fit the true crime typology in Apple's other categories.

In *Toward a Theory of True Crime Narratives* (2018), Ian Punnett explains why categorizing the true crime genre can be so complicated. He writes, "There is no overarching theory that determines what is and what is not true crime" (Punnett, 2018, p. 2). He explains:

> True crime and journalism share similar historical DNA, but true crime seeks to create emotional sensations regarding criminal events and transport moral

messages and social truths through entertaining narratives rich in detail and color. True crime eschews a slavish, chronological mono-dimensional discourse of news events in favor of narrative forms more commonly associated with fiction. . . . True crime is fact-based but, unlike journalism, it allows for a certain, quantifiable amount of "free play" to enhance the transportive qualities of a fictional narrative, as long as the text's teleology is striving toward nonfiction pedagogy . . . [True crime often has goals] to celebrate or subvert the actions of law enforcement, to express support for victims, and to educate readers/viewers/listeners about the lessons learned from aberrant stories. (Punnett, 2018, p. 93–94)

Punnett conducted a textual analysis of several popular true crime products, including documentary *Making a Murderer*, podcast *Serial*, and book *In Cold Blood*, to identify themes in the genre regardless of media format. His analysis yielded seven themes common across the true crime genre. Not every true crime product will exhibit all seven themes, but all true crime media will exhibit some. The first theme, identified as *teleology*, is shared across the genre and requires that crime narratives be true, or at minimum, purport to be nonfiction. This is different than narratives "based on a true story," as such may still be heavily fictionalized. While true crime stories may sensationalize or misstate facts, there is an effort to portray the story in a factual (even if not objective) way. Other themes which may be present are the seeking of justice (e.g., centering of victims, examining systems); subversion of the status quo (e.g., questioning verdicts or interrogating societal norms); locality (e.g., the geographic place and time of events are vital to the narrative); forensics (e.g., focus on the systematic and scientific elements of criminology); and vocative and folkloric elements (e.g., non-neutral narrators, emotional appeal, or a "lesson" imbedded in the story) (Punnett, 2018). While still limited and unable to completely explain the massive genre that is true crime, Punnett's research is the most thorough attempt at defining and theorizing a definition of "true crime" as a genre. It should be noted here that while this prior literature offers some guidance for setting boundaries of the population, which is useful especially for the initial demographic study, the interviews I conducted with true crime podcasters often challenged these boundary definitions.

English Language Podcasts 2005–2018

Informed by this research and the challenges of locating all true crime podcasts available, I set out on my initial 2018 search to identify a population of true crime podcasts. The process was based on methods used in previous ecological population studies—of computer firms (Kennedy, 2008), blogs (Lowrey, 2012), social networking sites (Weber et al., 2016), fact-checking sites (Lowrey, 2017), and ancillary organizations (Sherrill et al., 2022). I limited my demography to English language podcasts, as those were the ones I could most readily access.² The full process I used to arrive at this first demography can be found in my 2020 publication in *Journalism Practice* (Sherrill, 2020), but I will briefly summarize these early findings.

Through searching a combination of Reddit threads (True Crime Podcasts, 2016), published lists of new true crime podcasts (i.e., Nelson, July 30, 2018; Vulture Editors, November 1, 2018), the Apple iTunes podcast charts, and TopPodcast.com's database, I identified several hundred true crime podcasts. Perhaps the most rewarding find of this search was a Reddit thread linking to a user-created database of true crime podcasts. This database, created by a true crime fan named Erin Hendricks, included many independent and short-lived podcasts unavailable in previous searches. I came to know Hendricks a few months after finding the database when I discovered we were both members of several true crime discussion social media groups where she was lovingly nicknamed "the Fairy Podmother." This database consists of an open, crowd-sourced spreadsheet, moderated by Hendricks (personal communication, February 28, 2019) for accuracy, and includes true crime, true crime parody, supernatural, and conspiracy theory podcasts. After disregarding the non-true crime podcasts, I found nearly 100 additional podcasts through this database. These multiple sources—databases, Reddit threads, and so on—were included in the analysis in order to avoid the pitfalls of over-citing surviving organizations and undercounting early failures (Amburgey & Rao, 1996; Baum, 2000). True crime podcasts of any type, including companion podcasts to true crime television shows and other podcasts, were included. The earliest population entry was December 14, 2005, while the most recent was November 7, 2018.

As I continued to study the growing true crime podcast ecosystem, I began to notice a methodological complication—very new podcasts rarely showed up in any of my searches. This makes sense when algorithms and search engine optimization are considered, but it led me to doubt the validity of my demography. In March 2019, after I had conducted several interviews with true crime podcasters, I repeated the search process for podcasts through November 2018. I did this for several reasons. First, Hendrick's true crime database had gone through several updates and added podcasts not listed in the earlier version. These podcasts included many from the latter half of 2018, as well as the addition of English-language podcasts from New Zealand and South Africa. Second, I had discovered the difficulty in finding very new podcasts unless they had backing and promotion from a podcast network. Podcasts become much easier to find in searches several months after their debuts, and, as I suspected, I was able to identify previously undiscovered podcasts from the later months of the initial search. Finally, based on suggestions from early interview participants, I expanded the original search criteria related to Punnett's (2018) typology to include terrorism, cult crimes, and political and financial crimes. When I updated my search with the new criteria and the cushion of four months of possible publicity for new podcasts, my total for all true crime podcasts that first aired prior to November 28, 2018, was 1,152 podcasts (see table 4.1).

English Language Podcasts through April 2022

Because of the exponential growth of the podcasting medium across genres, as well as the continued pop-culture ubiquity of the true crime genre, I expected the population to have grown exponentially since my first analyses. Even without the cultural salience of the podcast medium, any industry or technology with such low barriers to entry and elasticity of its markets is likely to grow quickly as people discover its utility. With this in mind, I set out to reconduct my demographic analysis through the end of May 2022

Table 4.1   True Crime Podcast Population Demography Conducted March 2019

Source	Search Terms Used/Documents Analyzed	Unique Podcasts Identified
True Crime sub-Reddit list (True Crime Podcasts, 2016)	N/A	169
iTunes Top 100 English language charts July 2011–November 2018[a]	Podcast description terms, including cold case, disappearance, investigate, true crime, and unsolved	26
TopPodcast.com Top 200+ database	"crime," "criminal justice," "conviction," "forensic," "fraud," "incarceration," "innocence," "investigate," "justice," "missing person," "murder," "politics + crime," "prison," "white collar"	355
WhatPods.com true crime podcast recommendations list	N/A	10
True crime podcast sub-Reddit thread posts	811 posts from first post (February 2015) to most recent (March 2019)	94
The True Crime Podcast Database	N/A	466
Additional podcast recommendation lists (i.e, Nelson, July 30, 2018)	Google search terms "true crime" + "podcast"	32
Total true crime podcasts as of November 28, 2018		1,152

[a]The Wayback Machine archive (https://archive.org) was used to search the earliest iTunes charts available; charts include Australia, Canada, New Zealand, South Africa, United Kingdom, and United States.

using additional tools and my new knowledge. One of these new tools was the podcast indexing site Listen Notes (Listen Notes, Inc., 2022), which captures new podcasts almost as soon as they are posted online. Because Listen Notes cross-references with other podcast databases, it was unnecessary to repeat each step from the previous demography.

I also compared my findings with Hendricks's most recent iteration of the True Crime Podcast Database, and I spoke to her again to learn how the database had evolved. She told me that Listen Notes (2022) was her best source, and she kept up with new entries using keyword tracking through a premium subscription account. These accounts allow subscribers to harness the power of the Listen Notes API (a set of programming commands that allow users to search within a set of parameters). Hendricks told me that she currently tracks keywords including "cold case," "cult," "mystery," "unsolved," "homicide," "crime," "missing person," and "serial killer" (Hendricks, personal communication, April 15, 2022). Hendricks also said that she subscribes to the Podnews newsletter and watches the Apple charts for additional podcast foundings. As of April 2022, the True Crime Database included true crime podcasts that debuted before late 2021, and I found 1,179 additional podcasts in Hendrick's database alone.

After this 2022 round of demographic analysis, I am reasonably confident that my sample of 4,611 unique true crime podcasts (both active and inactive) is a reliable—though almost certainly incomplete—representation of the population (see *Appendix: True Crime Podcasts 2005–2022* and table 4.2).

Population Analysis and Density

While the sheer number of true crime podcasts is fascinating in itself, these numbers alone don't tell us much about the health of the population. In order to better understand the development of true crime podcasting since the time of the earliest podcast identified, January 1, 2005, to the most recent, May 29, 2022, I calculated population density over time to look for patterns.

In order to calculate population density, births or "foundings" were recorded for each podcast as the date of the first episode. Mortalities or "deaths" were calculated as podcasts that had either announced they were ending or who had not posted an episode in six months or more (unless there was an announced date for the next episode or season to debut). These births and deaths are shown in figure 4.1.

Once the census was complete and births and mortalities were recorded, the growth and density of the population were calculated and graphed. Density was calculated by recording cumulative frequency of entries minus cumulative mortalities per six-month interval (see figure 4.2).

It is important to note one major clarification to the density illustrations in figure 4.2. Around 2016, limited series podcasts began to emerge en

Table 4.2   True Crime Podcast Population Demography 2005–2022

Source	Search Terms Used/Documents Analyzed	Unique Podcasts Identified
Previous demography (see table 4.1)	N/A	1,152
Apple Top Podcast charts (formerly iTunes)	Podcast descriptions related to cold case, criminal justice system, cult, disappearance, incarceration, innocence, investigate, justice, missing person, murder, political crime, prison, terrorist crimes, and true crime	239
The True Crime Podcast Database	N/A	1,179
Listen Notes API	"crime," "criminal justice," "conviction," "forensic," "homicide," "incarceration," "innocence," "investigate," "justice," "missing person," "murder," "mystery," "prison," "serial killer," "true crime."	2,041
Total true crime podcasts as of April 18, 2022		4,611

Source: Created by author.

masse. These are podcasts, usually produced by legacy media outlets or, more recently, podcast networks like Wondery, that are intended to cover a particular case or topic in-depth for a limited run (usually between 4 and 20 episodes). Since these podcasts are created to last for a limited time only, the ends of their runs are not accurately categorized as "mortalities" or organizational failures. Instead, these limited series podcasts were counted only as foundings, as their existence adds to the total number of podcasts in the genre. The growth of these limited series podcasts is illustrated in figure 4.3.

These demographic illustrations offer insight into several trends in the population and also raise some additional questions. First, it is clear that the population's growth was slow but steady until the second interval of 2015, when podcast foundings began to rise steeply. Very few true crime podcasts were founded in the early intervals, ranging from 0 to 11 foundings per interval from January 2005 to December 2012. Between July 2012 and June 2014, foundings slowly began to tick up, ranging from 4 to 30 foundings per interval. In mid-2014, several technological innovations in podcasting, discussed in more detail in the next chapter, emerged. The true crime podcast population began to grow exponentially at this point, with double-digit numbers of podcasts being founded in each interval from January 2013 to December 2015. By June 2016, hundreds of true crime podcasts were being founded in each interval, from 142 from January to June 2016 to peaking at 764 in January to June 2019. In addition to the technological advances and the notoriety

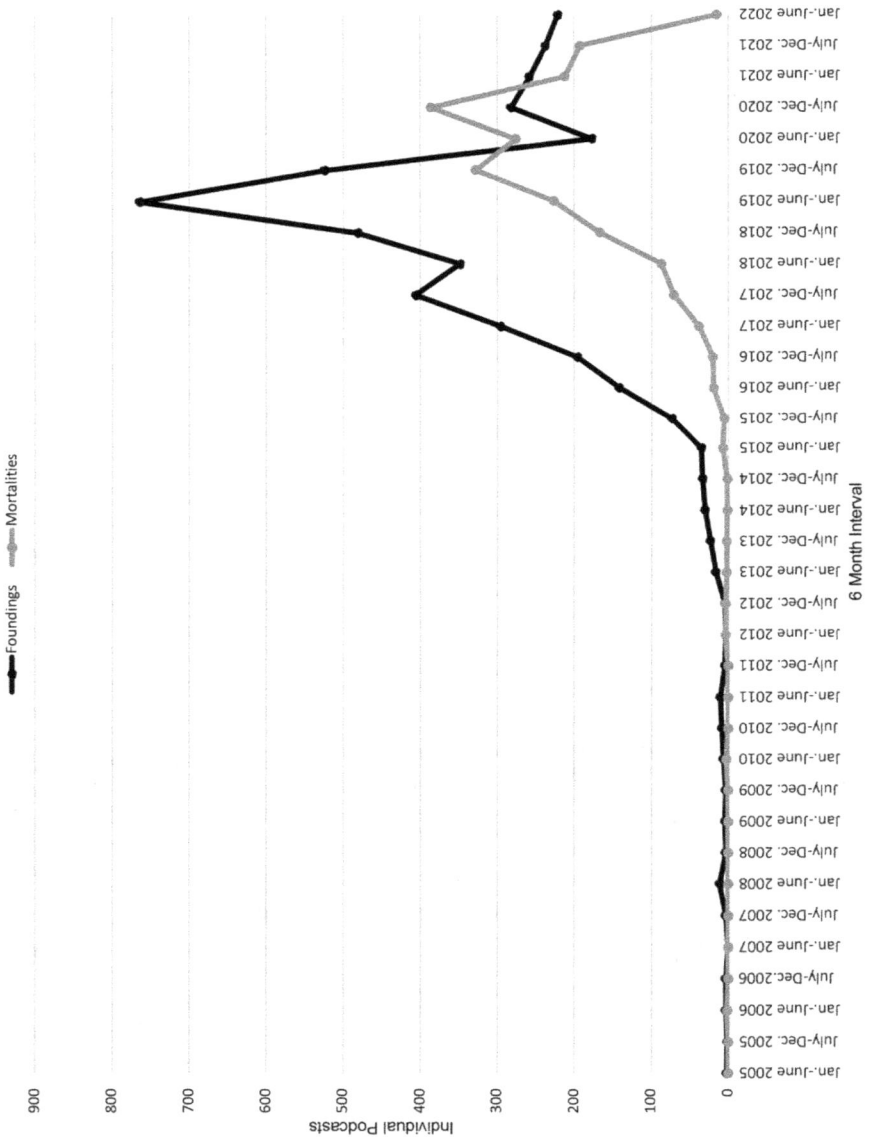

Figure 4.1   True Crime Podcast Ecosystem 2005–2022 Foundings and Mortalities.

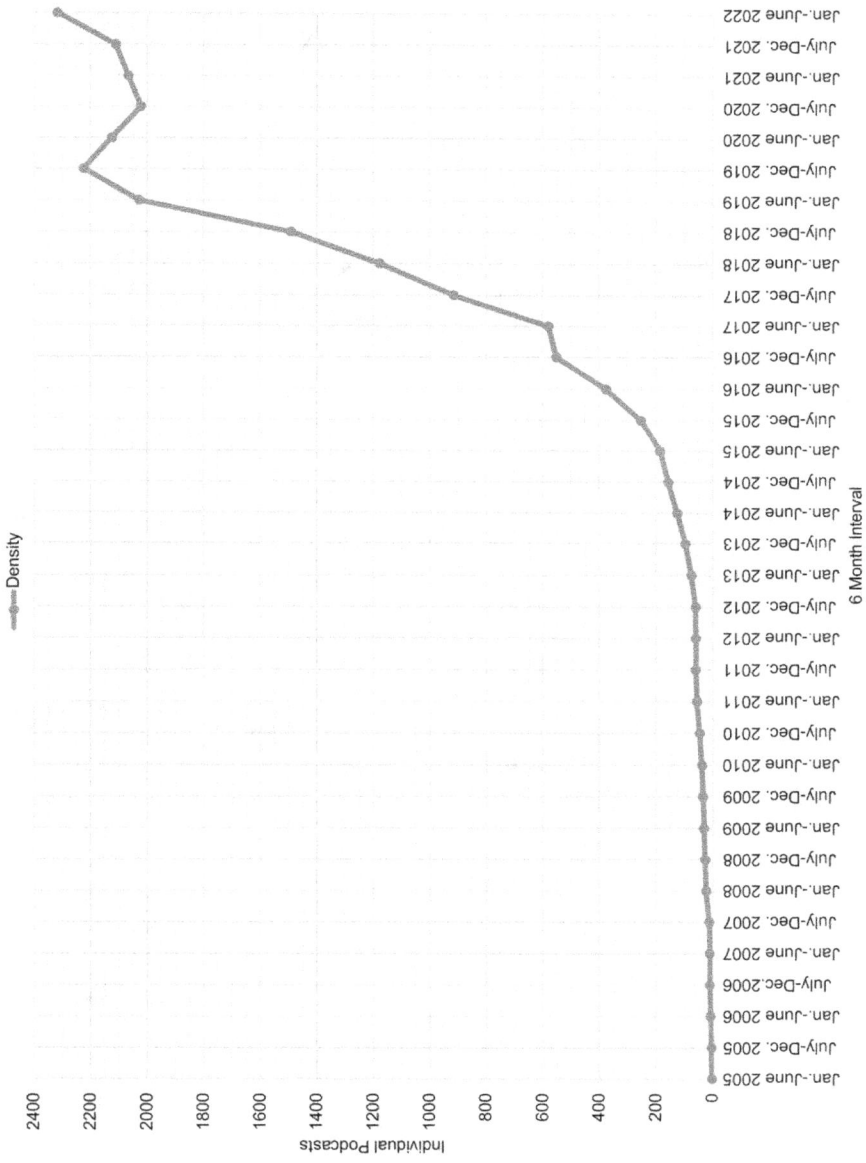

Figure 4.2 True Crime Podcast Ecosystem 2005–2022 Density.

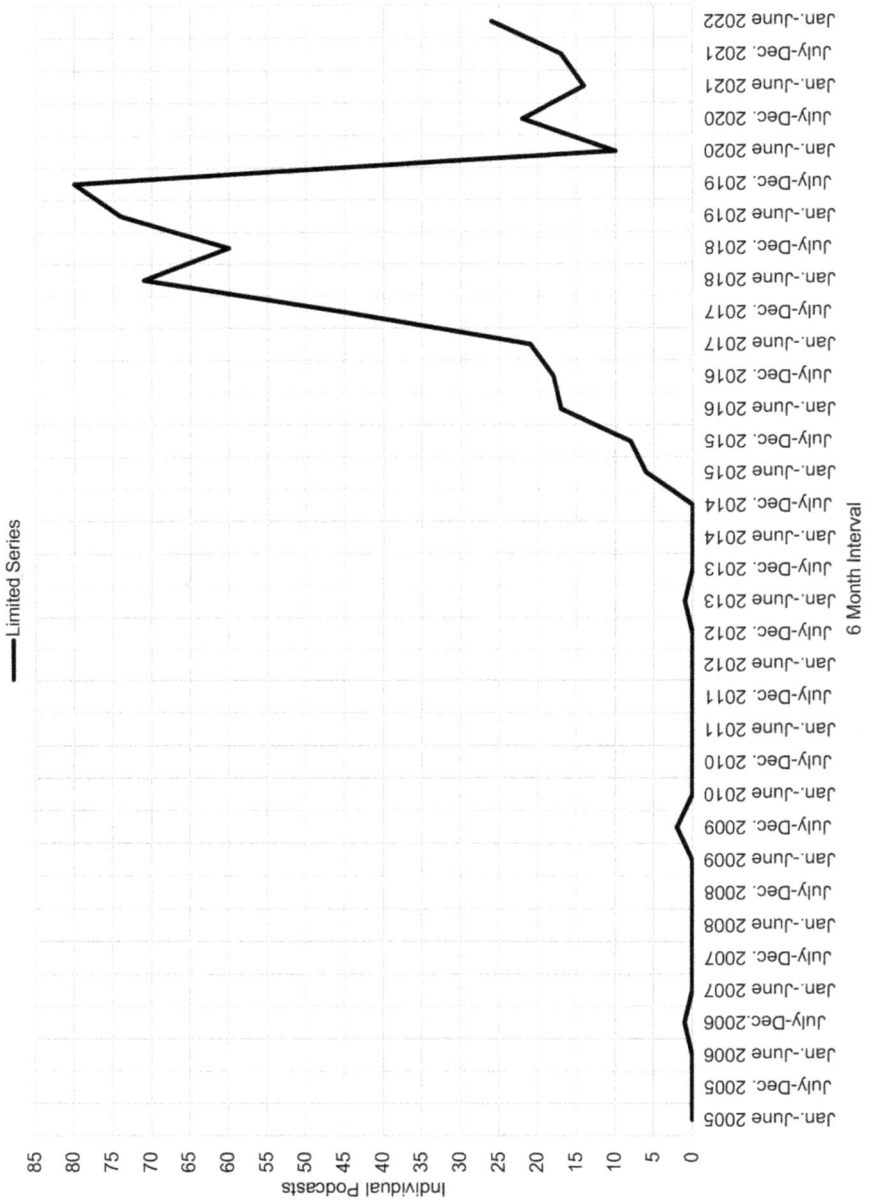

Figure 4.3   True Crime Podcast Ecosystem 2005–2022 Limited Series Podcasts.

brought to the medium by *Serial*, it's possible that another disruption may have influenced the explosive growth of true crime podcasts between 2017 and 2019—the March 2017 release of *S-Town*, one of the few true crime podcasts to achieved notoriety comparable to *Serial*. The limited series, produced by several individuals who had also worked on *Serial*, told the story of a gay man in rural Alabama and explored issues of sexuality, crime, mental illness, and small-town politics. While *S-Town* has faced its share of criticism, including claims that it is "a stunning podcast [that] probably shouldn't have been made" (Romano, April 1, 2017) based on ethical and privacy issues, it drew in listeners who were looking for the next *Serial* and open to a story less focused on murder and the legal process.

As the foundings of podcasts continued to surge, so did mortalities. This is logical when the sheer volume of podcasts is considered. While creators may have been inspired by podcasts like *Serial* and *S-Town*, actually producing and editing content on a recurring basis likely proved more challenging than expected. Add to this the fact that podcast advertising was still nascent in this period, so many independent podcasters were likely spending large amounts of money and time to see very little return on investment. Foundings remained steady until the first interval of 2020 or roughly the start of the COVID-19 pandemic. In both intervals of 2020, mortalities vastly outpaced foundings, leading to the first drop in density since the emergence of the population. Limited series podcast foundings also dropped significantly in 2020.

There are several factors likely at play in this period. First, the COVID-19 pandemic and lockdowns throughout the world affected creators' ability to investigate, collaborate, and monetize, both slowing population growth and accelerating podcast failures. Beyond the drop in births and rise in mortalities, I found other hints of the pandemic's effects when looking at episode dates for podcasts in 2020 and 2021. Multiple podcasts mentioned COVID-19–related schedule disruptions, and several podcasts posted notices that a host or producer had died from the virus. This in line with Broussard's et al. (2022) findings for podcasts in the sports genre during 2020—producers faced challenges from losing listeners who regularly consumed episodes while commuting to the toll of the pandemic on their own mental health. It is likely true crime podcasters faced the same challenges, perhaps compounded by the already dark content of their podcasts. This theory is bolstered by the ratio of foundings and mortalities in 2021 and 2022—foundings have outpaced mortalities, and density is back above pre-pandemic levels.

A second possible explanation is that this time period may have begun to reflect the effect of liabilities of adolescence (Baum, 2000) on the population. Essentially, after periods of exponential growth, the population may have begun to stabilize, with older, more established organizations continuing to thrive and new organizations still being formed, but with younger organizations floundering to find resources and their own specialist identities. Only time will tell if this is the case. Finally, it is possible that some of this slow in growth is the result of methodological challenges. Much like my earlier demography, even with new tools like the Listen Notes API, it is possible that I missed many newer population entrants. As said before, only time and additional demographic analysis will make this clear.

INTERVIEWING THE PODCASTERS

While the population analysis can tell us a great deal about trends and growth in the true crime podcast ecosystem, understanding how those trends have been utilized to spread knowledge about social causes required actually talking to the people involved in the industry. For this purpose, I elected to conduct in-depth, directed qualitative interviews. While these conversations were a welcome excuse to chat about podcasts with other true crime lovers, I wanted to ensure that my findings would be theoretically sound.

Methodology and Participant Recruitment

The method of directed qualitative interviews involves crafting interview questions around a set of themes informed by theory (Creswell, 2014). It is both deductive, as it is guided by the implications of the known theory, and inductive, as the possibility of emergent themes or unexpected theoretical implications is left open (Kvale, 2007). In addition to emergent themes, these kinds of interviews may reveal disconfirming evidence for theoretical concepts. In-depth interviews have been used by scholars of ecology (e.g., Raff, 2000; Lowrey, 2012), social movement theories (SMTs) (e.g., Kurzman, 1996), and in synthesis research (e.g., Carroll & Hackett, 2006).

I created an interview protocol with questions guided by prior literature. I also looked to my demographic analysis—the map of the growth of the true crime podcast industry over time—as well as to my prior content analyses showing evidence of changing true crime podcast legitimacy (Sherrill, 2020) to form my questions and codebook. I obtained institutional review board approval prior to recruiting interviewees, including approval for interviewees to consent to non-anonymized reporting of my findings. I decided early in my process that I did not want to do anonymous interviews. Everyone I spoke to is a public figure who has produced, recorded, or been involved with the public dissemination of these podcasts, therefore their name is already associated with the work and in the public eye. I also knew that true crime podcast fans would instantly identify most of these podcasters based on even vague descriptions. In a few instances, interviewees shared sensitive but useful information (such as comments about behind-the-scenes harassment or unethical behavior from others in the podcast community); in those cases, I've presented their comments anonymously (see table 4.3).

I used a *phenomenological* approach—that is, one that seeks to better explain or contextualize aspects of a "central phenomenon" and to "describe the essence of the experience" involved in said phenomenon (Creswell, 2007, p. 89). I recruited participants *purposively* (Creswell, 2007; Plano Clark & Creswell, 2008) based on their involvement in the production of selected true crime podcasts. Phenomenological studies may use as few participants

Table 4.3   Interview Participants

Participant	Role	Podcast(s)	Affiliation
Chip Brantley	Co-host	*White Lies*[a]	NPR
Rabia Chaudry	Co-host	*Undisclosed*[c]	Independent
	Co-host	*The 45th*[b]	
	Host	*Nighty Night*[b]	
	Host	*The Hidden Djinn*[b]	
Sarah Delia	Host	*She Says*[a]	WFAE Charlotte
	Host	*Still Here*[b]	
Samara Freemark	Producer	*In the Dark*[c]	APM and Minnesota Public Radio
Scott Fuller	Host	*Frozen Truth*[a]	Independent
	Host	*What Happened to Jodi?*[a]	10Cast Network
	Host	*FindJodi*	
	Host	*Status: Pending*	
	Host	*Dead & Gone in Wyoming*	
		The True Crime Files	
Amber Hunt	Host	*Accused*	Cincinnati Enquirer
	Host	*Aftermath*[a]	Obsessed Network
	Host	*Crimes of the Centuries*	
Colin Miller	Co-host	*Undisclosed*[c]	Independent
Mike Morford	Co-host	*Criminology*	Independent
	Co-host	*The Murder in My Family*	
		Crimesphere[c]	
Steven Pacheco	Host	*Trace Evidence*	Independent
Bill Rankin	Host	*Breakdown*	Atlanta Journal Constitution
Jami Rice	Host	*Murderish*	Independent
	Co-host	*Judgey & Juryish*	iHeartPodcasts
	Co-host	*Dirty Money Moves*	
Ottavia Zappala	Host	*Missing Alissa*[a]	Independent

Note: a = limited series; b = not true crime; c = mortality.
Source: Created by author.

as one (Dukes, 1984) and as many as 325 (Polkinghorne, 1989), but more commonly, including 10–20 subjects (Creswell, 2007). After contacting over 2 dozen podcasters, 12 agreed to an interview. Additionally, I sent an email questionnaire to participants prior to the interviews both for background information and to encourage them to begin thinking about concepts they might want to share during the interview (e.g., see Guest et al., 2013; Meho, 2006). This questionnaire was not a survey but rather an extension of the interview, allowing participants time to give detailed responses to conceptual questions such as "How would you define true crime as a genre?" The questionnaire answers were coded along with interviews, and those answers are included in the interview analysis.

In contrast to quantitative reliability and validity, qualitative research is focused not on generalizability of findings but rather on employing consistent strategies across the research project (Creswell, 2007, 2014). Other researchers (e.g., Eisner, 1991; Lincoln & Guba, 1985) prefer terminology such as "credibility" or "trustworthiness." In either case, establishing validity for qualitative findings involves a process of transparency and rigor on the part of the researcher. (Creswell, 2007). I performed my analysis using the technique described by Creswell (2014) for directed qualitative interviews. I first read through the transcripts without making any coding notes to get a holistic view of the material in the interviews. I made general notes at this stage, identifying interesting quotes and emerging themes. Next, using the codebook as a guide, I coded the interviews by identifying themes line by line, using margin notes to mark themes and interesting quotations. I also noted emergent themes and disconfirming information.

I also asked one interview participant, Brantley, to look over one of my coded transcripts as a "member check." Member checks or "member validation" is done to ensure the research has "verisimilitude" for those involved in the phenomenon (Creswell, 2007, 2014; Kvale, 2007); that is, does the understanding of the researcher match the understanding of those involved in a phenomenon? A peer debriefer was also asked to read the analysis of three interviews and offer feedback. I integrated suggestions from both the member check and peer debrief into the final round of analysis.

The Podcasters

The podcasters I interviewed represent a range of experiences and voices. Because my focus was on the criminal justice reform movement in the United States, I only spoke to U.S.–based podcasters.[3] I specifically chose podcasters with "goal-oriented" podcasts; there are many types of true crime podcasts in the ecosystem, but I was not interested in true crime comedy or serial killer stories or conspiracy theories. Instead, I wanted to understand how the producers whose work has real-life effects on real cases understood their place in that ecosystem. My interviewees included:

Chip Brantley of *White Lies.* Chip Brantley co-hosts the podcast with Andrew Beck Grace, and both hosts are journalists and teach podcasting and journalism at the college level. At the time I spoke to Brantley, his reporting was complete, but the podcast was still in pre-production. The podcast addresses topics ranging from systemic racism to public memory to the lingering legacy of Civil Rights era violence on a small town's residents. *White Lies* was a finalist for the 2020 Pulitzer Price for Audio Recording (Pulitzer, May 14, 2019).

Rabia Chaudry and Colin Miller of *Undisclosed.* Rabia and Colin co-host the *Undisclosed* podcast along with Susan Simpson. All three hosts are lawyers, and the podcast reflects their experiences: it is incredibly detailed and information dense, and listeners are as likely to learn the intricacies of precedent and habeas petitions as they are to hear details of a crime scene. On March 24, 2022, *Undisclosed* posted its final episode, titled "It's a Wrap." Over the course of their run, the podcast covered 24 cases and offered hope to multiple wrongly convicted defendants. In late 2022, after the release of Adnan Syed and new state's evidence in Hae Min Lee's murder, *Undisclosed* announced they would return with new episodes.

Sarah Delia of *She Says.* Sarah Delia is an Edward R. Murrow award-winning radio journalist based in North Carolina. She began the *She Says* podcast after covering a 2015 sexual assault. As Delia worked with the victim, she saw first-hand the hurdles that victims face in finding justice—discrimination because of perceived "lifestyle" factors, misogyny, police apathy, and lack of belief from the public despite the rise of #MeToo—and was inspired to chronicle how victims of sexual crimes were treated by the system. *She Says* has since released a second season focused on sexual abuse within the Catholic Diocese of Charlotte.

Samara Freemark of *In the Dark.* Freemark is the producer of *In the Dark,* an investigative journalism podcast from American Public Media and Minnesota Public Radio that has won multiple awards for investigative journalism, including two Peabody Awards. The show is hosted by journalist Madeleine Baran, and, in its second season, became a part of a high-profile U.S. Supreme Court case, *Flowers v. Mississippi. In the Dark* focused on criminal justice issues beginning in season one as it covered the 1989 murder of Jacob Wetterling, including how seriously allegations of molestation are taken, lack of cooperation between law enforcement agencies, and how local officials are held accountable to the public. In season two, the team covered the case of Curtis Flowers, a Black Mississippi man who spent 23 years in jail while being tried six times for the same crime. In the course of their reporting, *In the Dark* assembled massive amounts of data on race and jury selection. This data was vital to Flowers's victory in the U.S. Supreme Court. *In the Dark* was cancelled by American Public Media in 2022, leading to widespread criticism of the company's decision (Nesterak, July 6, 2022).

Scott Fuller of *Frozen Truth*. Scott Fuller is a podcast veteran, having worked in the medium since 2003. He has been the head of programming for multiple U.S. radio stations, and launched the eight-episode true crime podcast *What Happened to Jodie?* on December 4, 2017. *Frozen Truth* covers Fuller's investigations of several missing person cold cases. In February 2021, Fuller announced a commitment to continuing to cover lesser-known missing persons and began season four of *Frozen Truth*. Fuller also hosts *FindJodi*, a podcast covering the continued investigation of the 1995 disappearance of television news anchor Jodi Huisentruit with the advocacy group FindJodi.com, and *Status: Pending*, a podcast about unsolved cases.

Amber Hunt of *Accused*. Amber Hunt is a long-time crime reporter and journalism instructor, as well as the coauthor of several histories and true crime books. *Accused*, produced by the *Cincinnati Enquirer* and *USA Today* and hosted by Hunt, won the 2018 Pulitzer Price for local reporting. Season one of the podcast covered the 1978 murder of Elizabeth Andes, and the subsequent civil and criminal trials of her boyfriend, Bob Young, who alleged being forced to confess under coercive interrogation. *Accused* covered the details of the case, presented possible alternative suspects in the killing, and investigated the role that improper interrogation and investigation techniques play in cold cases and wrongful convictions. The podcast has since released four seasons, covering wrongful convictions, mysterious deaths, and police misconduct.

Mike "Morf" Morford of *Criminology*. Mike Morford is a true crime jack-of-all-trades. He became known as "True Crime Guy" through his blog and is known as an expert on the Zodiac and Golden State Killer cases. He has hosted or co-hosted multiple true crime podcasts, including *Crimesphere*, *The Murder in My Family*, *3 Men and a Mystery*, and *Zodiac Speaking*, and has been a guest on many episodes of other true crime podcasts. *Criminology* is set apart from many episodic true crime podcasts because of its serious tone and careful attention to survivors and victims' families.

Steven Pacheco of *Trace Evidence*. Steven Pacheco was one of the podcasters I spoke to who was not a professional journalist, lawyer, or crime writer. Instead, his podcast, *Trace Evidence*, was created out of his own true crime fandom and desire to shed light on unsolved cases with empathy toward the families and friends of the missing. Many of the cases Pacheco covers have received renewed attention, including increased rewards, identifications of unknown victims, arrests of suspects, and, in a few cases, the crimes have been solved.

Bill Rankin of *Breakdown.* The *Breakdown* podcast is the brainchild of long-time court reporter for the *Atlanta Journal Constitution*, Bill Rankin. Inspired by *Serial*, Rankin first covered the 2007 arson and murder conviction of Justin Ross Chapman in Bremen, GA. Rankin focused on the systemic issues at play in the case, including class disparity and Georgia's overloaded public defender system. The renewed interest in the case led to pro bono representation for Chapman and his eventual release from prison. Subsequent seasons of *Breakdown*, with Rankin as well as other hosts, have continued to explore criminal justice issues in Georgia in detail, ranging from police responses to mental health crises, jury selection and instruction, hate crimes prosecution, and the role true crime podcasts may play in influencing jury pools. *Breakdown*'s sixth season was awarded the American Bar Association's Silver Gavel Award.

Jami Rice of *Murderish.* *Murderish* is another independent podcast produced by a true crime fan, Jami Rice, who started the podcast while working as a real estate broker. Rice was inspired to begin the podcast after serving as the jury foreman in a 2017 murder trial. Her podcast covers murders, missing persons, and features interviews with high-profile true crime experts. In 2022, *Murderish* released two episodes about the murder of Hae Min Lee, the victim at the center of *Serial*'s case.

Ottavia Zappala of *Missing Alissa.* Zappala is a reporter with a background in both journalism and criminology. *Missing Alissa* covers the missing person case of Alissa Turney, a 17-year-old who disappeared in Phoenix, AZ, in 2001. Zappala reinvestigated the case, working with Alissa's younger sister, Sarah (now also a true crime podcaster), to make a case that Alissa was not a runaway but was instead a likely victim of her stepfather. While Sarah Turney's efforts, including a viral TikTok campaign, later became the driving force in the arrest and charging of Michael Turney in 2020, *Missing Alissa* turned up the investigative heat in the cold case. Zappala has continued to work as a journalist and appear as a guest on other true crime podcasts.

TRUE CRIME PODCASTS AS ENTERTAINMENT, JOURNALISM, AND ADVOCACY

In the next few chapters, the interviewees' insights are presented. During our conversations, I heard podcasters talk about their perceptions of the ecosystem's growth, and I'll show how these perceptions allowed me to better understand the density spikes in the population analysis. The interviews also clarified how podcasters—even those driven primarily by journalistic or advocacy goals—think about their shows as maintenance organizations with resource needs. There's also evidence of these podcaster's awareness of their advocacy potential, even for those who feel constrained by journalistic norms of objectivity. I'll also share how these podcasters, many of them true crime fans themselves, interpret and grapple with true crime's less savory side.

So, like any good true crime storyteller, now it's time for me to let you see the evidence for yourself.

NOTES

1. Kelli Boling is the author of several academic articles about true crime podcasting and is a journalism professor. Ian Punnett is an academic and radio broadcaster and the author of *Toward a Theory of True Crime Narratives*.

2. Apple now ranks international true crime podcasts in multiple countries where English is not the dominant language, including Spain, Brazil, Turkey, Thailand, Czech Republic, Mauritius, Malta, Bulgaria, Oman, and China. These charts also include English-language mega-hits, such as *My Favorite Murder*, which ranks in the Top Twenty true crime podcasts on several international charts. Countries like South Korea and Spain have podcast adoption rates higher than or equal to the United States, United Kingdom, and Canada (Moran, 2022).

3. As true crime podcasts have grown in popularity, international examples of podcasts focused on criminal justice reform topics have also emerged. The Canadian Broadcast Corporation has produced many of these podcasts, including *Someone Knows Something*, a deep dive into unsolved and missing person cases, and *Missing and Murdered*. *Missing and Murdered*, by journalist Connie Walker, focuses on the stories of missing indigenous women in Canada and the United States, and its second season, *Finding Cleo*, is often mentioned in true crime podcast fan groups as one of the best in the genre. *West Cork*, the first serial true crime podcast from Audible, covered the murder of a French woman in a small Irish village, and has been compared to the Georgia-based *Up and Vanished* but with "more professionalism and polish" (Hutchins & Hutchins, February 8, 2018). The Ireland and United Kingdom–based hosts of *West Cork* explore many of the issues we see in U.S.-based true crime—questionable investigative techniques, the unreliability of witness testimony, gender and domestic violence, and police misconduct. Australian newspaper, *The Sydney Morning Herald*, called *West Cork* "one of the greatest true crime podcasts since *Serial*" (Divola, June 17, 2021). Australian true crime podcasts have had their own moments in the spotlight. *The Teacher's Pet*, from *The Australian* newspaper, reinvestigated the case of the missing wife of a former rugby star, uncovering evidence along the way of sexual abuse in Australian schools. Much like the *Breakdown* podcast in the United States, *The Teacher's Pet* became a part of its subject's trial in 2019 when the courts cited it as overly prejudicial and requested the feed be made "temporarily unavailable" (Crampton, Oct. 6, 2020). Other Australian podcasts, like *Bowraville* or *Zealot*, have tackled complicated social issues in true crime, like the role racism plays in the criminal justice system or how many cult crimes never see justice because

of the cover of religious belief. *SKRIM*, a Scandinavian true crime podcast with two Norwegian hosts, has covered police murders of Black citizens, similarly to many of the U.S. criminal justice reform focused podcasts. True crime podcasts from India, South Africa, the Philippines, Spain, Singapore, Brazil, and China have all also had international success. As the international true crime podcast population continues to grow, I expect to see more explorations of non-English language true crime as catalysts for social change.

Chapter 5

Ecology and Podcasts as Maintenance Organizations

Everybody's got a podcast, for better or worse.

—*Rabia Chaudry*

Categorizing all of the formats and focuses or "organizational forms" (i.e., Polos et al., 2002) of podcasts in the true crime ecosystem would be, to put it mildly, quite an undertaking. In a randomly selected 100 of the podcasts in my demography, there are podcasts related to sports crimes, criminal women, unsolved and missing persons cases, political crimes, famous crimes, cult-related crimes, and investigative journalism. Some podcasts are dedicated to a single victim or perpetrator, others are companion podcasts to true crime television shows, single-story-per-episode podcasts, or talk show–style podcasts with occasional true crime tangents or episodes. Others can be categorized by the identities of their hosts or target audience. There are podcasts by detectives, medical professionals, first responders, lawyers, professors, and high school teachers. There are multiple examples of podcasts centered on queer identities, with punny names like *Be Gay, True Crime*, or *A Crime Most Queer*. There's an entire sub-genre of true crime podcasts with alcoholic drinks or drugs in their titles like *The Murder and Wine Club*; *Wine & Punishment*; *Weed, Wine, and True Crime*; *Whiskey Dicks and Jane*; *Case Closed, Beers Open*; and *Bud Trials*, just to name a few. And there are many, many true crime podcasts hosted by comedians. There seems to be some kind of true crime podcast for almost any kind of true crime fan.

This diversity of forms and target audiences exemplifies the role of organizational identification and speciation (i.e., Weber, 2017) in the true crime ecosystem, just two of the organizational ecology concepts at play in how populations of organizations relate to one another. This population can be characterized by many of the concepts of organizational ecology, and so this paradigm is useful for better understanding both this media format and how ecology theory can be applied to digital media forms.

The larger genre of true crime shapes both the niche these podcasts occupy, as well as their perceived organizational form, identity, and legitimacy (Barton, 2009; Dimmick, 2003; Lowrey, 2012). As the popularity of true crime podcasts continues to grow, we are also able to see how these organizations co-opt and confer legitimacy. Even a cursory analysis of popular media demonstrates this process. While the true crime genre was associated with "sleaziness" or poor journalism for much of the twentieth century, *Serial*'s winning of the Peabody Award signaled a cultural acceptance of true crime as a legitimate form for both entertainment and journalism (Punnett, 2018). Despite the popularity of the genre over time (i.e., Capote, 1966) crime entertainment was still viewed as somewhat prurient or not as "real" journalism. By contrast, *Serial* was a creation of established, respected public radio organizations, and its offspring were able to gain legitimacy from their symbolic and associational ties with the mega-hit. Later entrants to the population, like *Undisclosed*, co-opted *Serial*'s popularity to grow their own audiences and mobilize resources. When *Truth & Justice* began, its host shared information with *Undisclosed*, gaining legitimacy through inter-organizational transaction of resources. I found even more evidence of these ecological processes in my content analysis of newspaper articles about true crime podcasts (Sherrill, 2020). As journalists described true crime podcasts, they often compared the podcasts to "accepted" true crime media forms: documentaries, books, movies, and even plays. Many of these articles also referenced other more successful podcasts, such as *Serial* and *My Favorite Murder*, providing evidence of isomorphism in the growing population.

My interviews with the podcasters offer more illustrations of the concepts of organizational ecology, including niche development, environmental opportunities and constraints, negotiation of organizational form and identity, competition, density, disruption, and legitimacy. These podcasters—regardless of their backgrounds, affiliations, or goals—recognized the maintenance needs of their organizations, including audience and financial resources. They told me about their experiences with building legitimacy and the negotiation of ethical boundaries inherent in covering such sensitive topics. Their insights into the industry allowed me to more fully conceptualize the true crime podcast population, as well as to better situate *Serial* as both a product of and catalyst for explosive true crime media growth.

TYPIFICATION OF TRUE CRIME PODCASTS

I began each interview by asking the podcasters to describe their podcasts in their own words. This was important to me, both to make sure I characterized their work as they saw it, as well as to use these descriptions as a starting point for exploring ecological concepts of niche, isomorphism in the population, organizational form and identity, and the goal orientations addressed in the next chapter. There is evidence of both specialization and shared characteristics in these descriptions, as well as references to Punnett's (2018) true crime themes, including teleology, seeking justice, subversion of the status quo, forensics, and vocative elements.

- Chip Brantley (*White Lies*). "It is an investigative podcast about a Civil Rights cold case. . . . We've always thought of it as sort of an audio documentary about a Civil Rights cold case that touches on sort of broader themes of race in America. . . . As much about . . . the stories we tell ourselves as it is about solving the crime."
- Rabia Chaudry (*Undisclosed*). "Investigative true crime wrongful conviction podcast. . . . The point is not just to talk about the story but to really investigate the case . . . It's very, very involved, it's very detailed, it's pretty gritty."
- Sarah Delia (*She Says*). "It's about the criminal justice system and how it works. . . . Our intention was just telling her story, but also talking to a lot of experts along the way to help us explain to people how this really archaic system functions or it doesn't."
- Samara Freemark (*In the Dark*). "We are not *necessarily* a criminal justice podcast, like we can do work later that is in a different field, but the core of what we do is investigative journalism and that's always been the case. . . . We don't think of ourselves as much as a true crime podcast as a criminal justice podcast."
- Scott Fuller (*Frozen Truth*). "What I try to do is tell a story. It's the story of a missing person, and that's been the case for all three seasons, but that wasn't necessarily the original intention. . . . My purpose was to try and solve the mystery . . . I'm trying to tell a story more so than produce an *In Cold Blood* kind of true crime podcast."
- Amber Hunt (*Accused*). "We're an investigative podcast that focuses on unsolved murders."
- Colin Miller (*Undisclosed*). "We are not a journalism podcast, where I think a lot of the true crime podcasts are produced by people with a journalism background. We're three attorneys who are discussing not only the narrative but also bringing our legal insight. . . . We're just really digging

into the legal minutiae and trying to find ways to use these cases to find relief for the people we're dealing with but also to explain legal concepts to our listeners."

- Mike Morford (*Criminology*). "100% serious, very serious . . . It's a very serious type podcast, not a lot of banter. Not a lot of small talk. We've pretty much very to the point in that podcast."
- Steven Pacheco (*Trace Evidence*). "My podcast focuses on only the unsolved cases in true crime . . . I guess what differentiates my podcast from other true crime is that I try and put a lot more focus on the victim."
- Bill Rankin (*Breakdown*). "Like I've done all my journalism career, I'm just trying to tell a story in an engaging and compelling way . . . that hopefully gives people a better understanding of the criminal justice system."
- Jami Rice (*Murderish*). "*Murderish* is a true crime podcast. . . . It's a mixed bag podcast, in that I have some storytelling episodes, I have some interviews, but it's all related to true crime . . . I don't cover missing persons cases where there's no conclusion."
- Ottavia Zappala (*Missing Alissa*). "We call it a narration, like longform type of podcast. . . . It's not just a story, it's an investigation."

These descriptions illustrate not only the diversity of forms within the true crime podcast niche but also show the commonalities between many of these podcasters, such as a desire to teach listeners about the criminal justice system and to tell engaging stories.

COMMUNITY AND POPULATION

While their initial descriptions of the individual podcast types were varied, all participants agreed that they were in some way attached to the true crime podcast population. Several interviewees also noted the population's place within larger ecological communities. Nearly every interviewee compared true crime podcasts to other kinds of true crime media, including examples such as Netflix's *The Keepers* documentary and Capote's *In Cold Blood*. This is in line with quantitative findings from my prior research which show that news media also compare true crime podcasts to other true crime media in 61% of the articles analyzed (Sherrill, 2020). Several participants also noted that true crime podcasts are a part of the larger general podcast community. Both Chaudry and Rankin specifically noted the emerging population of political podcasts as connected to (and often overlapping with) the true crime population. This comparison isn't surprising considering the strong ties between political processes and criminal justice policy.

Niche, Isomorphism, and Heterogeneity

In organizational ecology, niches include both the environmental conditions required for populations to grow as well as the role of the population in a larger community (Dimmick, 2003; Hannan & Freeman, 1989). Within niches, populations may share "clusters of features," and population members may exhibit both *isomorphism*, or similarity, as well as some *heterogeneity*, or differentiation (Carroll, 1985; Weber, 2017). While all the podcasters acknowledged being a part of true crime media definitionally, they each described their podcasts as a specific type or sub-niche. Several podcasters used terms such as "shades of true crime," "subgenres," and "segments" to describe the population. Rankin said: "There's so many. Too many? And they're from all shapes and sizes." Many podcasters explicitly defined their podcasts as unique. For example, Zappala stated, "I think my model is different than the majority of podcasts," also saying of many other true crime hosts, "They're not journalists." Others differentiated themselves by production style. Fuller described his "public radio style" of going on location to record as rare among independent podcasts, while Freemark pointed out that devoting the resources of an entire professional investigative team to a serialized podcast is done by few other podcasts. Others, like Chaudry, noted that the specific goals of their podcasts (in her case, working specifically to correct wrongful conviction cases) separate them from the vast majority of true crime shows. Others admitted they were very similar to other podcasts but pointed out differentiating characteristics, such as *only* doing unsolved cases (like Pacheco) or *refusing* to do unsolved cases (like Rice). Morford summarized the variation by saying, "That's the thing about podcasts—there's so many different kinds of styles for different listeners."

While all of the podcasters were able to point out some kind of competitive or brand differentiation for their individual shows, interviewees as a whole indicated that there were substantial similarities across the population and that this similarity plays at least some role in their own productions. Often this is couched in terms of "inspiration" rather than direct mimicry. *Serial* was most often mentioned, though several podcasters also noted Freemark's show, *In the Dark*, as an inspiration. Rankin noted that his show began as an explicit desire by his editor to produce a *Serial*-type investigation. Several of the other participants also mentioned using more successful and popular podcasts as models. "I think all of us podcasters take little pieces from podcasts that we love and that we admire and incorporate those pieces into our show, but we do it our own way," said Rice. Delia described how she modeled her own podcast after *Serial*:

> *Serial* was a huge influence. I went back and listened to the first season to figure out how they formatted the podcast episodes . . . My mom makes lots of dresses,

and so I kind of think of it like a pattern. *Serial* was kind of like the dress I was taking apart to look at the pattern that was used to make it.

The podcasters also mentioned that other podcasts offered examples of both stylistic and professional standards to emulate, particularly for those podcasters without a formal background in audio media. According to Miller:

> We are all sort of avid listeners of podcasts out there in the true crime field . . . I personally listen to them and learn from them and see things that they are doing that we might want to incorporate into our own reporting. . . . Through listening to their podcasts I've learned a lot from them about being professional journalists and how they sort of tackle things. That has helped us in developing our own podcast.

Fuller echoed this sentiment, referencing "standards" of reporting he tries to mimic from National Public Radio and Canadian Broadcast Corporation productions. Brantley said, "There are models that we aspire to just because of their overall competence and artistry and intrigue." Morford noted the fine line between emulating others' styles and direct mimicry:

> I have shows that I enjoy, shows that appeal to me, certain aspects that I like, that I respect, and I think are good ideas, and I might say something like, "I like the way they did that" and maybe I'll remember that when I'm doing something on my podcast, but I don't directly steal from anybody or anything that somebody's creating and sort of make it my own.

All of the participants noted at least one podcast they felt was similar to their own. This is again a finding in line with my prior research which found that 30% of the analyzed news articles about podcasts compared true crime podcasts to each other (Sherrill, 2020). Several participants questioned if isomorphism within the population was a positive development for true crime. "Now 2,030 true crime podcasts pop up every day and some of them are good and some of them aren't, and they all have these angles and you get this repetition," said Pacheco. Fuller agreed, noting, "There's something from every angle, and there's probably 10 different podcasts for every angle at least, or more." Hunt mentioned that the constant comparison of podcasts to one another added a layer of pressure on producers as listeners' expectations evolve. "We worried [listeners would say,] 'Oh, this sounds like shit compared to *Serial.*'"

Forms, Boundary Work, and Identity

Organizations within niches often include shared characteristics, like forms and identities. Identity may evolve through creating relational ties with other similar organizations within the population or by fitting within certain recognized social boundaries (Polos et al., 2002; Tilly, 1986). "Boundary work" is the term used to describe how organizations negotiate form and identity both internally and with outside agents, including what is "acceptable behavior" (Jacobs et al., 2008). For media organizations, form and identity also have implications for how organizations act as "functional alternatives" to other types of media, such as radio, television, or print media (Dimmick et al., 2011; Perse & Courtright, 1993; Rubin & Stepp, 2000).

In discussing the organizational and stylistic forms their podcasts take, participants positioned podcasts as both extensions of and functional alternatives to older media, particularly journalism, radio, and true crime television. Perhaps not surprisingly, podcasters with journalism backgrounds positioned their work differently than those without news backgrounds. They describe podcasting as both a way to "do" journalism and to help people understand how journalism works. Hunt said of her podcast and those similar, "It *is* journalism, it just happens to be in podcast form." Delia agreed:

This is hardcore journalism. What's more hardcore than investigating somebody's case where something has really gone wrong? . . . To me it just keeps coming back to the basic principles of journalism—is this accurate and am I being fair— and that's just the attitude we carried into it.

Rankin credited the *Atlanta Journal-Constitution*'s "big leap of faith" into producing *Breakdown* with proving to other print outlets that the podcasting format could work for long-form journalism. Both Brantley and Hunt mentioned that, as journalists, one of the most compelling parts of listening to journalist-led true crime is the "inside journalism" perspective the shows offer. Brantley, like previous critics (e.g., Columbia Journalism Review, 2016), suggested that *Serial* was a story about Sarah Koenig's process as a reporter more than a story about a crime, and described debating with his co-host how much of that perspective should be a part of their podcast format. Hunt said of *Accused*, "I was able to take people along the journey, so they could not only understand what I uncovered but they could understand what it is to do journalism . . . that's really valuable." Fuller, a radio journalist-turned independent podcaster, described a hybrid orientation between traditional true crime and his journalism background:

I have been tasked to talk to as many people as I can who were involved in it, and that's where the journalism comes in. Some of the people I'm going to talk to are victim's family members and investigators, and that's where the true crime comes in.

Fuller also stated that he sees the lines between traditional storytelling-true crime and journalistic-true crime podcasts becoming delineated as the population matures, evidence of boundary creation. He used television true crime as an example of such delineation, pointing out the differences between shows like *Forensic Files* and more sensational programs. "Cousins Who Kill!," he quipped, referencing a particular type of especially salacious true crime television. Independent podcaster Pacheco made a similar comment, comparing many true crime podcasts to tabloids filled with gruesome crime scene photos, noir novels with risqué covers ("a woman in a bra and a man with a knife"), or slasher films ("torture porn") in contrast to a more "traditional" *Dateline* or evening news style.

When I asked interviewees why podcasting was chosen over another technological format, several participants described it as a uniquely suited alternative to other ways of both telling stories and delivering entertainment. "I've seen people get out of radio and just go to podcasting," said Rice. Freemark remarked on the luxury of virtually unlimited time to tell detailed stories compared to the tightly managed segments of radio broadcasting. Delia described podcasting as the *only* format in which she could have seen her story working. "It was definitely not going to fit into like four and a half minutes in a radio segment, and also we wanted to talk about this really graphic thing that it's hard to talk about on the radio."

Closely tied to podcast form and style were the participants' evaluations of who their listeners are and the kind of gratifications they believe those listeners to be seeking. Listeners are also considered a resource and a part of collective identity, both discussed in more detail below. Overwhelmingly, participants described their audience as between 60% and 90% women, a statistic in line with prior studies of true crime podcast listeners (e.g., Boling & Hull, 2018). They also described having listeners of all ages and from multiple countries. Several participants used descriptors like "well educated," "diverse," "invested," and "engaged." Chaudry described listeners as people "who have investigative minds," while Hunt called them "people who appreciate solid journalism." Brantley, whose podcast was still in preproduction, says he tries to imagine his future listeners as himself: "People want true crime—they don't want to be lectured about race in America." In contrast, Fuller said he often feels "a disconnect" from the true crime fans in his audience. "I think they listen to 75% true crime podcasts. They kind of devour each of these podcasts and just move on." Rice and Pacheco brought up specific motivations for listeners' interest. "They're not into it for the salacious details. They're into it for the psychology," Rice said. Pacheco agreed: "[Listeners don't want] sensationalized aspects of true crime. They want the humanity of the story, and they want to discuss the mystery." While Pacheco stated that his audience specifically disliked comedy true crime, Rice noted, "I've learned my audience has a very good sense of humor." These listener evaluations also touched upon podcasters' awareness of implicit community guidelines. Hunt described this in terms of production choices. "We knew that people would not forgive us for bad quality just because we didn't know what we were doing." Hunt also mentioned that these guidelines made her keenly aware of the challenge of going from print to audio reporting, including whether she had "a personality that can carry the narration." Pacheco mentioned guidelines as knowing what listeners do *not* want to hear ("blow by blow . . . detailed grotesque"), while Morford noted the importance of translating listener feedback into "doing the kind of stuff to make your listener base proud."

Everyone I interviewed also discussed the creation of boundaries and norms within the population, as well as examples of violations of those norms. These norms differ somewhat based on the segment or sub-niche of true crime podcast, as noted earlier in the different interpretations of the place of comedy in true crime stories. As much of the boundary work and norm negotiation participants mentioned overlaps with the goal orientations of true crime podcasts, norm creation, violation, identity, and stakeholder negotiation will be discussed in more detail later.

THE COMPETITIVE SPACE: DENSITY, DISRUPTION, INERTIA, RESOURCES, AND RELATIONSHIPS

As populations grow or shrink, organizations experience ripple effects in resource availability (Baum, 2000). These changes in density may change the perception of the population for outside actors, prospective member organizations, and existing population members—for example, increasing or decreasing the population's legitimacy—as well as lead to speciation or the emergence of generalist and specialist organizations (Weber, 2017). Disruptions in the population may also change the nature of resource competition or may change how member organizations negotiate their competitive and collaborative relationships. Inertia often prevents organizations, especially larger and older organizations, from being able to respond quickly to their environments (Aldrich & Pfeffer, 1976; Hannan & Freeman, 1977), though relationships may help organizations navigate volatile environments. Other constraints, such as knowledge or resource gaps, may prevent organizations from adapting or lead to early mortalities. These relationships and constraints were brought up time after time in the interviews.

Density

Over and over again, participants noted very low bars to entry for new podcasts. The low entry barrier, low startup costs, and elasticity of the digital media environment appear to affect some of the calculations that individuals and organizations make when entering the population. Participants noted these factors in discussing the density of their competitive environment. "Everyone and their mom has a podcast," Delia joked, but added, "I think there's enough space for everyone—it's just an abyss of space and time." Pacheco noted the exponential growth of the population around the time he began his podcast in May 2017: "[You could say,] 'Name me five true crime podcasts' and people would rattle off the same five, and now you get five different ones from everyone you ask 'cause there's so many of them out there." Some participants see this easy entry as positive for the development of the population. "It's a low bar to entry, it doesn't cost much at all, you can edit stuff at home, it's free to put online, I mean, it can't get better," said Chaudry. Others expressed concern that low bars to entry diluted the quality of podcasts being produced. Pacheco said:

> I think there's a lot of people that just kind of looked at it and thought, "Well, this is interesting." And then saw people making money and thought, "Well, I can create a true crime podcast and just make money and I don't really care if I'm accurate or factual or respectful. It's just a job, and I just want to make cash doing it." Because of that you have all different levels of professionalism or lack thereof.

Fuller described the true crime podcast population as "really saturated" and "a crowded space" and theorized that "the true crime bubble is bursting." He noted, however, that as the popularity of all podcasts and the number of podcast users continues to grow (see also Edison Research, 2021), there might still be an expansion of the population, though with caveats:

> You only have so many TV channels and you have so many dials and frequencies on the radio. There's an infinite number of podcasts available to people. I think it will probably put some upward pressure on creators. You have to be good at what you do, and you're going to have to set expectations—whatever your genre—set expectations and meet them just like you have to in any other media format.

Not all of the podcasters agreed with the idea of oversaturation and declining quality.

> Maybe there will be a certain point at which it's oversaturated, and you start to get some projects where maybe people aren't taking it seriously, but really, the ones that I've seen out there and started listening to, they're pretty high-quality.

Brantley stated, adding that he believes the medium has not "matured" enough to predict its future direction. Freemark also agreed that increased density was a strength rather than a weakness of the podcast space:

I think it's all for the good when the podcast field grows. I don't think more people listening to *Serial* takes away from our audience. If anything, it's good for us. I think we get listeners when people listen to other podcasts and then get interested in the medium and want to listen more.

Several participants also noted the importance of the interstitial, or time-shifted and "multi-task-able," usage of podcasts in allowing continued population growth. "It's just the wave of the future because it's so easy to listen to podcasts while you're driving, while you're working, while you're doing housework," said Morford.

Disruption

I was surprised by how many participants offered unprompted examples of moments of environmental disruption in the population. While it is hard to pinpoint causation with certainty, it is interesting to note that disruptions mentioned in the interviews appear to coincide with density changes in the true crime ecosystem. Two participants noted technological shifts that influenced the rise of the general podcast population. Morford, a former car salesman, said he began to notice the shifts to satellite radio and Bluetooth technology in new vehicles in the early 2010s and cited the changing technology as one of the reasons he felt secure changing careers to full-time podcasting. At the same time, he noticed advertisers begin to appear on big-name podcasts (while true crime podcasts had not received much attention at the time, there were other very popular, long-running shows in other genres). Morford said:

I think advertisers said, "Hey, we can reach a lot more people, maybe at a lower price than doing traditional TV or radio." I think that was sort of a big realization for me. Just seeing, learning more about podcast revenue and advertising. That was when . . . I realized that it was something that that could be more mainstream.

Fuller pointed to a different technology—the Apple iPhone update that made the podcast application native to the iPhone home screen. This echoes Quirk (2016), who credited the iPhone update just weeks before *Serial*'s launch as the real motivator of the podcast explosion that happened in late 2014 and early 2015.

All but one of the participants cited *Serial* in some way, as either a major disruptor to the population or as a driver of their own podcast interest. Some of their comments included:

- Rice: "A lot of people say *Serial*, and I would be one of them. I bet three out of every five people would say, 'Oh, *Serial*.' Yeah . . . I had a really crappy commute, you know for the longest time, and I would come to work frustrated and a friend said, 'Why don't you listen to podcasts?' He's like, 'Give me your phone,' and he immediately subscribed me to *Serial*. He said, 'Listen to this and you will be hooked,' and he was right. I mean, I've never been the same since."

- Freemark: "*Serial* Season 1 was the big one. That's when podcasts became like an actual 'thing.' Yeah, that's like the big moment."
- Chaudry: "It's not that there was no podcasting before *Serial*, but *Serial* made it sexy. *Serial* made it cool. *Serial* made it A THING. I didn't know what a podcast was until *Serial* and for a lot of people, for many—I would say millions of people—*Serial* was their introduction to the world of podcasts. Yes. That is the most, I think, significant moment. I think they turned everything around for the industry."
- Miller: "[*Serial*] opened the floodgates to all these interesting true crime podcasts that a growing segment of the population have started listening to . . . true crime has been around for decades, and I kind of feel like before *Serial* came around, predominantly true crime seemed to be more sensationalized and it wasn't necessarily done with the integrity and nuance that I think is important to that type of reporting. . . . sort of right after *Serial* you start to see other podcasts like *Breakdown* and *In the Dark* and *Accused* and *Missing & Murdered* coming out."
- Hunt: "[*Serial*] opened the door for us."

The interviewees also mentioned other smaller disruptions. Both Rankin and Hunt credited their own and each other's podcasts with beginning the growing trend of newspaper-produced podcasts. While Rankin's *Breakdown* offered a format model for print reporter–driven podcasts, Hunt's *Accused* proved that newspaper podcasts could attract the listeners and advertising dollars to be monetarily successful. "We opened the door for other newspapers to feel they could invest in this medium," Hunt said. These newspaper-produced podcasts comprise the bulk of the limited-arc series podcasts. Rankin and Hunt's podcasts are largely credited with the introduction of this form, but the population analysis offers another perspective on this disruption. Rankin's *Breakdown* in 2015 marked the emergence of this form in podcasting's second decade, but it was, in contrast to the interviewees' assertions, not the first of its kind. In 2006, the *Lancaster New Era* produced a six-part podcast series on an Amish schoolhouse shooting called *Lost Angels*. While the series and its associated news stories won the 2007 Eugene S. Pulliam National Journalism Writing Award, the podcast received very little other attention, and the paper converted the podcast into a book at the request of readers (LancasterOnline, January 24, 2007; Staff and Wire Reports, March 5, 2007). This again illustrates the importance of environmental factors for the growth of organizations in populations. While 2005 may have been "the year of the podcast," by 2006, writers were declaring, "Podcasting is dead" (Iskold, August 28, 2007). By the time Rankin and Hunt's podcasts emerged nearly a decade later, conditions were ripe for new forms to emerge. From a social movement theory (SMT) perspective, the difference in the distribution and reception of *Lost Angels* in 2006 and *Accused* in 2016 also illustrates the importance of the correct mix of symbolic political and environmental opportunities (McAdam, 1999) for the growth of movement sectors.

Brantley noted another disruptor in *S-Town*, the limited series podcast from *Serial*'s producers that debuted on March 28, 2017. "*Serial* was a television show, but *S-Town* was a novel," he said, stating that *S-Town* changed the model for the way that true crime narratives could be told. Pacheco pointed to two major crime stories that coincided with related true crime podcasts and brought new attention and fans to the medium. The first was *Up & Vanished*, an independent podcast covering a missing person case in Georgia when the first break in the case in over 12 years occurred. The second was the capture of the Golden State Killer during *Criminology*'s coverage of the decades-long case. While neither podcast was directly involved in solving the crimes, Pacheco credits their "right place, right time" coverage as being hugely influential in bringing new listeners to the population and attention to the cases.

The interviews, when combined with the population analysis, shed light on multiple factors at work in the growth of the true crime podcast ecosystem. These descriptions of *Serial* as a kind of "pioneer" reflect the positions of previous popular and academic literature (e.g., Boling & Hull, 2018; Chaudry, 2016), but there are other more complicated environmental factors at work. The first, as mentioned earlier, were advances in streaming technology, a kind of resource. In 2005, podcast subscriptions were first added to the iTunes interface, leading to the first podcast boom (Patel, September 24, 2018), though, as one *Slate* writer said, podcasting was still "the nichiest of niche media" (Bowers, December 30, 2005). For the next several years, podcasting technology stagnated, and with it, the growth of true crime podcasts. Podcasts (of all kinds) began to be more easily accessible to consumers when, in 2011, Pioneer introduced the first phone app–connected car stereo (Garvey, February 10, 2015), as Morford mentioned. The demography confirms that population density began to rise quickly around this time. Other changes to podcast technology also coincide with these rises in density. In 2012, Apple introduced the first podcast app separate from iTunes, and in 2014, the podcast app became native to iOS8 (Resler, February 2, 2018). These changes are likely as responsible for the explosion of population growth in late 2014 as any "*Serial* effect." In June 2018, Google introduced its first native podcast app for Android (Tech News, June 30, 2018). Considering the continued adoption of the podcast medium since 2018, it is likely that this introduction to the Android platform has had positive effects on population growth as well. These technological developments have been shown to be important factors in the stage development of populations in previous research (e.g., Bryant & Monge, 2008), again suggesting that the true crime podcast population is moving from the emergence to the maintenance stage. These various disruptors are marked in figure 5.1.

Another imminent disruption was also brought up by several participants. Chaudry, Pacheco, Brantley, and Fuller all pointed out the emergence of true crime–focused podcast corporations and the shift of traditional media mega-corporations, such as Clear Channel, into the podcast space. Brantley voiced concerns that, much like social media, podcasting could eventually become controlled by a few corporations or a single channel, noting the immense power that Apple already has over podcast distribution. Pacheco also expressed concern over the possible disruption from big money and professional media entering the still largely independent space:

> It's coming to a point probably in the future where you're going to see independents dying out. It's becoming kind of a corporate thing. Even a lot of the independents now who are very popular are joining corporate networks and getting guaranteed contracts plus the advertising just to bring them in, and then their names are being associated with other things.

Their predictions about corporate podcasting seem to be rapidly coming true, as corporately produced, mostly generalist true crime podcasts coming out of these networks are an increasingly large part of the population. As of the first week of March 2019, 19 of the 33 true crime podcasts on the Apple iTunes Top 100 belonged to one of these networks (e.g., Wondery, Parcast, Gimlet; iTunes Chart, March 7, 2019). By early 2022, fewer than 20 of the Apple Top 100 true crime podcasts were independent. As of April 2022, 40 of the Apple podcasts True Crime Top 200 podcasts were produced by only four podcasts networks. While independent podcasts are far from an endangered species, contracts with podcast networks, like Exactly Right (from *My Favorite Murder*'s creators), or exclusive deals with subscription services like Audible and Luminary are increasingly common.

Participants suggested that the growing power of these networks may affect the choices made by podcasters, as well as podcasts' ability to advertise and monetize. An example of this phenomenon played out with a very public severing of ties between the Wondery Network and one of its top true crime podcasters. This podcaster, one of those described by some participants as a "norm violator" within the true crime podcast community, has a well-documented history of negative social media behavior, including posting violent or crude memes, doxing challengers, and sending inappropriate messages to female fans, in addition to producing graphicly violent podcast content (The

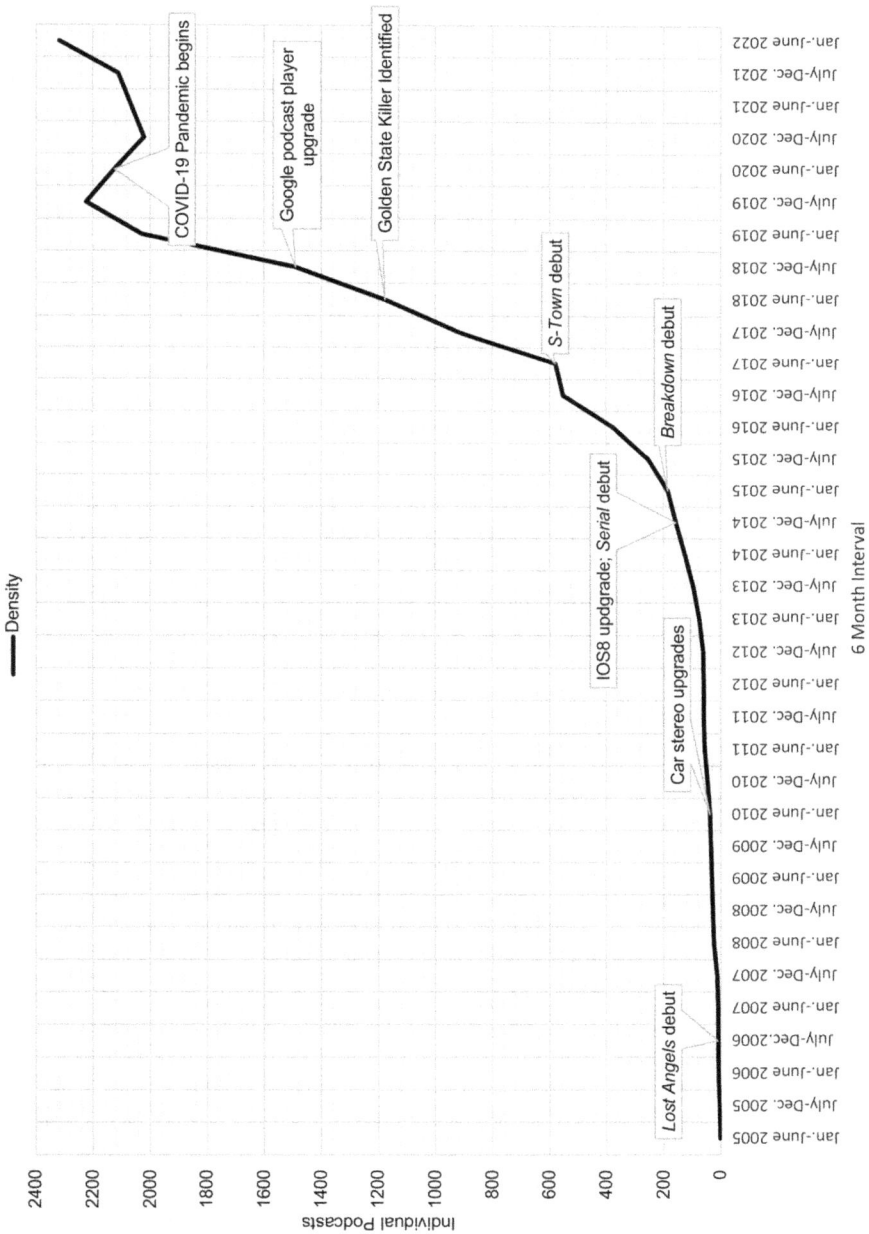

Figure 5.1 True Crime Podcast Ecosystem Density and Disruptions.

Society for the Re-education of *Sword and Scale* fans, 2018). In March 2019, Wondery Media tweeted that they would no longer carry the podcast on their network (WonderyMedia, March 9, 2019). This announcement came after a boycott of other Wondery podcasts by fans. Prominent podcasters (including several interviewed for this study) led a sustained social media campaign to pressure Wondery as well, including calls to drop the offending podcaster by other Wondery hosts.

This anecdote offers a real-world example of the way true crime podcasters and their fans negotiate and police the boundaries of the acceptable behavior in the population (discussed more in the next chapter). The day after the Wondery decision, Rebecca Lavoie (a prominent podcaster mentioned by several of the interview participants, who hosts several podcasts of her own and worked on the *Bear Brook* podcast for New Hampshire Public Radio) wrote a Facebook post describing why she had been so outspoken. Lavoie called the removed podcaster "a real liability to his partners and to our industry" (Lavoie [Facebook post], March 10, 2019).

While this is only one example in a vast population of true crime podcasts, it provides a snapshot of population members with clear ideas about what is "appropriate" behavior and content, as well as the collective identity and buy-in of fans of these podcasts and podcasters. Wondery's actions also offer a first glance at what kind of negotiations the emerging podcast networks may have to undertake and what kind of power they may have.

Inertia and Constraints

The interviewees offered insight into the kinds of organizational or environmental constraints that might lead podcast organizations to experience inertia and thus the inability to adapt to disruption. Their answers reveal several different kinds of restraints but do not offer direct insight into possible inertia in the population. Pacheco said podcasting has limited visibility to the general public, noting that while podcasting is a rapidly evolving field, those involved often forget that it is not fully mainstream: "Podcasting is weird in that a huge amount of people listen to it and about the same amount of people don't even know what a podcast is." While the most recent Edison (2021) statistics on podcast listening may disprove Pacheco's point, it is true that podcasts are still a niche medium in comparison to television or other legacy media.

The podcasters most often mentioned constraints such as lack of technical audio skills, lack of storytelling or investigative experience, or being overwhelmed by the amount of time required to sift through information and edit the final product, particularly for those podcasters without a full team or with other professional obligations. Pacheco called it "confusing" for a new podcaster: "Even if you ask questions or Google it you're going to get a million different answers about what the best microphone is, what the best program is, and I really just kind of learned you've got to figure it out yourself." Miller expressed similar frustration:

> We had no idea what we were doing whatsoever when we started our podcast. We're in different locations. My co-podcasters are in the D.C. area. I'm down in South Carolina, and we had to figure out how to do it remotely, how to edit it, how to do all the sound. When we started our podcast, it was a complete disaster.

While some podcasters discussed knowledge constraints, such as being unfamiliar with audio editing or distribution, others described actual threats to their physical or mental health as constraints to their continuing work. Zappala said that for those involved in investigating and producing podcasts in ongoing cases, personal safety may become an environmental constraint, citing a time she felt dangerous people involved in the case may have been coming after her. Fuller, Delia, and Brantley, all journalists as well as podcasters, mentioned mental health struggles as a kind of internal constraint that they experienced and saw in others involved in telling difficult stories. Brantley called the experience of researching an in-depth and often very dark case "overwhelming" for producers. "I can't tell you the kind of like, emotional and moral whiplash I've had on any given day talking to people," he said. Delia described her own emotions and expressed concern for others working independently or for small news organizations:

> That's very isolating especially when you're talking about a really dark subject. It's hard. We don't talk a lot about mental health in journalism . . . especially when you cover really serious stuff. I think that we do a good job with resources for journalists who cover wars, but obviously smaller shops don't have that culture or don't have those resources in place for people that need it. I was dealing with a lot of second-degree trauma from people's stories that were horrific. How do you go home? How do you process things? How do you just be a human?

Fuller similarly described the mental toil that telling true crime stories has had on him and others:

> You see the polished finished product, but you don't see the family members being angry with you . . . Some people get sued because of the result of their podcast. You don't see any of the negativity that comes your way. It's really kind of stressful. I don't know if it's something that I'll do forever.

Resources

While organizational resources are often thought of as economic, participants more often described knowledge, physical, and symbolic resources.

Several described experience from their time as print or radio reporters as an important resource, ranging from short stints as crime-beat reporters to over 25 years of covering courts. Both Miller, an evidence professor, and Chaudry, an immigration lawyer, credited their knowledge of the court system as a resource. Chaudry also noted that her personal case knowledge was an immense resource in *Undisclosed*'s first case. Both Hunt and Morford cited their history as true crime authors; Hunt, as the author of several true crime books, and Morford, as the creator of the exhaustive "True Crime Guy" website and blog (True Crime Guy, n.d.). Brantley noted the value of his print journalism background and his co-host's documentary film skills in collaborative storytelling. Pacheco also credited the transferability of his video storytelling skills to producing audio stories. Only one participant mentioned prior experience with podcasts before entering the true crime population: Fuller, who had experimented with a spoken-word podcast as early as 2005. Rice was the only participant to have no prior knowledge resources beyond fandom and a love of true crime.

The podcasters also acknowledged the importance of physical resources, namely, equipment, time, and capital. Delia, who began the podcast on her own time before formally proposing it to her employer, described a growing need for support as the impetus for pitching the project. "I didn't have any resources, really. I knew I was struggling to do it by myself. So I asked one of the smartest people, I think, at the radio station to help me with it." Even after the station took on the project, time and money were tight, and Delia called the process "lots of negotiation and struggle." Though Hunt's outlet had more resources, she still called *Accused* "cost intensive." Freemark also expressed how, even for professional investigative organizations like American Public Media, producing a podcast like *In the Dark* was "a resource heavy proposition." For Rankin, whose podcast required hours of courtroom audio, the availability of useable audio proved the most challenging resource to acquire. Due to laws in Georgia, courtroom audio (unlike transcripts) is often not allowed to be copied or shared, requiring Rankin to either be present on each day of a hearing to record his own audio or to rely on relationships with judges and court reporters to obtain older recordings.

While the resource inputs were described as obstacles by many participants, others described growing opportunities to bring in capital through podcast advertising. Fuller said that podcaster awareness of the increasing availability of advertising dollars is changing how aggressively producers research and pursue funding. Chaudry cited the importance of producing a quality product in order to tap into potential advertising revenue. She said:

> There's a lot of money coming and there's a lot of room for growth. Something
> I realized is that we get sponsors every week, advertisers every week. And

what I realized is like, it's like a roll of sponsors here. There's like 30 or 40 of them, and there are still thousands of companies out there who have not realized, tapped into their marketing potential yet . . . I really do think it's going to continue to grow. But like any other media, like any other art form, the cream rises to the top.

Pacheco also agreed that advertising dollars were an increasingly important part of the podcast industry, describing how finding advertisers had quickly allowed his podcast to become his primary source of income. He cautioned, however, that growth in ad revenue might also be a sign of the coming end of the free podcast and speed up corporate disruption of the population.

Participants also noted symbolic resources they believed were helping to grow the population or their own podcasts. Fuller mentioned growing awareness (i.e., the aforementioned cognitive legitimacy) of the podcast medium as a major resource. Others mentioned disruptions in other media populations, such as newspapers, as important for the growth of podcasting. Hunt said:

> We in the newspaper industry are constantly being told we need to think outside of the box. Maybe our jobs straight up depend on it these days because you know, the environment has been decimated. We get pink slips all the time. So I said, "Maybe we could do an audio component to go along with it?" And I just so happened to have bosses at that point that were completely amenable to that.

Brantley noted another kind of symbolic resource for podcasters tackling social issues, particularly topics that are race-related: societal privilege. His podcast deals with uncovering the truth about a Civil Rights era murder, and he described his unique ability to gain access to players in the story. As a white man from Alabama, he said he was able to earn trust of Southerners who are often (rightly, in some cases, he noted) portrayed as evil, one-dimensional characters by outsiders, thus allowing him to get closer to the truth of the more than 60-year-old murder. Brantley noted that this ability to go to places and speak to witnesses that other podcasters—for example, a Muslim woman of color like Chaudry—may not have the social capital to access acted as both a resource and "legitimated" him in the eyes of his often-reticent subjects.

Listeners were also cited as important resources. While Fuller and Rice both mentioned the importance of knowing their own style and recognizing that they cannot please everyone, both said they often receive helpful advice or case suggestions from listeners. Rice and Pacheco both pointed to listener interaction on social media as important. "I draw a lot of inspiration and motivation from my social media interaction with listeners," said Rice. Rankin and Miller both said listener feedback was helpful for understanding how to make writing style and case explanations clearer. Zappala and Chaudry credited listeners with providing new information or perspectives for cases, and Chaudry noted that listeners had provided connections to important stakeholders in several cases. For Delia, listeners became an integral part of her podcast, as she directly incorporated listener voicemails into *She Says*.

Relationship Networks

Inextricably tied to resources are the relationships across the podcasts and podcasters. These relationships exist both among the individuals involved, in the form of personal friendships and rivalries and as competitive or commensualistic relationships between organizations. Competitive relationships occur when organizations require some or all of the same resources, while commensualistic relationships allow organizations to complement each other, either through shared resources or by conferring legitimacy (Baum, 2000; Dimmick, 2003). Formal relationships, or relational density, in a population also decreases the mortality rate for that population (Amburgey & Rao, 1996).

Participants described both formal and informal relationship networks among podcasters, podcast organizations, and outside actors and organizations. Brantley called having a formal relationship with National Public Radio a "megaphone" for advertising, a relationship that allowed him and his co-host to focus on content rather than promotion. According to Chaudry, *Undisclosed* has worked closely with the Pennsylvania and Georgia Innocence Projects on their cases and has been integrated into the orientation for interns at the Philadelphia District Attorney's Office. Miller also noted the importance of formal relationships to *Undisclosed*, including inviting other podcast hosts to "guest star," and working with Rebecca Lavoie to improve the technical aspects of their podcast. Rankin was the only participant to say he had a little formal or informal interaction with other podcasters until well into his podcast career.

For Delia, who described often feeling isolated, forming friendships with successful podcasters helped her through both the emotional and technical stress of creating *She Says*. Brantley and Zappala said they reached out to other podcasters, particularly to learn about the advertising and promotion side of podcasting. Brantley also said he relied on other podcasters to help him navigate the transition from writing for print to writing for audio. While Pacheco said he has avoided formal relationships and prefers to work alone, he did say he had developed friendships and found advice through social media and events like Crime Con. Rice also described the role of informal relationships for her podcast:

> The community has been great. I have made what I think are lifelong friends, you know, who I would have never met had I not gotten into podcasting, other

podcasters, things like that. I speak to other podcasters on a daily basis. We speak about ideas, we talk about cases, we talk about different criminal laws.

Freemark said of formal relationships, "We don't collaborate directly," but she noted the closeness of informal networks of podcasters from audio journalism backgrounds. "It's a small field and a lot of people come from public radio. It is kind of a tight field." Fuller said his public radio background allowed him to keep going after several prominent podcasters ignored or denied his requests for mentorship. Morford was one of the podcasters who did help Fuller and was mentioned by several other participants as an important influence. Morford described his view of podcasters' relationships:

> For the most part, everybody in the true crime genre seems to interact with each other and is willing to do a reading of something, that kind of thing. Sometimes there's collaboration of two shows together for a topic. That's the cool thing about podcasting—you get to meet a lot of people and, for the most part, it's all positive and everyone is helping each other.

Relationships and Competition

When directly asked about competition, participants used words like "helpful," "supportive," "congenial," "collaborative," "community," and "friendly rivalries." Rice said:

> I also get very motivated when I see other podcasters doing well . . . it's a great community. It's, for the most part, very welcoming of others podcasters. . . . Yes, there are, you know, some out there that I've gotten to know who are sort of that kind of like, "me, me, me." You know, "I've got to be the best" and things like that. But for the most part, we all want to do well, but we also are very good about helping each other do well and grow our shows.

Miller expressed a similar sentiment: "It's not like we say, 'We want to be better than this other podcast, we want to figure out how to beat some other podcast' . . . there are a number of excellent true crime podcasts out there." Delia too described positive relationships with other podcasters:

> If I don't know how to do something, I find the person that knows how to do it and have a conversation with them, and I did that over and over and over again. I just found people to be really kind and gracious with their time. It's weird. I mean, I guess like, other people feel competition. I don't know.

Hunt positioned competition within the true crime podcast field in contrast to her experiences in journalism, including podcasts' relationships with media consumers:

It's a friendly comradery. Much more supportive field than some others—cough journalism cough. Journalists are very competitive with each other, and, for some reason, the podcast world seems to be much more supportive of each other. There seems to be more of an understanding that, you know, one's success can be everyone's success and people who like one tend to listen to others. You know, it's not like they go all, "I heard *Accused*. I'm not gonna listen to *In the Dark*." They binge this stuff that took me a year. They listen in a weekend and they're like, "Next!" The community has been really supportive. I get a lot of pick-your-brain kind of emails from others.

While these responses seem to paint a picture of a commensualistic, friendly confederacy of true crime podcasters, deeper probing and comments throughout the interviews suggest that there is more competition than participants may have wanted to admit. Rankin said that he had been so emotionally affected by competition with another podcast while working on *Breakdown* that he was not willing to talk about it in any way. Fuller said that while other podcasters were often friendly, as a whole, they tend to be very protective of information about monetization or downloads. He also described recognizing that, while he did not feel directly threatened by competitors, he saw evidence of more intense competition between other podcasters. Fuller said:

I try to keep everything at an arm's distance, but I hear stories about podcasters kind of feuding in a strange way. I know there's some of that negativity, but I'm not sure if that's competition or what . . . There's kind of a middle-school feuding cliquish element to the whole podcast community that I'd rather stay away from.

Pacheco described similar experiences:

When you first start off it's hard not to [feel competition]. You're looking around at these other podcasts who are better, doing something similar. As far as true crime, you might do a case that someone else has done before, so you feel this pressure of like, well, "I have to do it better than they do" or "I have to do it different" or whatever. You listen to other podcasts, and you see the way people respond to them. It's like anything else . . . the true crime community with podcasting is very strange in that many, many people are supportive, and we try to help each other out, but at the same time it's sorta competing for the same listeners. We're competing for the same advertising dollars, so there's certainly an underbelly to it that you learn the deeper you get into it. People who will maybe present themselves as though they're helpful, but they're not. And there's definitely people out there who are trying to submarine other people, so it's a little crazy.

Other participants seemed to distance their podcasts from competition by differentiating their resource needs. Hunt said that because of the way listeners use podcasts, consuming multiple similar shows quickly, she does not see competition for listeners as an issue. While Chaudry described *Undisclosed*'s relationships with other podcasts as "collaboration," she noted that it was possible that she did not see direct competition because of the show's unique format, citing only *Truth & Justice* as similar. Zappala stated that "90% of true crime is not a competitor" because of style and format differences. "Everyone has their own style of doing it where there's something different about every podcast, so I don't feel like I'm competing. I'm not worried about that," she said. Freemark sees growth in the population as positive for all true crime podcasters rather than as a worrisome increase in competition. She said, "I think what we do is pretty unique; I don't think we have a direct competitor. We just really don't think about it in those terms."

Brantley described competition as being not only within the true crime population but also with others in the podcast community and with standards he holds for himself:

> I think of competition as not so much to other podcasts that are trading in true crime or investigative work, but more just like listenability . . . one of my favorite podcasts is . . . a music podcast. I think about competition, and it's like, I want someone to have the same reaction to this podcast that I have to that. Where it's like, I can't wait to listen to it, regardless of the fact that it's not serialized . . . it has nothing in common with what we're doing, but that's how I think about competition more so than I think about, like you know, the type of thing we're making.

Many of the participants' other comments about competition and relationships are also related to their social movement orientations (SMOs). The "feuding" aspect is especially evident in mentions of how the "appropriateness" of true crime podcast styles and formats is negotiated and is discussed in more detail in the next chapters.

PODCASTS AS MAINTENANCE ORGANIZATIONS

All of the podcasters, even the ones deeply focused on advocacy goals, talked about their podcasts in organizational terms. These interviews provide evidence of the existence of niches, sub-niches, and boundaries in the population. Participants described multiple "types" of true crime podcasts, expanding Punnett's (2018) criteria to include political crimes, white collar and financial crime, terrorism, and exploration of cults in their definitions and recommendations (*Dear Franklin Jones*, a cult-centered limited series podcast, was a favorite of several participants). Some participants, like Brantley, directly stated a desire to subvert or expand how consumers understand true crime media.

Some of these podcasters, like Chaudry, Miller, Hunt, and Morford, described their roles within the true crime podcast community as encouraging the development of similar podcasts and promoting or mentoring newer podcasters. Other participants specifically cited the value of these relationships, describing having been helped along the way by more established podcasters. By playing a mentoring role, these podcasters and others mentioned (like Rebecca Lavoie) help to grow the population, establish boundaries of acceptable behavior and content, confer legitimacy on younger operations, and reduce uncertainty about the form, technique, and technology for would-be entrants to the population. From an organizational ecology standpoint, these network relationships (Dimaggio, 1986) allow for knowledge to be shared throughout the population, strengthening organizations and decreasing liabilities of newness. From a SMT orientation, these relationships facilitate the sharing of community resources for larger purposes (Greve et al., 2006).

The importance of these network relationships also supports the conceptualization of these podcasts as pre-organizations in an early stage of community and population growth (Aldrich, 1999; Bryant & Monge, 2008; Katz & Gartner, 1988). In this stage, relationships tend to be more collaborative than competitive as the population negotiates its way from the emergence to maintenance of organizational forms and relationships (Aldrich, 1999; Bryant & Monge, 2008). Participants' descriptions of the growing role of formal, corporatized organizations in the population suggest that true crime podcasting may be entering a more mature phase of community development.

Podcasters' definitions also challenged the delineation of journalism and true crime. Punnett draws a distinction between journalism and true crime, writing that true crime is differentiated by telling "moral messages and social truths through entertaining narratives rich in detail and color" (2018, p. 93) and by using "free play" in narration to transport true crime consumers. He contrasts this with structured, just-the-facts reporting. Participants, even those who considered their work to be strictly journalistic, all described their podcasts in almost Punnett's exact terms. They discussed using rich narrative and sharing "social truths" (e.g., systemic issues or statistics about victims) and described trying to draw in listeners or be "entertaining" in some way. Rankin, for example, said his podcasting, like his career in journalism, involved "trying to tell a story in an engaging and compelling way." Those who were resistant to the true crime label, like Freemark who preferred "criminal justice reporting," still positioned their work in relation to other true crime products. While many of these podcasts are inarguably journalistic, the insights from these interviews suggest that journalism podcasts focused on crime narratives are a sub-niche of true crime rather than a separate organizational form. At the same time, it is also clear that many members of the true crime podcast population are *not* journalistic. Participants drew clear distinctions in that regard and offered multiple examples of ways that other podcasts violate journalistic norms while telling true crime stories.

As shown by the population demography, beginning with the emergence of the first identified true crime–related podcast in 2005, the population has experienced a pattern of growth with no current evidence of slowing. This pattern extends across the sub-niches of the population, as evidenced by the uptick in limited-arc podcasts as well as regularly produced podcasts. As the population has grown, other media have recognized this growth and have focused more attention on true crime podcasts as legitimate organizational forms (see Sherrill, 2020). This is directly in line with organizational ecology's explanation of the relationship between population density and legitimation (e.g., Audia et al., 2006; Weber et al., 2016).

Podcasters interviewed specifically noted the extremely low barriers to entry into the podcast industry. This was repeatedly cited as a major influence on the growth of the population. As more people "discover" podcasts, they may attempt to make their own because the initial investment of time and equipment is so low. This also allows those with a movement-oriented goal, such as bringing to light an injustice in a case in which they have personal investment, to attempt mobilization with few resources. While this niche elasticity can be positive for increasing true crime podcast density, participants also noted that easy entry into the industry can decrease quality by allowing anyone to enter regardless of skill or ethics. This suggests the same double-edged sword described by Greve and colleagues (2006): more founding attempts can increase the legitimacy of a population, but at a certain point, may lead to lower acceptance and retention rates for new organizations.

The population analysis seems to cast doubt on one assertion made by several participants—the idea that the true crime podcast "bubble" might be bursting or that population density has reached a point of oversaturation. These participants mentioned the growth in true crime satire podcasts—like *The Onion*'s *A Very Fatal Murder* and *Done Disappeared*—as evidence of this. Traditional media outlets have also questioned this possibility, such as a *Guardian* article entitled, "Could *A Very Fatal Murder* kill off the true-crime podcast?" (Verdier, February 20, 2018). The growth trend of the population shows no evidence to support this observation. Not only is the density curve rising steadily across time, even during the COVID-19 pandemic, podcast foundings remained high. It seems more likely that the satire of the population's organizational form is evidence of a maturing population. Satire as evidence of the maturation of organizational forms has been noted in previous organizational studies, such as the evolution of satirical Mardi Gras krewes as both celebration and subversion of accepted forms (Islam et al., 2008). From the perspective of SMT, satire may also represent a budding countermovement or attempts to delegitimize movement goals, similar to the ways that comedic delegitimization frames were used against political movements like Occupy Wall Street (Young, 2013).

I did not find evidence of structural inertia in the population. There may be several reasons for this. First, structural inertia is a product of calcification of structures within established organizations (Aldrich & Pfeffer, 1976; Hannan & Freeman, 1977). While these podcasts may be established in terms of the relatively young podcast industry, they are still fairly new operations (or pre-organizations), suggesting that they may not have had time to calcify or are still in the organization-in-creation stage (Katz & Gartner, 1988; Lowrey, 2012). Second, many of the podcasts are operations with few (sometimes only one) staff members. Management hierarchies are not an inertial constraint in those situations. Final, while the lack of routinization and institutionalization of many true crime podcasts may be a liability in stable environments (Lowrey, 2012, 2017; Singh & Lumsden, 1990) in the constantly evolving landscape of digital media, remaining nimble is advantageous to podcast operations, which may further discourage processes that lead to inertia.

These findings also reveal the way that population members conceptualize competition. On one hand, some podcasters see their products as unique and not easily substituted. On the other hand, some participants suggested that true crime podcasts are almost interchangeable or "functional alternatives" (Dimmick et al., 2011) to each other. Perhaps because most true crime consumers have voracious appetites for these podcasts (as Fuller mentioned) and often discover new podcasts through other podcasts, producers described competition within the industry as more collaborative than competitive. These findings support Berry's (2006) description of the emerging podcast population as nonhierarchical and connected through conversations among producers and between producers and consumers. Participants also offered evidence of formal ties among podcast organizations, another factor that may lead to less contentious competitive relationships and lower mortalities (Amburgey & Rao, 1996). Again, these commensualistic relationships may also be a sign of a population in the early phase of community development (Bryant & Monge, 2008). In addition to illustrating the kinds of competition associated with organizational ecology, these relationships fit with resource mobilization theory's conceptualization of competition in social movement sectors (SMSs) (McCarthy & Zald, 2002). From a dual perspective of organizational orientation, the ability of listeners to participate in nonexclusionary membership as fans or constituents of these podcasts also lessens the effects of competition on podcast operations (Sandell, 2001). Participants did describe seeing evidence of more intense competition among other podcasters, particularly those they viewed as "norm violators." It is possible that these competitive podcasts are more oriented toward building audience and revenue than the podcasters interviewed or have less investment or interest in building community relationships.

The descriptions of growth of sub-niches within the true crime podcast population after *Serial* offer evidence of resource partitioning and speciation. Podcasters cited listeners as a resource and described "different kinds of styles for different kinds of listeners." From the ecological view of listeners, the division of "type" of listener by "type" of podcast illustrated both a division of resources and niche gratifications (Broussard et al., 2022; Carroll, 1985; Carroll et al., 2002; Dimmick, 2003; Greve et al., 2006). Several participants also described this partitioning in terms of their competition, such as Zappala's statement that "90% of true crime is not a competitor" because of the division of listener resources based on gratifications.

The emergence of specialist true crime podcasts illustrates speciation within the population (Weber, 2017). Participants described their podcasts in ways that suggest that most view their podcasts as specialist rather than generalist organizations. All of the participants' podcasts emerged post-*Serial* season one (arguably, one of the clearest generalists in the population based on its mass appeal) in order to exploit the growing true crime podcast fan base (a resource) and to take advantage of the exploding podcast industry. This is in line with Mezias and Mezias's (2000) description of the emergence of specialist organizations. Participants also described a desire to differentiate themselves from their competition, focusing on identification as "experts." Hunt said this explicitly: "We're not just some people off the street that decided that they wanted to do this for the sake of doing it." Podcasters position themselves in this way as "expert specialists," by, for example, promoting their credentials in law or investigation. This positioning may help increase their podcasts' legitimacy. Legitimacy may also be increased by listeners identifying with particular specialist "brands" (Carroll & Swaminathan, 2000), like *Truth & Justice*'s fan "Truth and Justice Army" or *My Favorite Murder*'s "Murderinos."

Participants also offered substantial evidence of isomorphism and mimicry across true crime podcasts. Most participants pointed to attempting to mimic *Serial* in at least some way and described using established or successful podcasts as examples of how to craft their own. Some described attempting to increase legitimacy by following the patterns of established podcasts (Deephouse & Suchman, 2008; Hannan & Freeman, 1977; Weber et al., 2016), or feeling honored by comparison to podcasts like *Serial* and *In the Dark*. At the same time, participants also described ways in which their podcasts exhibit heterogeneity or unique characteristics. This heterogeneity was most often discussed in terms of brand differentiation. Heterogeneity in this case may be an example of a still-new population discovering the optimal forms to insure retention within the population (Aldrich & Pfeffer, 1976; Baum, 2000; Carroll, 1984; Dimmick, 2003; Hannan & Freeman, 1977; Lowrey, 2012; Stinchcombe, 1965) or evidence of ongoing speciation (Carroll, 1985; Weber, 2017). Participants also described heterogeneity in terms of movement orientations, such as Chaudry's assertion that her show is unique for its specific, stated goal of correcting wrongful conviction cases. Others described their podcasts as similar to other podcasts, but different from other forms of "traditional" true crime media. This seems closely related to Greve et al.'s (2006) findings that diversity within goal-oriented populations may be a result of acting in opposition to dominant forms as a type of movement orientation or collective identity. Challenging dominant media traditions is also evidence of democratic media activism, particularly for those podcasters who utilize crowdsourcing and other horizontal forms of collective action (Carroll & Hackett, 2006).

My interviews also shed additional light on the way legitimacy has developed in the true crime podcast population. Podcasters that I interviewed noted an increase in popular knowledge of true crime podcasts in line with past research (i.e, Sherrill, 2020), pointing to multiple recent pop culture references, like movies and Saturday Night Live sketches.[1] The most recent Infinite Dial Reports support these results, finding over 116 million Americans listened to podcasts at least monthly in 2021 (Edison, 2021). While these statistics are not specific to true crime podcasts, they do support participants' observations of exponential growth in the podcast audience. These environmental factors (in addition to internal population factors, like density) are also in line with previous research on the development of legitimacy in populations in the emergence stage of community development (Bryant & Monge, 2008).

Participants described legitimacy in ecology terms, offering examples of how podcasts becoming "a thing" through increased density and attention was good for the sustainability of the population. Freemark specifically cited the growth of density in true crime podcasts as an important factor in the acceptance of the form. *Serial* was noted as important for both cognitive and normative legitimacy. From a cognitive legitimacy standpoint, *Serial*'s viral success brought new listeners to the podcast medium, either through hearing it promoted on National Public Radio and *This American Life*, or through social and popular media discussion. Chaudry particularly mentioned this, noting that *Serial* was her own introduction to podcasts. She, and others, also mentioned the importance of *Serial* for normative legitimacy, as it led to a mainstreaming of not only the often-maligned true crime genre but also wrongful conviction narratives. This mainstreaming of a criminal justice issue also offered evidence of the legitimacy of growing awareness of special movement organizations for true crime.

Legitimacy was also discussed in terms of appropriate identities for true crime podcast organizations. Participants described the tension between competing goals and identities. For some, this tension is between balancing journalism and entertainment. They described wanting to be factual and professional while still attracting and retaining listeners. This suggests an ecological orientation toward organizational maintenance. Others described a balance between advocacy for criminal justice–related goals, like bringing awareness to systemic mishandling of sexual assault cases, with journalistic ethics. Several specifically mentioned walking a line between their own bias and telling a balanced story. For these journalistically oriented participants, legitimacy seems to be a push and pull between their identity as journalists (e.g., working with the *Cincinnati Enquirer*) and their identification with criminal justice advocacy. Other tensions were present as well, such as how to balance humor and gravity or finding the line between providing valuable detail and veering into the grotesquely graphic. This suggests that in addition to organizational maintenance and movement orientations, there are identity-oriented motivations and tensions at work in the true crime podcast population. These tensions are constantly negotiated by participants, stakeholders, and publics, supporting the concept that organizational identity is a product of communicative social construction processes (Hsu & Hannan, 2005; Melucci, 1985; Weber, 2017). These tensions are even more evident when these podcasters talk about their advocacy motivations, as can be seen in the following chapter.

NOTE

1. Podcasting has shown up in multiple films and television shows over the past several years, including a 2021 comedy horror film titled simply *The Murder Podcast* (Bagley, 2021). *Saturday Night Live* has spoofed true crime in multiple sketches, but targeted podcasts pointedly, including a parody of *Serial* starring Cecily Strong as Sarah Koenig (Shetty, December 21, 2014).

Chapter 6

True Crime Podcasts and Social Movement Approaches

We're not just some people off the street that decided that they wanted to do this for the sake of doing it.

—Amber Hunt

In the post-*Serial* era, consumers can easily find all kinds of true crime, from the juicy and salacious to those focused on solving specific cases, freeing the wrongfully convicted, or reforming investigative procedures and policing. Many of these true crime media products invite and even encourage their audiences to take real-life actions or become involved in advocacy. Cecil (2020) addressed this shift in the genre in the first chapter of her book on true crime fandom:

> I have recently begun to see my former true crime obsessed self in some of my students . . . they eagerly ask me if I watched the newest true crime series to stream on Netflix. . . . These true representations of crime are becoming a part of their understanding of criminal behavior . . . these students can also log on to social media outlets such as Reddit, Websleuths.com, and other venues to chat about the details of their favorite true crime stories, and can even become a part of the investigation. For some, modern true crime is not a passive genre; it is interactive. (Cecil, 2020, p. 3)

When I selected podcasters for my interviews, I specifically sought those involved in this interactive subgenre of true crime. The goals of these podcasters ranged from educating audiences about systemic issues (like *She Says* and *Accused*) to advocating for the wrongfully convicted (*Undisclosed, In the Dark, Breakdown*) to finding missing persons (*Frozen Truth, Missing*

Alissa) to reevaluating historic unsolved cases (*Criminology, White Lies*). When I spoke to the podcasters, I asked about the ways they may take social movement theory (SMT) approaches to their work. These approaches can be observed in the way true crime podcasts create collective identity, exploit social and environmental opportunities, utilize mobilizing structures, and negotiate framing processes (Cohen, 1985; McAdam, 1999). I also looked for evidence of group efficacy and collective action (Bandura, 1995; Gamson, 1990; Klandermans, 1984; McAdam, 1999). Their answers gave me insight into these social movement factors, as well as legitimacy, organizational identity, and stakeholder negotiation, the concepts that stretch across both organizational ecology and SMT.

COLLECTIVE IDENTITY

The concept of collective identity is shared across the classical, resource mobilization, and political process paradigms of SMT and may be both a mobilizing force for collective action and an outcome of social movement processes (Cohen, 1985). Podcasters expressed both preexisting identity with true crime-related issues (e.g., empathy for victims, an orientation toward justice, and concern for criminal justice issues), and for some, a growing identification with true-crime-related social movements.

Many of the participants described themselves as life-long true crime fans, a fandom that evolved over time to care about both systemic and specific crime issues. Fuller described his love of *Forensic Files*. Other participants also specifically mentioned formative experiences with television and other true crime media:

- Morford: "I've always had an interest in true crime. It started when I was a kid. I used to watch *Unsolved Mysteries* and a lot of other shows plus a lot of different true crime channels. You know, the Discovery Channel and some of these networks."
- Pacheco: "I have been listening to true crime podcasts for a couple of years, but I was always into true crime. I watched *America's Most Wanted*, *Unsolved Mysteries*, all that kind of stuff growing up. It was always something I was interested in."
- Chaudry: "I mean, I grew up on the stuff. I loved it. I love those one-hour pass-time shows, but you know, it's not that I don't love it now."
- Rice: "I've always been into true crime, like since I was a pre-teen. I'd be reading books on serial killers, and different crime stories, watching TV shows about it, and movies, and then my interest continued."

• Zappala: "I have always been interested in cold cases and missing person cases, since I was a little girl."

Their prior fandom for true crime podcasts was mixed, however. While some, like Morford, expressed that they "only listen to true crime," others, like Rankin, Fuller, Rice, and Pacheco, described themselves as big fans of many kinds of podcasts, with true crime only being one of many interests. Others, like Chaudry and Zappala, were led to podcasts by particular true crime narratives, specifically *Serial*.

As mentioned in *Serial*, long before her involvement with podcasts, Chaudry was an advocate for Adnan Syed, based on her long-time friendship with his family. She credits her identity, as both a true crime podcast fan and host, with being directly related to her role in his case. Preexisting connections to a case or cause were mentioned by several other participants as well. "I wanted to do something I was passionate about," Morford said. Fuller began his first true crime podcast based on a case that he had been following—first as a journalist and later out of curiosity—for eight years. Pacheco said his drive to start a true crime podcast was based on his desire for more information on cases he cared about. "[I knew there] were other people like me out there." He continued:

I always found I wanted more information because at the time I thought a lot of podcasts were sort of giving you like the Wikipedia summary of the case. So I would always be asking myself questions during an episode and, at the end of it, I wouldn't have the answers. So I would research stuff myself to find out what I wanted to know. It just kind of became a decision of if I'm going to do this and research it anyway I might as well just make a show where I do a podcast the way I want it done.

Rice also expressed a desire driven by a personal connection to share stories with others who cared about true crime. She told me that

[I] sat on a first-degree murder trial last year for a murder that happened here close to my home . . . I wanted to tell the story and I had already been listening to podcasts. It was a kind of perfect storm of "I have a story to tell plus I love podcasts and kind of want to start one of my own."

While some participants, like Miller, became podcasters specifically to advocate for criminal justice causes, others developed their identity with criminal justice movement goals after beginning their podcasts. Morford described starting his podcast out of a desire for a career change and a love of telling stories but developed a passion for amplifying the voices of victims after interviewing Golden State Killer survivors. Zappala and Fuller told similar stories. Both began their podcasts to tell journalistically oriented missing person stories, but found themselves identifying with larger causes over time, like advocating for child victims. Delia's podcast and subsequent passion for exposing how the justice system interacts with victims of sexual assault began through covering a story on her crime beat. She developed a relationship with the victim of an assault and, through their conversations, saw a story that she felt demanded to be told.

Participants also mentioned how becoming involved in producing true crime changed their focus from specific cases to systemic issues. Fuller described how investigating the second season of *Frozen Truth* caused him to become an advocate for children in the foster care system:

> I came away a changed person . . . I thought this is a story that needs to be told . . . I've gone from a journalist fact-finder to find *her*, to find Ayla Reynolds, to an advocate for foster care system reform. And there again, you're straddling that line. After I uncovered that part of the story, I felt that it needed to be included.

Chaudry described a similar phenomenon of discovering how procedure and bureaucracy—even for those familiar with the criminal justice system—could become obstacles to finding justice, and her desire to advocate for systemic changes. The obstacles she mentions facing as an advocate are the same that Rankin described as external constraints as a journalist. Chaudry said:

> Thinking about this from an advocacy space—one of the things that's been shocking for me is a lot, in all these convictions that we work on, the perception, even as a lawyer, my perception was that what happens in the court room, the public owns it, right? Like, there's public access, there should be access to public recordings of all those proceedings. But it's not. And one of the most shocking things to me is that often times things happen in a courtroom, and, if there is a recording, you can't have it, or there is a recording and you can have it, but you can't air it. There are records that just disappear. How easy it is for huge holes in systems to remain forever and nobody ever try to do anything about it.

Podcasters credited interactions after entering the true crime podcast space with further developing their sense of belonging to a collective cause or motivating them to advocate for particular issues. Zappala said:

> I saw that I got a lot of response from listeners about some themes that came up in the later episodes, like domestic violence and sexual assault. So many people reacted to that in the next episode that I'm preparing to be talking more about it

. . . a lot of women have said "I've had a similar experience," and they write me emails about what happened to them.

Participants also mentioned that fans of their podcasts often share this identity as both true crime fans and people who care about crime-related issues. Chaudry described her listeners as "people who have investigative minds, who are also really interested in criminal justice issues and wrongful conviction as a phenomenon, and there've just very socially justice kind of oriented." These listeners often see the podcasters as allies in a shared cause and reach out to increase publicity. Rice said:

I've had listeners reach out to me on Facebook and say, "Hey, my cousin was murdered by so and so," and that person actually happened to be a serial killer, a lesser known serial killer, and I ended up telling that story on the podcast . . . I got an email from a listener saying that she sat on a jury for a horrendous murder out of New York State, and I'm going to be telling that story on the podcast as well.

What seems to take podcasters (and their listeners) from members of a fandom to a collective identity around social causes is a commitment to "justice." While commitment to justice is one of Punnett's (2018) defining aspects of true crime, obviously not all true crime focuses on a justice orientation. Over half of the participants mentioned justice or advocacy in some way. Others, while not directly using the word "justice," described desiring some acknowledgment of systemic wrongs through their work. Rankin offered journalistic podcasts like his own, *Accused*, and *In the Dark* as examples of media "focusing on failures in the system." Delia, while uncomfortable with "advocacy" in her role as a journalist, sees working toward better systemic understanding as the point of her work. "You do it to do good work, and if needed change comes from that work, then that's great to know. That's why you do the work."

Hunt, also a journalist, had no hesitation in referring to herself as an advocate and said that balancing journalistic ethics with advocacy in her cases had been a deep discussion over the production of the podcast. She described the position that she and her team took: "I'm comfortable being an advocate for a dead person. I mean, she was brutally killed, I'm comfortable with that. She did not deserve that. Nobody deserves that. I can be on her side. That's okay."

Both Rice and Brantley specifically described their views of podcasts' relationships to justice by allowing these stories to be told. Rice said: "There's been no justice in a case and then you've got a popular podcast that tells the story and boom! Now you've got a thousand eyes on it, and, all of a sudden, things start working again, and they're bringing justice."

Brantley proposed that the act of exposing truth through storytelling might in itself bring some kind of catharsis to people and communities involved in crimes: "We talked a lot about truth and reconciliation, and that's sequential. There's a sequence; you can't have reconciliation without truth . . . what part of justice is just getting a true account?" More about the role of justice and advocacy is discussed in the next chapter in relation to legitimacy and identity.

While many participants described identifying with movements to encourage broader knowledge of and involvement with systemic criminal justice issues, others suggested that not all true crime podcasters, even those who focus on criminal justice reform issues, have such altruistic motives. Both Pacheco and Brantley used the word "narcissistic" to describe both themselves and other podcasters. They suggested that, even if the intent of the podcast is good, the podcaster may still focus on glory or fame for themselves or be more concerned with growing the podcast than with helping a cause. Others, like Fuller, described how identifying too much with a cause or becoming too invested in a case could cause a podcaster to lose perspective and detract from any original movement motivations.

MOVEMENT ORIENTATION

Social movement theory approaches, particularly those within the classical paradigm, consider both symbolic and tangible action to be evidence of movement orientation (Buechler, 1993; Cohen, 1985, Diani, 2013; Eder, 1985; Melucci, 1985). Collective identity and issue awareness may in themselves be a kind of social movement, regardless of the existence of formal movement organizations (Cohen, 1985; Diani, 2013). From this viewpoint, collective identity can be both a goal and an input for those focused on driving social changes. I asked the podcasters about their perspectives on building symbolic and tangible action through their shows, and their responses reflect how listener input and deepening awareness of systemic issues drive their actions.

Collective Identity as Input and Goal

The podcasters gave examples of listener identification acting as an input for the growth of their podcasts as movement organizations, as well as how identification acts as symbolic or knowledge resources for podcasters with justice goals. Miller and Chaudry both credited help from listeners with the tangible successes of their podcast. Listeners connected the podcasters with an autopsy expert in the first season, leading to the discovery of valuable new case evidence. In other seasons, listeners have been responsible for tips and information throughout the investigations. Chaudry describes the willingness of her listeners to see themselves as involved in the criminal justice reform movement beyond *Undisclosed*, including a willingness to crowdfund other organizations. She said:

> There are so many people chiming in on our podcast. I mean whenever we plug—and we do this once or twice a year—we'll start off one of our shows with saying, "Hey, would you mind texting or whatever to this number and just giving five bucks to an Innocence Project or something." And literally, when we've done that in the past, these organizations will raise their funding for the year. There's a lot of trust. People have a lot of trust in the hosts of the podcasts they listen to.

Chaudry also described creating listener willingness to advocate—more evidence of collective identity—as a goal for justice advocates. Delia expressed the importance of giving voices to sexual assault victims to encourage listeners to become empathetic. By telling the stories of people who might not be considered "the perfect victim," Delia said she hoped to help people identify with the issues all kinds of victims of assault face. Brantley's definition of encouraging collective identity included the preservation of "institutional memory, the collective memory" to keep justice issues salient.

Tangible and Symbolic Action

While collective awareness and identity are necessary for all social movement approaches, both resource mobilization and political process paradigms include symbolic and tangible action as necessary components of "collective behavior" (Smelser, 1962). These actions may be facilitated through *technologies of mobilization* or forms of communication used to increase collective awareness within social movement sectors (SMSs) (McCarthy & Zald, 2002). In the context of resource mobilization and political process paradigms of SMT, "technology" refers not only to equipment or technological advances but also to the networks, relationships, and institutions that may facilitate the flow of knowledge, resources, and shared identification in a movement. These technologies of mobilization are also be referred to as *mobilizing structures* (McAdam, 1999; McCarthy & Zald, 1996, 2002). Participants pointed to many instances of both tangible and symbolic action through true crime podcasts and described the role of these podcasts as mobilizing structures.

Tangible action, like the high-profile cases mentioned throughout this book, has received more attention in popular press but can be harder to attribute solely to podcasts. The interviews provide evidence that the players involved in the true crime podcast population firmly believe, as Rice said, "It's real and it's happening." Participants not only mentioned these high-profile cases, such as Syed's new trial ruling following *Serial* and *Undisclosed* and new evidence in the Tara Grinstead case after *Up and Vanished*, but also offered concrete examples from their own experiences. Rankin described having judges in two cases bring up his podcast during jury selection as a possible influence to be considered during voir dire.[1]

Freemark, while hesitant to credit her podcast's investigation, said that Curtis Flowers, the defendant in *In the Dark*'s second season, had his case accepted for review by the U.S. Supreme Court, possibly based on information found during the podcast.[2] For Delia, hearing that survivors of assault have found strength to navigate the judicial system is tangible proof of results: "We had someone from Canada email us the other week like, 'I listened to your podcast and it inspired me to report my sexual assault to the police, and I never had the courage to do that before.'"

Miller scoffed at the idea that true crime podcasts' ability to create social change was even in question. "The things that we are reporting on have led to possibilities of relief for these people. That's the answer, proof of concept." Miller also described the ability of podcasts to take on reform issues without a narrative arc and still achieve tangible results:

> Early on, I recognized that I wanted to do sort of discrete episodes that looked at particular issues in the criminal justice system. And you know, through those episodes, for instance . . . one focused on compensation for people who are exonerated and wrongly convicted and a second was on looking at the lack of laws in this country that make it so that police officers can't claim consent as a defense when they engage in sexual acts with people in their custody . . . I'm working with a legislator here in South Carolina who is now basically filing bills on those issues next year.

Rice illustrated within-sector mobilization by comparing true crime podcasts to mobilizing true crime documentaries like *The Keepers*. Her description matches those found through content analysis (Sherrill, 2020), as many of the analyzed news articles also compared true crime podcasts to other true crime media. Rice described podcasts in particular as a tool for advancing podcaster's movement goals:

> The thing that I'm most excited about when it comes to podcasting, and to true crime specifically, is the power that podcasters have to really do good. To bring awareness to cases where justice has not been served or the case has not been solved. And I think that's very exciting.

Chaudry too used a "tool" analogy to describe the advocacy power of podcasts:

> I think it's a fantastic tool, and you have to use every tool in your arsenal. Social media is a tool, podcasting is a tool, any kind of media can be a tool. In terms of if it's the right method—if it works it's the right method. It's as simple as that. And it has worked . . . at the end of the day, if you can bring somebody justice, it's working. It's a tool. You can abuse it, and you can use it properly.

Participants offered more examples of *symbolic* action. Rankin credited both true crime and political podcasts with improving civic knowledge. He said, "There are people who normally wouldn't read the newspaper or watch TV news, and it's making them more informed." Several participants cited the attention that podcasts bring to both individual cases and to systemic issues as the most important and widespread form of symbolic action. Pacheco and Rice mentioned attention as the primary output of their podcasts and similarly-formatted shows, particularly for less well-known cases. Rice said,

> Podcasts have had a real impact on solving crimes and bringing justice to families just by telling these stories . . . if a podcast has a certain number of listeners, you know, a large audience, they can really make an impact on solving, let's say, a cold case or bringing enough attention.

Zappala too mentioned the ability to bring attention to "miscarriages of justice" through the viral popularity of podcasts—something that other forms of investigative journalism might not garner. Morford and Delia described the power of amplifying the voices of survivors. Morford said:

> When somebody opens up to you about something so personal, it's sort of moving because it's something that a lot of people don't like to talk about, and they share their stories with you. And then you share their stories with the world. It's an odd feeling. It's really a pleasure to do that, to give somebody a platform for them to talk. The interesting thing about podcasting is that you can help . . . . There's people learning about things that maybe they didn't know before, being outraged about things . . . the subject of rape and some of the Golden State Killer coverage we did—some people just didn't know how bad things were in that case and some of the stuff that was done—it brought up the subject of untested rape kits. I think as people learn about stuff they become more involved, more educated, and do things like contribute money to certain funds . . . there's a really good learning process to learn things and about causes you might not have known about before these podcasts.

Delia also expressed the importance of education about systemic issues through the stories of survivors, particularly as a way for men to understand women's experiences:

> There's a lot of power in hearing your story and saying it out loud even if no one knows who you are . . . [I had] men telling me they understand women's assaults better now. I got a lot of feedback that they were just horrified. It was an education for them about women being believed or not being believed. . . . When I look at the work that we are doing, it's really affecting people, and it's really doing things, and it's really making people look at these systems that are so important that we all don't know how to navigate.

Increasing knowledge and awareness of how the judicial system works was mentioned by almost all participants as the most valuable symbolic contribution of true crime podcasts. Depending on the podcast, this knowledge may deal with racial disparity, sexual assault, missing persons, forensic science, or even personal safety. Chaudry credits being a fan of podcasts herself with teaching her ways of protecting herself:

> They [particular podcasters] work with Crime Stoppers and they work with law enforcement, so they're not just saying, "Oh, let me tell you about this case from 1995 that's so crazy and so horrible," but they're saying, "Does anybody know anything? These are the numbers to call." Also, they're providing valuable information. I learned a lot from listening to true crime podcasts about how to keep yourself safe.

Chaudry went on to describe the impact of true crime podcasts to challenge the narrative of traditional depictions of "law and order" and criminal justice. She said:

> We've been watching TV, we've been growing up on this stuff, and on *Dateline* and these true crime shows, rarely did you see the police getting it wrong. Rarely do they point out like all the flaws in prosecution or investigation, and podcasts are very, very well able to. And people like the long format. They are willing to listen to a series, they're willing to pay attention and get it and understand why criminal justice advocates, criminal justice reform advocates, for years have been saying, "This shit is broken" . . . I've gotten tons of emails over the years from people who are middle aged, midwestern white people who say, "I never got it until I listened to your show. Now I get it."

Hunt also stressed the value of podcasts' ability to show the real judicial system. "We might not be able to really move the dial of a case, you know, our best efforts might not get us there. But at least we can do work that highlights flaws in the law enforcement process or the legal system or just inform people about parts of this process that they don't know about," she said.

Hunt also offered the strongest rationalization for recognizing true crime podcasts as structures for advocacy: the testimony of the people personally affected by the stories these podcasts address. She said:

> People who have been in this kind of situation, they know that the attention paid when they're adopted in this way is invaluable. There was a woman at our live show that said, "I would have paid a million dollars for this." I think it was her son that was murdered. . . . It's not so much that they want us to solve it. They just want to be heard and to have it looked at properly. When you feel like police have done too cursory of a job or have somehow failed you, or that your loved one is somehow forgotten, is just some statistic, it's hard to move forward with your life without feeling like you're betraying that person. So these podcasts at least, you know, they highlight issues that people need to know about. They pay attention to victims who are often forgotten and when they're done well, they can make a real difference in a case.

MOVEMENT PROCESSES

In the resource mobilization and political process paradigms of SMT, movements go beyond collective awareness and identity to organized, politicized forms (Diani, 2013; Huddy, 2001; Van Zomeren et al., 2008). These organized forms require group efficacy, symbolic and environmental political opportunities, and physical, monetary, and symbolic resources to survive (McAdam, 1999, 2017; McCarthy & Zald, 1977, 2002; Oberschall, 1973). *Framing processes*, such as mobilizing emotions, are used to negotiate boundaries and tactics by acting as the social construction of "shared meanings and cultural understandings . . . including a shared collective identity" (McAdam, 1999, p. ix). My interviews with true crime podcasters illustrated the ways these producers navigate movement processes and harness collective identity.

Symbolic and Environmental Political Opportunity

Participants described both symbolic and environmental political opportunities over the past several years that have allowed true crime podcasts to be effective as movement organizations. Brantley credited the surge in true crime popularity across media formats as one such opportunity that has allowed podcasters to capture audience. "Woo them with the true crime and then keep them there for the meditation on race in America," he said. Brantley and Chaudry both described the post-2016 U.S. presidential election climate as an opportunity. While Chaudry sees both the expansion of political podcasts and "resistance" rhetoric as related to and beneficial for true crime–related movements, Brantley pointed directly to the rise in conversations about race in America as an opportunity for his podcast: "Put yourself back in early 2017. We've just had an election, everyone is talking about white nationalism. There are things happening in the country that make that feel like a good conversation to have."

Hunt described environmental opportunities as a convergence of timing and resources. The effectiveness of her podcast was possible because of technological, forensic, popular culture, and media shifts (i.e., her print outlet was exploring new ways to monetize) at a point when the original suspects in the 1978 case were still alive and able to be investigated.

Miller, Rice, and Chaudry each credited an unlikely source of symbolic political opportunity—celebrities' social media. Both Rice and Miller referenced the impact of reality star Kim Kardashian's interest in criminal justice reform, specifically in the Cyntoia Brown case. Brown, an inmate in Tennessee, received a life sentence at 16 for killing a man who had paid her for sex and allegedly threatened her life. Miller credited Kardashian's tweets about Brown with drawing his interest to the case, leading to an episode of *Undisclosed* and Miller's involvement with 16 other legal organizations to petition on Brown's behalf. Brown was granted clemency in January 2019 (Gafas & Burnside, January 8, 2019). Rice mentioned pop star Rihanna's social media activism as influential for drawing attention to criminal justice reform issues, as well the conversation of other celebrities about *Serial* and Syed's case.

Chaudry too pointed to the relationship between true crime podcasts, pop culture, and celebrities becoming involved in advocating for issues of justice. She said:

> Where some podcasts have been useful is not just talking about a specific defendant, but talking about systemic issues. And that's caught the eye of certain celebrities. I mean, I think just yesterday Jay-Z [rapper, media mogul, and husband of Beyonce Knowles] announced a new initiative for criminal justice reform. I'm not saying that's been influenced by podcasts, but I think in general that podcasts are adding to the urgency of these issues and that's a good thing.

Participants offered other examples of taking advantage of environmental and symbolic political opportunities but also mentioned ways that outside political actors affected these opportunities. One example is the pushback from the state of Georgia in several cases covered by podcasters. While Rankin described using his existing relationships with judges and court officials to side-step courtroom audio rules, Chaudry and Miller both mentioned being stymied by state officials. One such case led all the way to the Georgia Supreme Court, which ruled against *Undisclosed*'s request for court audio (*Undisclosed LLC v. The State*, 2017).

Framing Processes

In the context of social movement processes, "framing" goes beyond the kind of linguistic frame analysis common in communication literature (e.g., Goffman, 1974). While the use of particular frames to shape a movement narrative may be a part of framing processes, social movement scholars describe the creation of collective action frames as "an active, processual phenomenon that implies agency and contention at the level of reality construction" (Benford & Snow, 2000, p. 614). Framing within a social movement paradigm is a phenomenon that involves action and choices on the part of the mobilizing organizer, as well as the negotiation and redefinition of goals and emotions through two-way communication with constituents. This process is closely related to what organizational ecology calls "bidirectional boundary work," the process through which an organization's audience and consumers help to define the identity of the organization (Gioia et al., 2000; Polos et al., 2002). These framing processes, including mobilizing emotions, group efficacy, and issue ownership, affect the evolution of collective identity into politicized forms capable of creating societal change (McAdam, 1999).

Participants offered examples of these framing processes. One such example is the "motivational framing" (Snow & Benford, 1988) movement leaders may employ to encourage constituents to feel efficacy and issue ownership. Miller described *Undisclosed*'s efforts to build efficacy among podcasts with criminal justice reform goals. He said,

> Podcasts can have a terrific role in advocating for social change. We've actively promoted other podcasts, again under the thinking that we want people tackling these issues in the criminal justice system. . . . We want our podcast to secure justice for people we think are wrongly convicted.

Miller's explicitly expressed goal orientation ("to secure justice for people we think are wrongly convicted") is also evidence of issue ownership. Several participants mentioned podcasters feeling either protective of certain issues or cases or of wanting to incorporate ownership of an issue into their listeners' collective identity. Pacheco said, "You'll cover a case, and someone will get mad because they had this proprietary thing, 'That's my case.' Well, it's really not anybody's case." Fuller also described feeling protective of his case and the victim's family as he came to know them. Delia felt that her audience owned the stories:

> I wanted people to feel like this was their podcast and that even though maybe their assault didn't involve drugs or didn't involve a stranger or whatever, that they had a voice and that everyone's story is different and that everyone's story is valid.

Mobilizing emotions were also important to participants. In some cases, these emotions were present in the way that podcasters chose to produce their podcasts. For Rankin and Freemark, a desire for accountability from elected officials and law enforcement served as motivation. Hunt said that the *Accused* team kept photos of the victims in their cases up in their work-room to be a constant reminder of the goals behind the project. In addition to humanizing their subjects, Hunt said the photos helped the team to be aware of ethical considerations as they worked. She said,

> Our bias was that we were clear that we wanted to move this case forward, that we wanted to help find a resolution. We want to help solve a murder. It wasn't because I wanted bragging rights. It was because this victim's family deserved it.

Pacheco mentioned trying to keep a similar emotional motivation behind his process working with missing person cases:

> This person was a person. So a lot of times people get wrapped up in the disap-pearance and not the, "this was an actual person that had friends and family and kids" or whatever, and so I try to make that come to life a little bit instead of just being the background to what happened.

Almost all participants described their work in terms of goals, generally related to criminal justice issues, and expressed shared identity as both true crime fans and supporters of systemic changes to the way justice issues are handled in the United States. They often described their listeners as compa-triots in those goals and as people with similar attitudes toward crime and justice. What these responses do not illustrate, however, is how widespread this orientation is across the ever-expanding true crime podcast population. In describing the violation of "norms" they see by some other podcasters (more in the next chapter), participants suggested that many true crime podcasts do not have goals beyond organizational maintenance as entertainment enti-ties. These responses illustrate that *some* members of the true crime podcast population operate from a social movement orientation, though that orienta-tion is often more aligned with an idea of spreading awareness for the cause of "justice" rather than a clear connection to a fully formed social movement.

MOVEMENT ORIENTATION, COLLECTIVE IDENTITY, AND MOVEMENT PROCESSES

The podcasters offered mixed support for the conceptualization of true crime podcasts as social movement agents or mobilizing structures. While the participants in this study all described orientations toward furthering "justice" in relation to true crime narratives, they were clear in noting that not all true crime podcasts share any such motivation. The strength of this justice orientation and its links to a social movement around criminal justice reform also differed among participants.

Collective Identity

These podcasters expressed an identity as (most often, lifelong) true crime fans. For many, this fandom led to an interest in particular cases. For others, personal connections pulled them into a case. Some participants described how individual cases led them to become advocates for systemic issues, like child victims or more thorough investigation of rape cases. A desire for "justice," whether through telling a victim's story or bringing attention to a systemic problem, often led podcasters to feel an obligation to uncovering "truth" in the service of justice, broadly.

For podcasters who are also journalists, there seems to be a fine line between a journalistic orientation toward the basic principles of fact-finding and information sharing as a good in itself and the desire to bring about change. Participants reported wrestling with journalistic ethics and their own biases. They were divided in how they justified their positions, with some falling firmly on the side of reporting without advocating broadly, while others clearly stated advocacy motivations. Some, like Fuller, cautioned that while advocacy could be ethical, becoming too close to stories could become detrimental both to advocacy causes and the podcaster's own credibility.

The importance of identity as part of a social change movement oriented toward criminal justice reform is evident in the way some podcasters spoke about themselves. They used words like "passion" to describe their podcasts and cited mobilizing emotions (McAdam, 2017) growing from their personal connections to a cause. Even those participants who considered themselves to be most oriented toward traditional journalism rather than advocacy expressed the desire to tell a story in a way that would lead listeners to feel a connection or call to action around an issue. This suggests the classical social movement paradigm which considers awareness and symbolic challenges to systemic norms "victories" (Eder, 1985; Melucci, 1985, 1995). Participants' expression of a commitment to justice is also in line with McAdam (1999, 2017) and Cohen's (1985) motivating factors for collective action in both the political process model and classically oriented SMT paradigms. In addition, participants expressed a sense of efficacy that their work could have tangible effects, nearly all offering, as Miller phrased it, "proof of concept" that their methods work. This sense of efficacy, commitment to justice (or, recognition of injustice), and politicized identity are strong predictors of effective social movements in the social identity model of collective action (Van Zomeren et al., 2008) as well as the political process model (McAdam, 1999; McAdam et al., 1996; Oberschall, 1973; Rule & Tilly, 1975; Tilly, 1978). This further supports claims that at least some of these true crime podcasts and their listeners are acting more as social movement agents and less as journalists or entertainers.

Whether participants' desire to create collective awareness of criminal justice issues regardless of formal attachment to a social movement sector represents a movement orientation depends largely on the SMT paradigm through which it is interpreted. As mentioned earlier, the classical approach conceptualizes the creation of collective awareness and identity as a type of movement on its own, regardless of the mode or organization of collective action that follows. It is clear from participants' descriptions of the growing interest in criminal justice–oriented true crime media, celebrity involvement, and popularity of criminal justice–oriented documentaries, as well as the increasingly bipartisan support for criminal justice reform (Fandos, December 18, 2018; Levine, July 1, 2021), that there is some kind of growing criminal justice social movement in the United States—at least from the standpoint of collective identity. How much credit for mobilizing that movement can be given to these true crime podcasts, however, is still up for debate.

From a resource mobilization or political process perspective, the work of goal-oriented podcasts can be conceptualized as *popular contention*, or action by non- or newly institutionalized forms (McAdam et al., 2003). Resource mobilization also offers a framework for possibly explaining how different podcasters fit into a social movement framework. Two of its four assumptions require the spread of knowledge about a movement and the friendliness of mass media toward covering the movement (McCarthy & Zald, 1979, 2002). While some of the journalists/podcasters may not be explicitly movement actors themselves, they provide the "friendly mass media" environment needed for more directly involved actors to thrive.

Prior scholarship has suggested that SMT frameworks like resource mobilization and the political process model can lead to erroneously conflating movement organizations with the movement itself (Johnston, 2014). Johnston describes movements as "big, change-oriented ideas" that unify various separate organizations and groups. It is networks of loosely connected and broadly defined agents that form a social movement, and no one, organized, elite contender is required. Diversity of forms under the umbrella of those "big ideas" may represent "symbolic outputs" for a movement. These "symbolic outputs" are especially relevant for populations of movement-oriented media organizations (Greve et al., 2006; Hannan, 1988). Interviews with podcasters point to this diversity, with some explicitly describing their podcasts as social change organizations, while others described their work as more loosely tied to "big ideas" like justice for victims, police accountability, and spreading knowledge about systemic criminal justice issues. Some participants, like Rice and Brantley, offered examples that echoed Carroll and Hackett's assertion that within social movements, "alternative media are not simply a political instrument but a collective good in themselves" (2006, p. 88). Participants' descriptions of creating collective identity by spreading awareness also reflect the classical conceptualization of modern social movement mobilization: "Occasions for identification have to be created—the public sphere has to be 'made'" (Habermas, 1989, p. 201). It seems safe to say that the public sphere for conversations about criminal justice has been made in the true crime podcast space.

NOTES

1. *Voir dire* comes from French for "to speak the truth" and is the process through which lawyers and judges determine jurors' and witnesses' fitness to serve or testify (Cornell Law School, n.d.).

2. While Freemark did not take credit during the interview, the Supreme Court likely accepted the case based on findings discovered over the course of a massive data journalism project by the *In the Dark* team. Their investigation discovered evidence of a pattern of racial discrimination in jury selection that has been reported as the reason the high court agreed to hear the case (Liptak, Feb. 18, 2019). In June of 2019, Flowers' conviction was overturned, and, in 2020, all charges were finally dropped. Flowers had served over 20 years without a conviction ever holding up on appeal (Slotkin, September 5, 2020).

Chapter 7

Podcasts as Legitimated Hybrid Organizations

It's inherently a medium where people have to be entertained. If people are not entertained in some way, they're not going to listen.

—Chip Brantley

When I first began talking to friends and colleagues about podcasts in the true crime genre as social movement mobilizers, I would be met with blank looks. "True crime?" my listeners would say. "You mean serial killer fans and reenactment shows?" I understood. As I've already mentioned in earlier chapters, the true crime genre's reputation for salaciousness has stuck around, often for good reason. A quick glance at the programming lineup for the Investigation Discovery or Oxygen cable networks makes this clear: show and episode titles like *Deadly Women: Twisted Desire*, *Your Worst Nightmare: He Seems Perfect*, or *An Unexpected Killer: Closet Murderer* abound. Then there are the documentaries and based-on-a-true-crime movies that seem to fully embrace the problematic "sexy serial killer" tropes. Take for example 2019's Ted Bundy movie *Extremely Wicked, Shockingly Evil, and Vile* starring former teen heartthrob Zac Efron. Many critics have pointed to the film as an example of the worst type of salacious true crime, including *Vox*'s Alissa Wilkinson who wrote that "*Extremely Wicked* gives off the distinct impression that it finds Bundy far more fascinating that anyone who suffered at his hands" (Wilkinson, May 3, 2019, para. 27). Among the podcasts in the demography, the same kind of sensationalist true crime titles abounds, with titles like *Sex, Love & Murder*, *All Killa No Filla*, or *Adventures in Murderland*.

As I talked to each of these podcasters, I began to see a clearer picture of how they understood their organization's form and identity, as well as what listeners would accept as "appropriate" behavior and content. While ideological goals were vital, they were pragmatic about the resources and costs associated with maintaining their organizations. Both organizational ecology and social movement theories (SMTs) include these concepts of organizational identity, legitimacy, and stakeholder negotiation. Identity is related to form and niche, and it may evolve over the life cycle of an organization. Identity evolves as the norms, or acceptable behavior, are negotiated within the organization, with other population members, and with outside agents (Jacobs et al., 2008; Tilly, 1986). Legitimacy, both for the maintenance of organizations and the acceptance of social movements, may be affected by how well the identity of an organization matches with the needs or goals of its population or movement sector. Both legitimacy and identity are influenced by negotiation with stakeholders and outside agents as the organization or movement evolves. I asked the participants about their perceptions of true crime podcasts to understand how those organizations exhibit hybrid characteristics. Podcasters discussed several concepts in ways that reflect both ecological and social movement paradigms, supporting that yes, *some* true crime podcast organizations do have hybrid orientations.

ORGANIZATIONAL NORM
CREATION AND VIOLATION

As discussed earlier, boundary work establishes the niche fit of organizations. The negotiation of norms within a population is a kind of boundary work and may also shape the identity of organizations. Participants gave examples of ways norms have been established for true crime podcasts as well as their perceptions of norm violations.

Several participants mentioned that norms may still be in flux for true crime podcasts and compared these norms to other media. "There are not a lot of stringent standards to telling these stories," Rice said, adding that the lack of standards separates a lot of true crime from what she would consider journalism. Pacheco made a similar comment, saying, "It's a very strange environment because there's no rules to it." Miller too described the lack of clear boundaries for podcasters, particularly in dealing with legal matters. He said, "I think rules are still being figured out in terms of how these are handled and how they sort of intersect with the legal system, but it's exciting."

More than one participant used the term "wild west" to describe the true crime podcast community. Because of the lack of formal standards, podcasters reported a kind of self-policing of the space, with other podcasters and listeners constantly negotiating what is "acceptable." Pacheco said:

> In terms of the community itself, there's a huge debate about the way [stories] should be handled, and you've got everything from the people who are very

comedic about the way they tell them to the people who are very serious. . . . Most of the debate is between podcasters . . . hosts try to self-moderate the world of true crime so that if they feel someone stepped over the line then some of the bigger names might say something publicly about it. But then the bigger names go back and forth, and you see these debates happening all the time between upper echelon podcasters.

Chaudry described this self-policing as a consideration for deciding which other podcast hosts to have as guests or to endorse on *Undisclosed*. She said, "We are very careful in our assessment of shows that we think might be exploitive to a case and the defendants and victims."

Interactions with listeners were credited with helping to shape the norms of the population by several participants. Miller noted that listeners helped his team negotiate the language barrier between seasoned attorneys and people with a strong interest in criminal justice but no formal training. Pacheco said listeners helped him understand what kind of content might require a "trigger warning" and how to be more sensitive when discussing topics like sex work or assault. Morford said the development of his "very professional, very serious, very respectful" style had also been shaped by listeners: "I'm very creative, and it's important to me to be fact based and detail-oriented and put a lot of work into it. and I think the end result, you know, it shows, and the listeners appreciate that."

Hunt said she trusted listeners to recognize high-quality podcasts and to support deserving population members:

People recognize the power of telling a story in this format. I don't necessarily agree with how every other podcaster approaches this. . . but I'm hoping . . . the quality ones rise, and the less savory ones hopefully fall away.

Chaudry and Pacheco both described the importance of podcasters doing investigations and interacting with open cases in careful and ethical ways, particularly, what information podcasters chose *not* to broadcast. These comments reflect some podcasters' focus on tangible outcomes of their work. Said Chaudry:

We don't do anything, we don't report anything that has not been cleared because we do not want to hurt the defendant's case. We don't care about the listenership, we don't care about the wow factor, we don't want to hurt that person's case.

Pacheco expressed the importance of podcasters recognizing their responsibility to "not make things worse." Of discovering unknown or titillating information about a case, he said,

I've got to hold that back. There are other people to be like, "No one else has heard this! We'll get more downloads if I put it out there!" So, it's a really sticky situation of being a true crime podcaster. It isn't always, "Let me tell you everything." Sometimes it's knowing what to tell and what not to tell.

The lack of clearly set boundaries for true crime podcasters is reflected in Freemark's hesitation to call *In the Dark* a "true crime podcast." While Freemark's show clearly fits the boundaries of the true crime population, based both on Punnett's (2018) criteria and the way it is marketed and discussed by media, listeners, and other podcasters, she insisted, "I think people are very clear on the distinction between what we are doing and like a traditional true crime thing." In explaining how she views the distinction between "traditional true crime" and her work, Freemark too noted the lack of clear standards and boundaries. She said:

In the same way as TV, there's like true crime TV stuff that's really just like, you know, lots of like dramatic music and focus on blood spattered walls and like reenactments of someone stabbing someone to death. And then, on the other hand, there's something like *Making a Murderer*, more like a criminal justice broadcast that like, is just reporting. In TV, we don't really lump those together. We understand the distinction there. I think in podcasting for some reason we have trouble drawing some of those distinctions which are distinctions which should be drawn. Again, there's work that's really based on the storytelling of crimes, and then there's work that adheres to more traditional journalistic standards, and so we do our best to be the latter of those. And again, we would never describe ourselves as a true crime podcast. Like, we would describe ourselves as criminal justice reporting.

While other participants were fine with their identities being defined as "true crime," they were quick to offer multiple examples of norm violations of what they see as "acceptable" ways of doing true crime. Some of these violations are more ecological, relating to boundaries between journalism and sensationalist media, while others relate to the movement orientations of podcasts, such as how goal-focused investigations are conducted. Delia described "bad" true crime as those with poor production and editing quality. Pacheco noted that some podcasts "steal" content from others and wondered how long it will be until the population begins to see pushback or lawsuits between members.[1] Hunt described being uncomfortable with podcasts that she saw as gratuitous or disrespectful:

I don't think that reflects well on the rest of us . . . I'm very careful. I saw another podcast doing a promotional type of act that was like "wine, cheese, and murder" and it's like, there's a real person in this case!

Zappala expressed a similar criticism, particularly pointing to the divide between podcasts by journalists and those by amateur reporters:

I think it's definitely just as professional as other ways of talking about news or issues as long as it's done by a professional. There's definitely a lot of those podcasts I was mentioning, I don't want to bad-mouth them, but a lot of times I find that they approach things in an unprofessional and disrespectful manner because they are not journalists and they just want to chat about cases . . . Yeah, of course it can be unprofessional. Some people enjoy it that way. I don't.

Morford too expressed dismay at the nature of many popular true crime podcasts, describing one of the most popular as "joking through Wikipedia." He continued:

For me personally—not to damn anybody that listens—it's hard for me to hear about these stories of what happened to people and make jokes. That's not me. And I think . . . it helps people laugh a little bit, you need some laughs, but for me it's just hard to mix the two. I think when I'm dealing with victims of crime or family members of victims, or the police, you treat them very seriously and professionally and with respect. We're putting our reputation on the line.

Chaudry described audience appetites and podcasters' quests for ratings as a possible driver for the kinds of true crime she personally finds disturbing:

I'm continuously kind of surprised. I shouldn't be because, when I think about it, there's a lot of podcasts out there that are not great in terms of substance but have a huge following. And sometimes it's kinds of annoying because it signals the kinds of public appetites that exist for things that are not great. Just recently there was a podcast that was announced a couple of weeks ago and I was shocked. Anyways, the whole podcast pitch is that "This is some of the goriest true crime incidents that have ever happened, and we're gonna air the goriest gore of it, and we're not gonna be squeamish, and we're gonna play the 911 calls, and we're gonna play the audio of people screaming." And you know what? Huge audience for this shit.

Several participants described podcasts that they saw as violating norms— either of the true crime population or of basic human decency. Brantley described some popular podcasts as "irresponsible and gross" in the way they treat their subjects. He described one top-charting podcast as having, "done more harm for journalism than anything I can think of." Brantley, along with several other participants, described how podcasters who are not mindful of their work can easily distort a case and exploit already traumatized families.

Several participants also used the colloquialism "murder porn" to describe this kind of exploitative true crime. Fuller said:

> I know for some people it's kind of an unhealthy fascination and obsession with murder and with really strange death and torture . . . If you're not advocating for the victim, you're probably not journalistically going after any information. You're simply showing the recreation of a series of what *South Park* the TV show called "murder porn."[2] It's hard to come up with a better description . . . at what point are you trying to help someone, are you trying to solve a mystery, and at what point is it just voyeurism?

The language choices of participants in describing things they view as norm violations or to be avoided in their work are noteworthy. Three participants were very concerned with professional versus unprofessional behavior from podcast hosts, often using examples of journalistic norms as standards of professionalism. Several participants also used words like "exploit," "exploitative," or "exploitativeness" to describe the ways "unprofessional" podcasters treat victims or families. Other examples of participants' descriptions of "inappropriate" ways to tell podcast stories included "salacious," "sleazy," "sensational/sensationalized/sensationalist," "voyeurism," "grotesque," "lurid," "harm," and too much focus on "blood and guts" or "gore."

There were two very successful podcasts and their hosts who were brought up repeatedly by multiple participants as extreme examples of norm violations. While none of the participants were comfortable going on the record with criticism in the interview (though several have been open in their criticism on public forums), their comments are worth discussing anonymously. One of these podcasts was started in 2013 and has continued to be one of the most well-known and widely listened true crime podcasts. It was at one time a member of one of the largest corporate podcast networks and had major advertising contracts.[3] While participants commented on the strength of the podcast in terms of accurate information and technical quality, they questioned the ethics of its host. Interestingly, this host was also one of the people many participants described as a negative or "feuding" influence within the informal personal networks of podcasters. Participants suggested that this host and the host of another podcast described as particularly "exploitative" are involved in true crime because of its current popularity and revenue potential rather than any real passion for victims or causes. Said one participant,

> For the most part, the fans will listen and enjoy it, but among other podcasters they will look at certain people and say, "That guy doesn't really care about the case or about the victim, he just wants to make money. He's just making things up or doing whatever."

Other participants lamented that the monetary success of these norm-violating podcasters might lead other people to mimic their style in hopes of duplicating that success. On the other hand, a listener boycott of the podcast network and social media backlash against insensitive (particularly misogynist and transphobic) comments by one of these podcasts were mentioned as examples of listeners helping to define "appropriate" boundaries. Another participant suggested that podcasters—even successful, relatively famous ones—are not prepared to deal with the possibility of millions of listeners without having the public relations support a traditional media outlet might provide. At the end of the day, one participant said, even the most demonized host is "just a guy doing a podcast."

Stakeholder Negotiation

As noted earlier, listeners, victims, and families of victims are considered stakeholders for true crime podcasters, as resources, consumers, and movement compatriots. Participants discussed the ways in which these stakeholders and others connected to cases (i.e., prosecutors, judges, and police) influence the creation of boundaries and the podcast production process.

Podcasters often described negotiation with law enforcement and judges as important for the investigation of cases. Rankin credited his prior relationships with judges and court reporters from years of work for the *Atlanta Journal Constitution* with allowing him access to audio and court documents that other podcasters (like *Undisclosed*) were unable to get. Delia said that she and her producers met with local police often, both to include law enforcement's side of the story and to build rapport in hopes of gaining information. Chaudry too noted the value of working with law enforcement despite her cases often involving police or prosecutorial misconduct:

> We do our best to reach out to the law enforcement involved, the prosecutors that were involved, to current prosecutors, to the people in the system who either had an impact on the case or can have an impact. We always did that. A lot of times, they don't want to talk. Sometimes we get lucky. . . . We have been told that whenever we go about reporting about or investigating on these cases, stakeholders are listening, the D.A. will be listening. Ex-judges will be listening. People are paying attention.

Hunt was quick to note that while she was happy to work with police, her journalistic investigation was a separate endeavor. "We are not an arm of law enforcement. They need to do their own damn jobs," she said. Zappala said that the mayor of Phoenix had become involved in the case after her reporting in his community, and that law enforcement and families were her greatest resource. She credited the sister of the victim and the help of a retired detective as the most important elements in her choosing and sticking with the Alissa Tourney case. Several participants described the particular negotiations involved with working with families of victims. Rice said, "I was very mindful of the way I told the story because I realized that—and I always know—that there's a chance that victims' families are listening to these stories."

Hunt told me, while as a journalist she never allowed the family any editorial oversight, she worked closely with families and often gave them information before airing the podcast to prevent hurtful on-air surprises. Brantley said that being mindful of promising too much to families was an important consideration. He told me, "You're entering into people's already kind of fractured and damaged lives often, and you're offering some sort of like, redemption." Pacheco described families as "open to getting attention" and "very appreciative" but noted that he avoided talking to close stakeholders until after he had done his own research, as he found stakeholders to often be too biased to provide good information.

Participants also brought up the legal complications associated with open or pending cases. Miller described the negotiation of attorney-client privilege, pointing to how *Serial* had been used to argue in court that closed documents could be considered public record because of the podcast. Miller also said that his team stressed to defense attorneys and possible subjects that while a podcast might help someone wrongfully convicted, it might be just as likely to have negative effects on their case. Fuller, whose podcast deals with cold cases, said that negotiation with law enforcement had not been difficult, as he found them so desperate for any leads that they were happy to share information and work directly with him.

Brantley mentioned negotiation with stakeholders as sometimes involving interacting with people he might normally avoid. Getting to a story, he said, means the podcaster must "treat them with dignity." He said:

> You have to go and sit down and have all-you-can-eat catfish dinners with KKK members. And like, that's not a thing that flies very well in the world right now, but it is part of this work. You have to sort of sit and listen and hear other people whose views you find despicable, but you're not there to tell them they're wrong and to virtue signal. You're there to get them to tell you the truth.

Legitimacy

The stakeholder negotiation process may both increase the perceived legitimacy of true crime podcast organizations and be aided by preexisting legitimacy. As demonstrated in past content analyses (e.g., Sherrill, 2020), cognitive legitimacy or the "taken for granted" understanding of true crime podcasts appears to be widespread. Participants offered anecdotes illustrating this. Both Hunt and Fuller talked about recent pop culture references to true crime podcasts, including a recent *Halloween* franchise movie and *Saturday Night Live* sketches. Brantley described sensing the ubiquity of true crime podcasts by how often he hears students outside his office having conversations about podcasts like *S-Town*.

Normative legitimacy, or the societal acceptance of the "appropriateness" of true crime podcasts, is also relevant to their organizational and movement orientations. Podcasters offered examples of how listeners, podcasters, and outside agents negotiate normative legitimacy. Fuller told me that while traditional media outlets may not be ready to see podcasts as peers, he believes that audiences have already made that switch. He said:

> I think the media—like TV, radio, newspaper, mainstream media—still thinks of itself as a bit above podcasting. In terms of the audience, I think most of the audience is willing to accept you as a news source if that's what you're giving them. People aren't given enough credit for being able to listen to something and say, "This is being done in a really good way and here's why" and "This is being done in a comprehensive way" . . . I think listeners can figure that out.

Fuller also described the way that law enforcement had treated him as evidence of the growing legitimacy of true crime podcasts:

> Law enforcement takes podcasts seriously almost out of fear. They understand what the medium has done to some others. They've made some agencies look pretty silly on different podcasts, and they don't want that. So, as far as law enforcement is concerned, when I've ever approached any agency, they got back to me as if I were a producer for *Dateline*. Just in this last year. That probably wouldn't have been true 10 years ago.

Different kinds of outside agents were described as helping to legitimize true crime podcasts as well. Several people mentioned the Apple iTunes chart as valuable for conferring institutional legitimacy, though also voiced concerns that Apple's "gatekeeping" might keep good podcasts from being discovered. Pacheco said that top charts as well as "best of" articles constantly being filled with the same few network-connected podcasts despite the size of the population suggested that algorithms, corporate negotiation, and advertising ties may be keeping independent podcasts from reaching legitimacy. Pacheco also pointed out that Apple's lack of a True Crime podcast category until nearly five years after the *Serial* fervor may show that the genre is "still likely not completely accepted."

Participants noted examples of celebrities and political figures conferring legitimacy to their podcasts, the podcast medium, and the true crime genre.

Former Alabama Senator Doug Jones was interviewed by Brantley for his podcast, and, as already noted, Zappala credits the mayor of Phoenix for increased police cooperation in her case. Several participants mentioned major celebrities—like Oprah, Conan O'Brien, Alec Baldwin, and Anna Farris—starting their own podcasts as evidence that the medium was continuing to grow. Rice said, "They're doing really well in their lives, but they're turning to podcasting for some reason."

Participants also described the involvement of important associations and figures in legitimizing the advocacy and justice missions of their podcasts. Hunt called actor John Cryer her "biggest fan" and credited his enthusiasm for *Accused* with helping to grow its audience. Chaudry mentioned the involvement of celebrity defense attorney Kathleen Zellner with *Truth & Justice*'s sixth season as proof of the value of that podcast's wrongful conviction work. Rankin said that winning the American Bar Association Silver Gavel Award for court reporting proved that *Breakdown* was doing superior journalism in podcast format. Morford described the attention his podcast received after being mentioned in a *Time* magazine article for its coverage of the stories of Golden State Killer victims:

> When *Time* magazine recognizes that there's people out there that are in-depth about these things and they talk about it, I think it shows you how serious and how much attention there is out there for good stuff in podcasts.

Miller, who also described the impact of celebrity interest in true crime as a resource, credited celebrity attention with helping true crime podcasts gain legitimacy. "It's great that celebrities have gotten interested in true crime and are advocating changes, and I treat that with respect. I think that is something that's a good thing," Miller said. Three podcasters also said they had been approached by television networks about their true crime podcasts, but were contractually prevented from disclosing details.

Co-option

For many podcasters, legitimacy was co-opted (Deephouse & Suchman, 2008; Downing & Pfeffer, 1975) by relationships with established organizations. While a conference of legitimacy comes from recognition (like winning an award) by established agents, co-option (also called *co-optation*) involves a relationship, either formal or informal, with already legitimized agents (Downing & Pfeffer, 1975). Rankin, Hunt, and Freemark mentioned their jobs at the *Atlanta Journal Constitution*, *Cincinnati Inquirer*, and Minnesota Public Radio as allowing their endeavors to be seen as legitimate from day one. Brantley said he felt the same advantage in working with National Public

Radio. "Just to be totally honest, the show could totally suck, and it would still reach a lot of listeners because it's NPR," he said, noting that National Public Radio has the power to negotiate with Apple iTunes on his behalf. Others described co-opting legitimacy by teaming up with well-connected individuals while producing their shows. Miller mentioned the importance of retired law enforcement officials for his cases, while Rice talked about gaining listener trust by interviewing retired FBI profilers, *Dateline* hosts, and interviewing Debra and Terra Newell, the real-life survivors known from mega-podcast-turned Bravo television series *Dirty John*. Chaudry described both benefiting from co-option of legitimacy by being a spin-off of *Serial* and conferring legitimacy to others by promoting podcasts with what she called "the *Undisclosed* bump."

Threats and What Is "Appropriate"

As already discussed in terms of identity and boundaries in earlier chapters, true crime podcasters must decide how to balance the entertainment aspects of the medium with journalistic or social justice goals. Participants also described this negotiation in terms of legitimacy and being seen as credible or trustworthy organizations.

Hunt talked about the ethical debates that went into deciding how far her show could lean into advocacy while still being seen as journalistically legitimate:

> It felt more appropriate to embrace the biases rather than to bury them . . . we also didn't want to then sway too far, you know anti-police. For example, I love cop sources. Some of them are amazing, you know they've broken cold cases just, you know, by shoe leather detective work. But in this case, I—obviously and very clearly—don't think that they did a thorough job. So, we just had to talk all of that out.

Brantley too acknowledged ethical struggles with how to treat sources in his investigation as both a journalist and someone out to solve a mystery. He said,

> This touches on the real ethical struggles with true crime . . . I believe there is sort of an underlying condition of this work, which is that you have all the power whether you think you do or not. You have all the power, and you have to weigh the invasion of privacy and any inevitable exploitation of other people's stories and voices against the story that you're doing.

While not a journalist by trade, Rice acknowledges a similar quandary over the right way to tell very personal and sometimes graphic stories. She used the example of *The Keepers*, a 2017 documentary series about the murder of a nun and the molestation of children by a priest in Baltimore, as an example of the "appropriate" way to treat crime stories and victims: "Yes, you heard a lot of the salacious details, and some of those were very hard to hear, but it was just done in such a respectful and artistic manner that I think gives true crime a very *good* reputation."

Fuller also described podcasts as unique opportunities to explore issues or take positions on cases that might be frowned upon by traditional journalistic outlets. He specifically mentioned the narrative format of podcasts as a way to tell journalistic stories through a new lens, such as *In the Dark*'s exploration of the power of U.S. sheriff's departments. He said:

> One of the things that I think true crime can do that journalism can't . . . is advocate for victims or their causes. If you're looking at criminal justice reform, people look at *Serial* and may see a true crime podcast. The real thing in that story is that they're pursuing an angle of a certain part of the criminal justice system, and they're just using a case to bring it to light.

Both Rankin and Rice acknowledged negotiating how much humor they could use and still be considered part of "legitimate" true crime rather than one of the norm violators discussed previously. Rice said that interaction with listeners through social media taught her that fans shared "a dark sense of humor" and could tolerate a certain amount of comic relief. Rankin described being aware of the balance in his delivery as well. "I try to make it entertaining, if I can," he said.

> I try not to be serious all the time. I try to make people laugh a little bit because I'm dealing with such serious, sad, sometimes morbid topics. So, I try to see if I can find a moment to bring a little levity to that.

Countermovements

Previous social movement research has shown that as political actors, either established elite or newly mobilized movement actors, act to create social changes, there may be evidence of countermovements working in opposition to the movement actors (Amburgey & Rao, 1996; McAdam et al., 2003). The emergence of countermovements may imply that a movement is seen as a legitimate politicized form (McAdam et al., 1988; Meyer & Staggenborg, 1996). Countermovements may also play a role in movement-framing processes (Benford & Snow, 2000). Organizational ecology scholars have described ways that countermovements to movement-connected organizations may also affect the evolution of niches and population density through altering resource availability (Amburgey & Rao, 1996; Carroll, 1984). While the podcasters did not offer evidence of an organized countermovement, they did describe incidences of pushback against their work or its goals.

Freemark described virulent pushback to *In the Dark*'s reporting and attributed it to a desire by elite opponents in the Curtis Flowers case to bury evidence of misconduct. She said that she expected to have received the same pushback regardless of the format of the reporting. "I don't think that's related to the impact of podcasts. That's just people that don't want something dug into," she said. Hunt said that as her podcast gained more attention and success, she began to receive criticism accusing her of being motivated by making money off of cases rather than a true desire for justice.

Fuller said that he does not see an organized countermovement yet, but felt that more pushback against true crime, particularly investigative podcasts, was possible if creators are not responsible and diligent in their reporting: "It hasn't really happened yet, but if somebody irresponsibly goes about doing this and puts someone in danger or puts themselves in danger, if some unfortunate event happens because of a podcast, then that might change that."

Pacheco expressed concern that podcaster biases may have a chilling effect on movements associated with true crime podcasts and that pushback seems inevitable. He pointed out that podcasters can easily manipulate an audience by only telling one side of a story. He said, "It's very weird to try and figure out who's being honest and who's not." He also described being troubled by negative attitudes toward law enforcement he sees from others in the community and being concerned by the possibility of growing political polarization dividing the true crime audience:

> They're [true crime podcasts] having an effect on social change. Whether or not that's positive or negative is up for debate depending on what side of it you're on. . . . One thing I see but never really gets talked about in true crime—because you think it really doesn't have a place in there, but it does—is the politics of it in terms of liberal versus conservative, Republican versus Democrat, whatever. There's a back and forth there where you've definitely got true crime podcasts out there that lean very liberal, so they're going to approach a case and look at the law from a liberal point of view. And then you have more conservative ones that are going to look at it from their point of view. And you can listen to two podcasts cover the same case and get to very, very different impressions just based on their personal political or social beliefs.

Pacheco described the rise of social movements like the Women's March and #MeToo as forcing podcasters to think about their language choices and treatment of victims, but he added that the opposition to those movements had also inspired listener pushback criticizing him for any perceived "political correctness." Pacheco also noted (but would not name) podcasters he saw as intentionally crafting shows to counternarratives that are victim- or justice-focused, including explicitly trying to offend listeners or other podcasters who express concern.

Podcasts that may represent these "countermovements" were not included in any of my interviews, though several were contacted. These podcasts range from those created to push back against advocacy-focused true crime (e.g., *Rebutting a Murderer*) and those who specifically describe themselves as intentionally violating the norms or "political correctness" expected from other true crime podcasts (e.g., *Sword & Scale*; hyper-gory *Monstruo*). It is likely that producers of these podcasts would conceptualize their roles and listener gratifications in very different ways than those expressed by the podcasters I interviewed.

The emerging sub-niche of law enforcement–perspective podcasts could also be considered a type of countermovement within true crime podcasting, particularly those that explicitly pushback against wrongful conviction and police misconduct narratives. I contacted several podcasters from this sub-niche for interviews, but none responded to my requests. Some of the earliest podcasts discovered in the demography, like those produced by the FBI, fall into this category. Additionally, there are podcasts produced by investigators (*Gone at 21*), military prosecutors (*Military Justice*), retired police officers (*Slim Turkey*), and detectives (*The Murder Squad: Jensen and Holes*). These podcasts (and there are many more) offer different perspectives from those produced by civilians, and their producers may have different conceptualizations of norms, boundaries, and goals.

EVIDENCE OF DUAL ORIENTATION

While the true crime podcast population shows evidence of both an organizational maintenance and social movement orientation through the creation of identity, boundaries, legitimacy, and stakeholder negotiation, participants also *explicitly* talked about their work in dual terms. For some participants, those orientations blended seamlessly, such as Miller's description of being motivated by sharing "the message in a quality way," whether to influence movement outcomes or to acquire listeners and advertising. Morford said that he got into podcasting because he recognized that it was a way to turn his passion for sharing true crime and victims' stories on his website into a viable career.

Other participants described a "grappling" process or tension between motivations, whether that motivation was to produce journalism or entertainment in addition to sharing their cause. Pacheco described his own ethical debates over making a profit from missing persons cases and the multiple identities podcasters have to negotiate:

> There's a certain degree—at least for me when I'm doing it—where it's hard like, to do advertisements sometimes because . . . there's a part of me that feels like "Am I exploiting this person by making money by telling their story?" And that's something that I kind of wrestle with on every case that I do . . . I'm telling this terrible story about this terrible thing that happened, and then I'm getting money for doing that. That can be challenging emotionally and mentally . . . I think as a podcaster you're constantly stuck in the middle. Are you someone talking about true crime, or are you a journalist? Are you a detective? It's kind of a blending of all of those and you're not officially any of them.

The participants who were professional journalists as well as podcasters also reported feeling pulled by dual motivations. While they described their work as the job of professional journalists and journalism organizations, they also pointed to positions of advocacy in their podcasts. Brantley said of his podcast, "I don't feel like an advocate at all," but later contradictorily expressed that his goal was "to arrive at some definitive answer . . . I feel like an advocate . . . for truth and reconciliation." He also described wrestling with the dichotomy of telling serious, journalistic stories in an entertainment medium:

> It's inherently a medium where people have to be entertained. If people are not entertained in some way, they're not going to listen. They're going to stop listening. I think—of course "entertaining" is its own loaded word that we could debate—I think for us, we struggle with this a ton. Like, how much do you play on what draws you as a listener? Like *Serial*, that sort of drama, the mystery, the stakes, all the sort of narrative hooks, the way the narrative hooks us—how do you reconcile that with what is a very serious mission?

Delia described wrestling with the role of advocating for the rights of assault victims without becoming seen solely an advocate rather than a journalist:

> *She Says,* I know it didn't just impact Linda, the main character in the story. I know it had an impact on so many women and men too. That's meaningful. That's what you want as a journalist, for your work to be accurate, educational and to have some kind of meaning without an agenda . . . as a journalist, I do not want to be seen as an advocate, but I also want to listen to people, and I want to connect with people.

For Fuller, the lines between journalist, advocate, and entertainer have been especially blurred. Through his coverage of the Ayla Reynolds disappearance, Fuller grew to know the family so well that he was asked by a family member to draft public relations statements for them. He described how the closeness to victims' families and investigators affected him and his view of the true crime podcast space:

> I am straddling the line between journalist and advocate at that point, and I'm taking sides. . . . You lose your objectivity, and you start looking at the case through the prism of something that is different from where you started . . . It's a weird space . . . You've got victims' rights, and you've got people whose lives have been destroyed trying to heal themselves through helping others, and then you've got everyone who's kind of watching behind the scenes for whatever reason.

Other participants talked about the evolution of their podcasts as a business model after the success of their goal-focused first seasons. Hunt said, "The focus has always been on the victim . . . we're going to keep doing what feels right because that's what worked the first time." Chaudry expressed surprise that her passion project, the follow-up to *Serial* with the goal of sharing all the facts in Syed's case, had turned into a job:

> We kind of threw ourselves into podcasting just for Adnan's case, not ever thinking we're going to continue to do this. Not ever thinking that this was going to become like work. The first time I went to a podcast conference, Podcast Movement, it was like, "Oh my god, this is a real industry." It's really growing and evolving. . . . It's just exploding. There's a lot of money flowing into it.

The interviews made clear that even those podcasters who push against the idea of advocacy also express goal-oriented motivations. These tensions and dual motivations illustrate that podcasters themselves think of their work from both ecological and social movement perspectives. Additional tensions exist between journalistic orientations, like telling a factual story in a non-biased way, and orientations toward entertaining the audience and advocating for producers' personal or shared causes.

HYBRID ORGANIZATIONS IN THEORY AND IN PRACTICE

These findings, along with those in the previous chapters, shed light on how these true crime podcasts entities and their producers—some driven by journalistic motivations, some to create successful entertainment products, some advocacy focused, and some hybrid organizations—negotiate and develop their identities and orientations. While some producers start their podcasts with explicitly social movement motivations, many develop these through interactions with listeners and relationships with other producers. These interactions and relationships shape the boundaries of the population and allow podcasters to take positions and advocate for causes in ways that are accepted as legitimate and "appropriate" by their peers, constituents, and outside agents, like courts and law enforcement.

The podcasters also discussed the ways that the form and boundaries of true crime podcasts are negotiated. The interviews reveal that the form the podcasts take (e.g., narrative style, case per episode versus series, investigation or storytelling, and victim or perpetrator focused) is often a product of negotiation and reevaluation through communication with listeners, other podcasters, and stakeholders. This is consistent with Polos and colleagues' (2002) explanation of organizational form and boundaries as a product of social and cultural construction rather than only of niche fit. This is also an example of organizational identity being determined by how the organization is "seen" by its publics as well as how it sees itself (Albert & Whetten, 1985). McAdam (2017) described this as a central role of social movement communities as well, as constituents act to shape the actions of movement leaders and organizations. This negotiation process with listeners, often through social media feedback, also gives podcasters insight into the gratifications that listeners may be seeking (Dimmick, 2003), an important factor both for organizational maintenance through attracting and retaining audiences and for meeting the demands of listeners who identify with movement goals. The interviews also support Florini's (2015) findings that podcast fan communities tend to overlap with each other, further encouraging podcasters to support the flow of community resources.

These findings also allow us to bridge theoretical "symmetrical gaps" between organizational ecology and SMT. Perhaps most significantly, the interviews provide evidence that organizations oriented toward maintenance (survival, growth, and success within their niche) make use of "submerged networks" of relationships (Melucci, 1985; McAdam, 1999) to shape their organizational identity in much the same way previous research has shown social movement organizations (SMOs) do. The podcasters interviewed also provided evidence of the ways that relationships—both competitive and commensualistic—affect how producers acquire and utilize resources and become seen as legitimate both within and outside of the population.

Substantial evidence exists for the ways that true crime podcast organizations operate from both organizational ecology and SMT paradigms, as well as examples of other factors at play, such as contention between journalistic and entertainment motivations. The demography and interviews, as well as my previous content analysis of media mentions of true crime podcasts (Sherrill, 2020), offer triangulated corroboration for how this population has grown, its increasing size and legitimacy, and the ways that population members understand and interact with changing environmental conditions.

Theoretical Overlap in Legitimacy, Density, and Resource Mobilization

The interviewees addressed the development of normative legitimacy in terms of the "appropriateness" of true crime as both a revenue-producing media product and a driver of social movement goals. They included examples of how this "appropriateness" is negotiated among podcasters, stakeholders, and listeners. Participants, like Pacheco, noted that they believe listeners are able to discern between "good" and "bad" podcast content and can be trusted to evaluate the value of sources as "legitimate" or "illegitimate." Podcasters also described how stakeholders, like law enforcement and families, have deemed true crime podcasts legitimate by being willing to share resources or partner on cases.

Podcasters' remarks also offered evidence of conferences of legitimacy by outside agents, such as podcasts receiving the Pulliam or Peabody awards, as well as cooption of legitimacy through establishing formal and informal relationships with respected entities by networking with one another. However, instances of low normative legitimacy for true crime podcasts were also described, such as Apple and other podcast rankers' reluctance to add a "True Crime" category for so long. It is also possible that perceptions of low legitimacy of true crime podcasts are related to the population's stage of development—that is, legitimacy grows as communities "come of age" and move from emergence to organizational maintenance (Bryant & Monge, 2008).

Similar to the scholarship of Sandell (2001) and Greve et al. (2006), these findings also show that participants viewed population density and legitimacy as important for the social movement orientations of true crime podcasts, mentioning specifically how the growing visibility of true crime podcasts brings more attention to certain cases or causes. Podcasters supported the evidence of growing population density and legitimacy in other ways as well. Participants often referred to true crime podcasts becoming "a thing," citing the viral acceptance of pioneer podcasts like *Serial* and *S-Town*. Others, like Pacheco, Fuller, and Hunt, described how listeners supported the growth in the density of the population by expanding their awareness and consumption beyond a select few true crime podcasts.

Participants described resources in terms of physical, knowledge, and symbolic resources. Economic factors were mentioned, particularly for the more in-depth, investigative journalism–oriented podcasts like *In the Dark*. More often, participants described time and technical support, rather than money, as their biggest resource challenges. The relational networks of these podcasters were often used to fill these gaps, such as partnering with a more experienced podcaster for editing or promotional support. While advertising was discussed, it seemed to be a still largely untapped resource for many of these podcasters. Participants described balancing the ethics of making a profit through stories of others' suffering but also pointed to the small number of advertisers investing in podcasts.[4] This lack of advertising support in the midst of the true crime boom may have been indicative of low legitimacy, either from advertisers not recognizing the power of the podcast industry (cognitive) or of being uncomfortable associating with the subject matter (normative). Participants suggested that the lack of advertising resources could also have been symptomatic of their lack of business knowledge—most podcasters entered the population with little or no idea how to monetize.

Symbolic resources were described in terms of access or privilege by several participants. Rankin noted that his history with court officials allowed him access that other podcasters (and journalists) do not have. Brantley described societal privilege as a symbolic resource for his podcast, as his demographic identity helped him to gain access and trust from people who had previously been unwilling to cooperate, or who could be literally dangerous to another kind of podcaster. While Chaudry did not mention it in the interview, she has publicly discussed a lack of this kind of symbolic resource as a detriment to her podcast (Chaudry et al., 2015). She has described how, as a Muslim woman of color, she has been unable or felt unsafe entering the communities involved in some cases, leading her to lean on co-hosts to take on those tasks. This conceptualization of privilege as a symbolic resource has been noted in social movements literature as an important component of rational movement mobilization, as at least some members must have the symbolic capital to "take risks" in order to accomplish movement goals (Olson, 1968; Jenkins, 1983).

The positioning of listeners as resources by the podcasters offers support for both organizational maintenance and social movement mobilization orientations. Interviewees described listeners in terms of their contributions to knowledge and boundary negotiation, as well as for supplying information about cases. Generally, the participants in this study downplayed the idea of listeners as a commodity, noting that they were not focused on metrics or download numbers beyond a general sense of curiosity about geographics. Instead, participants tended to discuss listeners from a social movement–oriented view. In these descriptions, listeners are described as compatriots or constituents, suggesting that podcasters see listeners in the way Gamson (1990) defined movement members—as collective actors whose interests affect the decision-making process. Participants who describe themselves as part of a social change movement, for example, Chaudry, describe their listeners as similarly committed. This suggests that these podcasters may be viewing social change through the classical approach paradigm of social movements, that is, as Buechler put it, their "central process is the social construction of a collective identity that is symbolically meaningful to participants" (1993, p. 228). In the classical view, and as some participants described, the creation of awareness and identity is both a goal and an outcome. From this perspective, when listeners become aware and then voluntarily associate with discussion about systemic issues, that identity is itself a kind of symbolic action (Cohen, 1985; Diani, 2013). Conversely, this *politicized* identity (Van Zomeren et al., 2008) also develops as a result of action, such as the influx of new supporters *Undisclosed* received after its efforts helped lead to new appeals in the Syed case.

Institutionalization and Professionalism

Additionally, podcasters described the value of knowledge resources, and many cited knowledge acquired from other industries, like law and journalism. Most described self-teaching or informal network relationships as their introduction to how to "do podcasting." From an ecological standpoint, this points to the existence of few formal institutions and organizations for learning podcasting, especially when compared to an industry like journalism. Formal or "ancillary" organizations within an industry contribute to the spread of innovations, the development of organizational norms, and the increase of legitimacy of organizational forms (Aldrich & Ruef, 2007; Lowrey, 2012; Lowrey et al., 2019; Sherrill et al., 2022). However, as mentioned by several participants, organizations focused on podcasting (and true crime podcasts) have emerged, signaling a growing institutionalization of the population. Most of the formal organization seems to be in the form of conventions (e.g., Pod X, Crime Con, and True Crime Podcast Festival) or panels and lectures at other media conferences (e.g., South by Southwest, Broadcast Educators Convention, and National Broadcasters Association), though media schools are increasingly focusing on adding podcasting courses or labs (e.g., Banville, Aug. 31, 2015; NYU Journalism, 2019; Berkley Graduate School of Journalism, 2022). The effects of institutions on organizational practice have also been tied to the development of norms for social movement sectors (e.g., Lounsbury, 2001), adding another rationalization for the development of formalized knowledge organizations related to the population.

MAINTENANCE, MOVEMENTS, AND MOVING FORWARD

When I began studying true crime podcasts as organizations, I set out to understand how these operations act within organizational ecology and SMT paradigms, as well as to better understand the motivations of podcast producers and to expand theory, or fill "symmetrical gaps." The findings I've presented here support a dual orientation for this population and provide evidence that identity—both organizational and collective—is an important factor for the success of both maintenance and social change–oriented organizations.

True crime podcast organizations operate in many ways as maintenance-oriented organizations, as might be expected from an organizational ecology standpoint. The true crime podcast population displays characteristics of density, niches, and boundaries. Density and legitimacy show evidence of being directly related to the growth of one another. Podcasters I interviewed described niches and sub-niches and offered examples of the ways organizations negotiate their fit within those niches. There is evidence of isomorphism in the population, as well as resource partitioning and disruptions leading to speciation. Listeners were described both as a commodity to be obtained to maintain the organization and as sources of knowledge and collective identity.

From a SMT perspective, at least *some* members of the true crime podcast population operate from movement orientations. They depend on collective identity and seek to grow their constituency by spreading awareness of systemic issues among their audiences. While these podcasts do not seem to belong to a single defined movement sector as McCarthy and Zald (1979, 2002) and resource mobilization theory would define, many of them do exhibit an orientation toward correcting or spreading awareness of criminal justice issues that fall within a larger movement orientation (Buechler, 1993; Johnston, 2014; Melucci, 1985). They share community resources, and listeners have non-exclusionary membership with multiple podcast fan/constituent identities (Greve et al., 2006; Sandell, 2001). These factors suggest that identity and political process paradigms of SMT offer better theoretical explanations for true crime podcasts' social movement orientations than do resource mobilization approaches.

These findings also expand the theoretical synthesis between organizational ecology and SMT. Participants offered multiple examples of both listeners and relational networks working to shape organizational boundaries through communication and negotiation. This bi-directional boundary work provides more support for prior conceptualizations of audiences' role in defining organizations, their niches, and niche boundaries (i.e., Gioia et al., 2002; Polos et al., 2002). These findings are also evidence that the "submerged networks" of relationships observed in SMOs (Melucci, 1985; McAdam, 1999) can also be at work in maintenance organizations, helping to fill one of the "gaps" of organizational ecology, the formation of identity through intrapopulation network relationships. These network relationships help new entrants to the population understand norms and boundaries, attract listeners, and become identified as legitimate members of the community. My findings also give further support to Greve et al. (2006) and Sandell's (2001) explorations of dual-oriented populations. True crime podcasters' entrepreneurial attempts are often encouraged by a personal goal orientation, such as a desire to help in a particular case combined with a sense of efficacy, suggesting that personal goal orientation and identity goals have a place in the explanation for niche emergence and development. Participants' explanations for the explosion of true crime podcasting as a legitimate form and population with rapidly increasing density offer evidence of widespread identity with and belief in the effectiveness of these podcasts. While it is early in its emergence, the institutionalization of true crime podcasts (and podcasts in general) may also hint at support for McCarthy and Zald's (2002) suggestion that institutionalization and professionalization occur in social movement industries (SMIs) similar to the way they occur in other industries.

Finally, it is clear that multiple motivations beyond organizational maintenance and social movement goals may be at work for true crime podcast producers. These producers expressed journalistic orientations toward sharing facts and information and described a desire to subvert the true crime genre. The interviewees in this study suggested that current delineations of both journalism and true crime may be too limiting and that new digital forms and communities, like those of true crime podcasts, may require scholars to use new lenses for exploration and interpretation.

NOTES

1. In 2019, Ashley Flowers, of chart-topping podcast *Crime Junkie*, was accused of plagiarism for not citing source material in her storytelling (Sprangler, Aug. 15, 2019). Despite the allegations and pulling several episodes, Flowers remains one of the highest paid podcasters in the industry (Lee, June 20, 2022). Other high profile crime and crime journalism podcasts have also faced controversy: *Caliphate* (Folkenflik, Dec. 18, 2020); *Son of a Hitman* (Inside Radio, February 25, 2021), *The Prosecutors* (Sommer, June 8, 2022), *and The Murder Squad* (Ehrlich & Marks, July 22, 2022), to name just a few.

2. *South Park*, an animated show for adults, focused on absurdist humor and social satire, aired an episode in their 17th season entitled, "Informative Murder Porn." In the episode, a group of elementary school children become increasingly concerned by their parents' fascination with true crime television shows involving reenactments of spousal homicides. The children dub the genre "murder porn" and set up parental controls to prevent their parents from watching true crime (Parker et al., 2013, Oct. 2).

3. The podcast named was dropped by its network in 2019 after the host publicly posted a violent misogynist message on International Women's Day. The podcast is now available through subscriptions only.

4. Some of the interviews were conducted as early as 2019. In the years since, the podcast advertising market has exploded, offering advertisers better returns on investment than many traditional marketing channels (Moran, April 4, 2022).

Chapter 8

Still Obsessed

Lessons from the True Crime Podcast Ecosystem

I don't know why I was surprised, but I didn't expect to cry so much when Adnan Syed's sentence was vacated on September 19, 2022. After 23 years behind bars, the man whose story inspired millions of listeners—and this research—was finally going home (Daniels & Davies, September 19, 2022).

In the days since, news story after news story, as well as hundreds of social media posts, pointed to the role *Serial* and Sarah Koenig played in bringing Syed—and other alleged victims of miscarriages of justice—into the public eye. But for every acknowledgment of *Serial* and Koenig's work, there were criticisms pointed at *Serial*'s lack of acknowledgment of police missteps and the role of systemic racism in the case, and a sense that Koenig "abandoned" her subject in the years since the original podcast aired. Many of these criticisms ring similar to what the podcasters I interviewed told me about their struggles, fears, and negotiations in finding the balance between entertaining listeners, following journalistic norms, and advocating for victims through—and of—the criminal justice system.

And yet, despite these emerging criticisms, it is still clear that *Serial*, sometimes called "the granddaddy of them all," had a tremendous influence on true crime as a whole, and especially on the true crime podcast ecosystem. *Serial*, after all, as Rebecca Lavoie told Slate's *In Case You Missed It* podcast, "gentrified the true crime industry" (Slate, September 24, 2022). True crime was no longer a closeted guilty pleasure—it was cool. I would argue, however, that while *Serial* was unquestionably a viral phenomenon, a cultural phenomenon, and an inspiration for all of the interview participants, it emerged as part of the natural evolutionary process of the population, and new forms have since developed to compete with it, existing older podcasts, and one another. True crime podcasts did not inexplicably become, in the words of Rabia Chaudry, "suddenly sexy." Instead, from an ecological standpoint, environmental disruptions in the form of technological innovations (Weber, 2017), as well as growing collective identity around movement causes, were important factors that allowed for speciation processes to work quickly after *Serial*'s emergence.

These speciation processes have created a vast world of true crime podcasts of varying success and quality, and those included in the analysis and interviews here offer only a snapshot of the dueling motivations of a cross section of the true crime podcast population. I explicitly chose to interview podcasters for their ties to criminal justice reform advocacy, or through referrals to podcasters in those relational networks. This excluded many of the sub-genres of true crime podcasts that may have weak or no ties to advocacy goals. This means my sample excludes perhaps the most popular sub-niche of true crime podcasts, true crime comedy (such as arguably big-as-*Serial*-sensation *My Favorite Murder*). There are none of the gore-centric podcasts in this sample, nor any of the emerging crop of corporate-produced podcasts. It is very likely that the inclusion of different types of true crime podcasts may have offered more evidence of generalists and specialists in the population, as well as different motivations and gratifications of creators and listeners.

Throughout this research, I've focused on these podcast operations as organizations, both from the ecological and movement orientation. Because of that focus, I've neglected one of the largest criticisms of true crime (and, recently, of *Serial*)—the centering of overwhelming white and privileged voices and victims. While I did not set out to complete a critical-cultural study, it seems irresponsible not to mention this omission. The participants in this study are overwhelmingly white, and most are highly educated (e.g., lawyers, professors, and journalism professionals). While some of their advocacy does lend itself to less privileged groups—for example, wrongly convicted men of color—much of their work, and true crime in general, falls into the trap colloquially called "missing white woman syndrome" (Demby, April 13, 2017). Cecil (2020) addressed this, comparing how massively popular podcasts cover missing and murdered white women (like Tara Grinstead of *Up and Vanished* or Maura Murray of *Missing*) to the type of coverage given to missing Black and indigenous women. Sommers (2016) and Moody et al. (2014) specifically looked at the overrepresentation of white, female missing person cases in news media, and other scholars have examined how media misrepresent people of color as both victims and perpetrators (e.g., Crichlow & Lauricella, 2018; Dixon & Linz, 2000; Gilliam et al., 1996). While some podcasters have tried to specifically address this disparity (McHugh, August 31, 2017), it seems important for both producers and scholars to continue to challenge these stereotypical crime narratives, particularly while the clearance rates for U.S. homicides and other crimes remain racially disparate.[1] Other scholars have described the unique ability of true crime podcasts to amplify marginalized voices (Doane et al., 2017; Tiffe & Hoffman, 2017), but more work is needed to understand who this population may actually be serving, which voices are truly being amplified, and its effects on survivors and families. Cecil cautioned true crime fans and producers that, even as norms and ethics are negotiated within true crime, "The genre is still rooted in fear, which feeds anxieties about crime and victimization. And for some people, it has become an invasive and painful medium that re-traumatizes them for the sake of entertainment" (Cecil, 2020, p. 138).

So what's a true crime storyteller or fan to do? We are, across global pop culture, clearly obsessed with true crime narratives, and there's no evidence of that obsession abating any time soon. Through listening to the podcasters I've interviewed, following the work of other scholars like Cecil (2020), Boling (2019), and McHugh (2016), and staying attuned to the voices of victims' families and friends—often as guests on true crime podcasts—I've arrived at a set of ethical standards for my own true crime consumption. Through becoming more mindful consumers or producers of true crime media, I truly believe the power of fanship and collective identity can be used to direct our guilty pleasure toward creating lasting, meaningful, real-world changes.

First, fans and creators must be cognizant of the motivating factors that drive them to create or consume true crime media. For journalists, motivations may be driven by the norms of their profession—to tell an important story, to expose the malfeasance of the powerful, or to hold systems accountable to the public. For podcasters, even those in the journalism profession, those normative lines may become blurred. The podcasters in my interviews repeatedly pointed to the importance of being consistently aware of the real-world effects of their storytelling. On the other hand, they also pointed to producers they believed to be motivated by fame or fortune and the questionable storytelling that often resulted. As fans, recognizing our own motivations is equally essential. What, as one of my interviewees asked me, do they say about us? Titillation and morbid curiosity are normal human emotions, and yet, those aren't the motivations that lead to collective identity and real-world change. As I've immersed myself into researching the true crime world, I've found my own motivations changing. I'm no longer simply curious—I feel compelled to support the work of ethical producers and their causes, and find myself increasingly turned off by podcasts that simply tell a tale for the sake of the gory story. I want *more*—more understanding of the intricacies of the law, more opportunities to become involved in advocacy, more knowledge of systemic issues to share with others. By demanding this more—from ourselves and the creators we support—it is more likely that, in the words of Rabia Chaudry, "the cream rises to the top."

Second, true crime fans and creators must be cognizant of the potential our obsessions have to reopen wounds or even cause new harm to the people in these crime narratives. Criminologists like Elizabeth Yardley have written extensively about the ethics of true crime storytelling, particularly about its effects on "secondary victims," or people closely connected to both victims and perpetrators (Yardley et al., 2015). These secondary victims have been on full display in the media around Syed's release, from heartwarming photos of the Syed family reunited to heartbreaking interviews with Hae Min Lee's family, who, just like when she disappeared in January of 1999, are left without answers. Lee's brother, Young, has been outspoken since *Serial*, openly criticizing his family's lack of representation in the production and even going to the *Serial* sub-Reddit to call fans "disgusting" and admonish them: "Shame on you," Lee wrote, "I pray that you don't have to go through what we went through and have your story blasted to 5mil listeners" (Reddit, 2015). On the day Syed was released, Young Lee addressed the court. "This is not a podcast to me. This is real life—a never-ending nightmare for 20-plus years" (Levenson, September 19, 2022, para. 14).

True crime storytelling, just like traditional journalism, delves into painful subjects. Sometimes, that means private citizens' lives become public information. Sometimes, that means wounds are reopened. The podcasters I spoke to admonished other creators to remember these secondary victims and their wounds in every step of storytelling. Part of that remembrance means being cognizant of the real feelings of real people affected by crime, as well as the potential for unpredictable virality in the true crime podcast world. As Brantley put it, "You have all the power, and you have to weigh the invasion of privacy and any inevitable exploitation of other people's stories and voices against the story that you're doing." For fans, this means critically evaluating the podcasts to which we subscribe, as well as how we interact with others in fan communities, like social media discussion groups. In the true crime storytelling that has positive real-world impacts—on correcting wrongful convictions, solving cold cases, or identifying long-unknown victims—the potential for justice and hope must outweigh the pain and horror than can also come from the remediation of tragedy.

Finally, the insights I gained from these podcasters—journalists, advocates, storytellers, and some secondary victims themselves—remind me, as a true crime fan, that being motivated to collectively identify and act is what separates the good true crime from the morbid and the ugly. It leaves fans with a mission. To donate. To call a member of Congress. To lobby against unjust systems. To work in our own communities and to seek healing, for ourselves and for others. The worst of true crime leaves me feeling helpless and afraid; the best, excited, connected, and energized. While these insights can't alone create a world of more just systems and more ethical creators and consumers, they remind us that our individual consumption has impacts. By giving our time, our attention, and our resources to the storytellers who take the real-world effects of their work seriously, we—as "Murderinos, " crime junkies, and fans—can amplify the potential for real-world good in our true crime obsession.

NOTE

1. According to the Murder Accountability Project (2018), murders of white women are most likely to be solved (79.37%), while those of black men are least likely to be solved (65.79%). Murders of black women and white men each have a 73% clearance rate. Additionally, it is estimated that nearly half of all homicides of Native Americans are not accurately reported to federal agencies.

References

48 Hours. (2018, April 28). *Has the golden state killer been caught?* https://www .cbsnews.com/news/james-deangelo-golden-state-killer-caught-michelle-mcna-mara-48-hours-update/

Albert, S., & Whetten, D. (1985). Organizational identity. In L.L. Cummings & B. Staw (Eds.), *Research in organizational behavior* (Vol. 7, pp. 263–295). JAI Press Inc.

Aldrich, H.E. (1999). *Organizations evolving.* Sage.

Aldrich, H.E., & Fiol, C.M. (1994). Fools rush in? The institutional context of industry creation. *Academy of Management Review, 19,* 645–670.

Aldrich, H.E., & Pfeffer, J. (1976). Environments of organizations. *Annual Review of Sociology, 2,* 79–105. https://doi.org/10.1146/annurev.so.02.080176.000455

Aldrich, H.E., & Ruef, M. (2007). *Organizations evolving.* Sage.

Amburgey, T., & Rao, H. (1996). Organizational ecology: Past, present, and future directions. *The Academy of Management Journal, 39*(5), 1265–1286.

Associated Press. (2017, Sept. 15). *Vignarajah, prosecutor tied to 'Serial' case, running for office.* The Daily Record. https://thedailyrecord.com/2017/09/15/maryland -serial-podcast-prosecutor/

Atlanta Journal Constitution (AJC). (2015). *Breakdown* [Audio Podcast]. http://www .myajc.com/voices/breakdown/

Audia, P.G., Freeman, J.H., & Reynolds, P.D. (2006). Organizational foundings in community context: Instruments manufacturers and their interrelationship with other organizations. *Administrative Science Quarterly, 51,* 381–420. https://doi.org /10.2189/asqu.51.3.381

Bagley, W. (Director & Writer). (2021). *The murder podcast* [Film]. Brodacious Films.

Bandura, A. (1995). Exercise of personal and collective efficacy in changing societ-ies. In A. Bandura (Ed.), *Self-efficacy in changing societies* (pp. 1–45). Cambridge University Press.

Banville, J.G. (2015, Aug. 31). *How and why journalism schools should teach podcasting.* Media Shift. http://mediashift.org/2015/08/how-and-why-journalism-schools-should-teach-podcasting/

Barton, K.M. (2009). Reality television programming and diverging gratifications: The influence of content on gratifications obtained. *Journal of Broadcasting & Electronic Media, 53*(3), 460–476.

Baum, J. (2000). Organizational ecology. In S. Clegg and C. Hardy (Eds.), *Studying organization: Theory & methodology* (pp. 71–108). Sage Publications.

Baum, J., & Shipilov, A. (2006). Ecological approaches to organizations. In S. Clegg, C. Hardy, T. Lawrence, & W. Nord (Eds.), *The Sage handbook of organization studies* (pp. 55–110). Sage Publications.

Baum, J., & Singh, J. (1994). Organizational niches and the dynamics of organizational founding. *Organization Science, 5*(4), 483–501.

Benford, R., & Snow, D. (2000). Framing processes and social movements: An overview and assessment. *Annual Review of Sociology, 26*, 611–39.

Berkley Graduate School of Journalism. (2022). *Podcast bootcamp* [graduate certificate course]. University of California. https://multimedia.journalism.berkeley.edu/workshops/podcast-bootcamp/

Berry, J. (2015). A golden age of podcasting? Evaluating *Serial* in the context of podcast histories. *Journal of Radio & Audio Media, 22*(2), 170–178.

Berry, R. (2006). Will the iPod kill the radio star?: Profiling podcasting as radio. *The International Journal of Research into New Media Technologies, 12*(2), 143–162.

Breton, A., & Breton, R. (1969). An economic theory of social movements. *American Economic Review Papers and Proceedings of the American Economic Association, 59*(2), 198–205.

Boling, K. (2019). True crime podcasting: Journalism, justice or entertainment? *Radio Journal: International Studies in Broadcast & Audio Media, 17*(2), 161–178. https://doi.org/10.1386/rjao_00003_1

Boling, K. (2020). Fundamentally different stories that matters: True crime podcasts and the domestic violence survivors in their audience. (Publication No. 22582900) [Doctoral dissertation, University of South Caroline]. ProQuest. https://www.proquest.com/openview/512cbf61827827c7b38d5a3c5721d6ad/1?pq-origsite=gscholar&cbl=18750&diss=y

Boling, K., & Hull, K. (2018). *Undisclosed* information—*Serial* is *My Favorite Murder*: Examining motivations in the true crime podcast audience. *Journal of Radio & Audio Media, 25*(1), 92–108. https://doi.org/10.1080/19376529.2017.1370714

Bottomley, A. (2015). Podcasting: A decade in the life of a "new" audio medium: Introduction. *Journal of Radio & Audio Media, 22*(2), 164–169.

Bowers, A. (2005, Dec. 30). *The year of the podcast.* Slate. http://www.slate.com/articles/podcasts/podcasts/2005/12/the_year_of_the_podcast.html

Browder, L. (2010). True Crime. In C. Nickerson (Ed.), *The Cambridge companion to American crime fiction* (pp. 205–228). Cambridge University Press.

Broussard, R., Sherrill, L.A., & Funk, K. (2022, April). Pandemic podcasting: Covering sports when the world stops. Presented at the Broadcast Education Association Conference, Las Vegas, NV.

Brown, W.J. (2015). Examining four processes of audience involvement with media personae: Transportation, parasocial interaction, identification, and worship. *Communication Theory, 25*(3), 259–283. https://doi.org/10.1111/comt.12053

Bryant, J.A., & Monge, P. (2008). The evolution of the children's television community, 1953-2003. *International Journal of Communication, 2*, 160–192.

Buechler, S. (1993). Beyond resource mobilization? Emerging trends in social movement theory. *The Sociological Quarterly, 34*(2), 217–235.

Buechler, S. (1995). New social movement theories. *The Sociological Quarterly, 36*(3), 441–464.

Burger, P. (2016, Aug. 24). *The bloody history of the true crime genre.* JSTOR Daily. https://daily.jstor.org/bloody-history-of-true-crime-genre/?utm_source=internal-house&utm_medium=email&utm_campaign=jstordaily_08252016&cid=eml_j _jstordaily_dailylist_08252016

Burrell, G., & Morgan, G. (1979). *Sociological paradigms and organizational analysis.* Heinemann.

Cameron, D.R. (1974). Toward a theory of political mobilization. *The Journal of Politics, 36*(1), 138–171.

Canel, E. (1997). New social movement theory and resource mobilization theory: The need for integration. In H. Dilla Alfonso and M. Kaufman (Eds.), *Community power and grassroots democracy* (pp. 189–221). Zed Books.

Capote, T. (1966). *In cold blood.* Random House.

Capewell, J. (2017, Feb. 24). *Arrest made in decadelong cold case after podcast renews national attention.* Huffington Post. https://www.huffingtonpost.com/entry /arrest-made-in-decadelong-cold-case-after-podcast-renews-national-attention_us _58a737a3e4b037d17d277dd4

Caronia, L. (2005). Mobile culture: An ethnography of cellular phone uses in teenagers' everyday life. *Convergence, 11*(3), 96–103.

Carroll, G. (1984). Organizational ecology. *Annual Review of Sociology, 10*(1), 71–93.

Carroll, G. (1985). Concentration and specialization: Dynamics of niche width in populations of organizations. *American Journal of Sociology, 90*(6), 1262–1283.

Carroll, G., Dobrev, S., & Swaminathan, A. (2002). Organizational processes of resource partitioning. *Research in Organizational Behavior, 24*, 1–40.

Carroll, G., & Hannan, M. (1989). Density dependence in the evolution of populations of newspaper organizations. *American Sociological Review, 54*(4), 524–541.

Carroll, G., & Swaminathan, A. (1992). The organizational ecology of strategic groups in the American brewing industry from 1975 to 1990. *Industrial and Corporate Change, 1*(1), 65–97.

Carroll, G., & Swaminathan, A. (2000). Why the microbrewery movement? Organizational dynamics of resource partitioning in the U.S. brewing industry. *American Journal of Sociology, 106*(3), 715–762.

Carroll, W., & Hackett, R. (2006). Democratic media activism through the lens of social movement theory. *Media, Culture & Society, 28*(1), 83–104.

CBS Baltimore Staff. (2022, March 10). *Mosby approves additional forensic testing in case of Adnan Syed, man at center of 'Serial' podcast.* CBS Baltimore. https://

baltimore.cbslocal.com/2022/03/10/mosby-approves-additional-forensic-testing-in
-case-of-adnan-syed-man-at-center-of-serial-podcast/

Cecil, D.K. (2020). *Fear, justice & modern true crime.* Lynne Rienner Publishers, Inc.

Chan-Olmstead, S., & Wang, R. (2022). Understanding podcast users: Consumption motives and behaviors. *New Media & Society, 24*(3), 684–704. https://doi.org/10.1177%2F1461444820963776

Chandler, D. (1997). *An introduction to genre theory.* http://www.aber.ac.uk/media/Documents/intgenre/intgenre.html

Chaudry, R. (2014, June 24). *What a Muslim American learned from Zionists.* Time. https://time.com/2917600/muslim-american-zionists/

Chaudry, R. (2016). *Adnan's Story: The Search for Truth and Justice After Serial.* St. Martin's Press.

Chaudry, R. (2016, Nov. 21). *Why two top Muslim and Jewish groups joined forces to fight bigotry—and why some are trying to stop them.* Tablet. https://www.tablet-mag.com/sections/news/articles/why-two-top-muslim-and-jewish-groups-joined-forces-to-fight-bigotry-and-why-some-are-trying-to-stop-them

Chaudry, R., Miller, C., & Simpson, S. (Producers). (2015). *Undisclosed* [Audio podcast]. http://undisclosed-podcast.com/

Chicago Public Media. (Producer). (1995). *This American Life* [Radio show]. https://www.thisamericanlife.org/

Clayton, A. (2018, April 2). *ITX client Ed Ates parole approved.* Innocence Texas. https://innocencetexas.org/news/itx-client-ed-ates-free-on-parole

Columbia Journalism Review. (Producer). (2016). *The Kicker* [Audio podcast]. http://www.cjr.org/business_of_news/podcast-serial-stown-this-american-life-de-corre-spondent.php

Cohen, J. (1985). Strategy or identity: New theoretical paradigms and contemporary social movements. *Social Research, 52*(4), 663–716.

Cornell Law School. (n.d.). *Voir dire.* Legal Information Institute. https://www.law.cornell.edu/wex/voir_dire

Cosimini, M., Cho, D., Liley, F., & Espinoza, J. (2017). Podcasting in medical education: How long should an educational podcast be? *Journal of Graduate Medical Education, 9*(3), 388–389.

Crampton, C. (2020, Oct. 6). *How a podcast paused a murder trial.* Vulture Hot Pod. https://www.vulture.com/2020/10/teachers-pet-podcast-murder-trial.html

Creswell, J. (2007). *Qualitative inquiry & research design: Choosing among five approaches* (2nd ed.). Sage Publications.

Creswell, J.W. (2014). *Research design: Qualitative, quantitative and mixed methods approaches* (4th ed.). Sage Publications, Inc.

Crichlow, W., & Lauricella, S. (2018). An analysis of anti-Black crime reporting in Toronto: Evidence from news frames and critical race theory. In M. Bhatia, S. Poynting, & W. Tufail (Eds.), *Media, crime and racism* (pp. 301–316). Palgrave Macmillan.

Cwynar, J. (2015). More than a "VCR for radio": The CBC, the Radio 3 podcast, and the uses of an emerging medium. *Journal of Radio & Audio Media, 22*(2), 190–199.

Daniels, O., & Davies, E. (2022, Sept. 19). *Adnan Syed, featured in 'Serial' podcast, released from prison.* The Washington Post. https://www.washingtonpost.com/dc-md-va/2022/09/19/adnan-syed-conviction-vacated-judge/

Deephouse, D., & Suchman, M. (2008). Legitimacy in organizational institutionalism. In R. Greenwood, C. Oliver, R. Suddaby, and K. Sahlin (Eds.), *The Sage Handbook of Organizational Institutionalism* (pp. 49–77). Sage Publications.

Demby, G. (2017, April 13). *What we know (and don't know) about 'missing white women syndrome.'* NPR. https://www.npr.org/sections/codeswitch/2017/04/13/523769303/what-we-know-and-dont-know-about-missing-white-women-syndrome

Diani, M. (2013). Organizational fields and social movement dynamics. In B. Klandermans, C. Roggeband, & J. Van Stekelenburg (Eds.), *The future of social movement research: Dynamics, mechanisms, and processes* (pp. 145–168). University of Minnesota Press.

DiMaggio, P.J. (1986). Structural analysis of organizational fields: A block model approach. In B. Staw, & L. Cummings (Eds.), *Research in organizational behavior,* (vol. 8, pp. 335–370). JAI Press.

Dimmick, J. (2003). *Media competition and coexistence: The theory of the niche.* Lawrence Erlbaum Associates.

Dimmick, J., Feaster, J.C., & Hoplamazian, G. (2011). News in the interstices: The niches of mobile media in space and time. *New Media & Society, 13*(1), 23–39.

Divola, B. (2021, June 17). *Is West Cork one of the greatest true crime podcasts since Serial?* The Sydney Morning Herald. https://www.smh.com.au/culture/tv-and-radio/is-west-cork-one-of-the-greatest-true-crime-podcasts-since-serial-20210611-p58061.html

Dixon, T., & Linz, D. (2000). Race and the misrepresentation of victimization on local television news. *Communication Research, 27*(5), 547–573.

Doane, B., McCormick, K., & Sorce, G. (2017). Changing methods for feminist public scholarship: Lessons from Sarah Koenig's podcast *Serial. Feminist Media Studies, 17*(1), 119–121. https://doi.org/10.1080/14680777.2017.1261465

Downing, J., & Pfeffer, J. (1975). Organizational legitimacy: Social values and organizational behavior. *Pacific Sociological Review, 18*(1), 122–136.

Drew, C. (2017). Edutaining audio: An exploration of education podcast design possibilities. *Educational Media International, 54*(1), 48–62.

Dukes, S. (1984). Phenomenological methodology in the human science. *Journal of Religion and Health, 23*(3), 197–203.

Eder, K. (1985). The "new social movements": Moral crusades, political pressure groups, or social movements? *Social Research, 52*(4), 869–890.

Edison Research. (2018). *The infinite dial 2017.* Edison Research and Triton Digital. http://www.edisonresearch.com/infinite-dial-2018/

Edison Research. (2019). *The infinite dial 2019.* Edison Research and Triton Digital. https://www.edisonresearch.com/infinite-dial-2019/

Edison Research. (2021). *The infinite dial 2021.* https://www.edisonresearch.com/the-infinite-dial-2021-2/

Ehrlich, B., & Marks, A. (2022, July 22). *A true-crime star lost his podcast over misconduct allegations. Then, more women came forward.* Rolling Stone. https://www

.rollingstone.com/culture/culture-features/billy-jensen-murder-squad-misconduct-allegation-investigation-1384950/

Eisner, E.W. (1991). *The enlightened eye: Qualitative inquiry and the enhancement of educational practice.* Macmillan.

Evans, C. (2008). The effectiveness of m-learning in the form of podcast revision lectures in higher education. *Computers & Education, 50*(2), 491–498.

Fandos, N. (2018, Dec. 18). *Senate passes bipartisan criminal justice bill.* The New York Times. https://www.nytimes.com/2018/12/18/us/politics/senate-criminal-justice-bill.html

Florini, S. (2015). The podcast "Chitlin' Circuit": Black podcasters, alternative media, and audio enclaves. *Journal of Radio & Audio Media, 22*(2), 209–219.

Folkenflik, D. (2020, Dec. 18). *'New York Times' retracts core of hit podcast series 'Caliphate' on ISIS.* NPR. https://www.npr.org/2020/12/18/944594193/new-york-times-retracts-hit-podcast-series-caliphate-on-isis-executioner

Freeman, J. (1973). The origins of the women's liberation movement. *American Journal of Sociology, 78*(4), 792–811.

Funk, M., & Speakman, B. (2022). Centrist language, camouflaged ideology: Assembled text-based content on mainstream and ideological news podcasts. *Journalism Studies, 23*(11), 1415–1433. https://doi.org/10.1080/1461670X.2022.2094820

Gafas, M., & Burnside, T. (2019, January 8). *Cyntoia Brown is granted clemency after serving 15 years in prison for killing man who bought her for sex.* CNN. https://www.cnn.com/2019/01/07/us/tennessee-cyntoia-brown-granted-clemency/index.html

Gamson, W. (1990). *The strategy of social protest* (2nd ed.). Wadsworth.

Garvey, M. (2015, Feb. 10). *The evolution of playing music in your car.* Complex. https://www.complex.com/music/2015/02/the-evolution-of-playing-music-in-your-car/

Generation Why. (Producer). (2012). *Generation why* [Audio Podcast]. https://genwhypod.com/

Gilliam, F., Iyengar, S., Simon, A., & Wright, O. (1996). Crime in black and white: The violent, scary world of local news. *Harvard International Journal of Press/Politics, 1*(3), 6–23.

Gioia, D.A., Schultz, M., & Corley, K.G. (2000). Organizational identity, image, and adaptive instability. *Academy of Management Review, 25*(1), 63–81.

Goffman, E. (1974). *Frame analysis: An essay on the organization of experience.* Harvard University Press.

Goldberg, K. (2018, Feb. 14). *The Serial effect: How true crime came to dominate podcasts.* Discover Pods. https://discoverpods.com/serial-effect-true-crime-dominate-podcasts/

Greer, A. (2017). Murder, she spoke: the female voice's ethics of evocation and spatialisation in the true crime podcast. *Sound Studies, 3*(2), 152–164. https://doi.org/10.1080/20551940.2018.1456891

Greve, H., Pozner, J., & Rao, H. (2006). Vox populi: Resource partitioning, organizational proliferation, and the cultural impact of the insurgent radio movement. *American Journal of Sociology, 112*(3), 802–837.

Guest, G., Namey, E., & Mitchell, M. (2013). *Collecting qualitative data.* Sage Publications.

Habermas, J. (1989). The transformation of the public sphere's political function. In *The structural transformation of the public sphere* (T. Burger, Trans., pp. 181–235). Polity Press.

Hammersley, B. (2004, Feb. 11). *Audible revolution.* The Guardian. https://www .theguardian.com/media/2004/feb/12/broadcasting.digitalmedia

Hancock, D., & McMutry, L. (2017). "Cycles upon cycles, stories upon stories": Contemporary audio media and podcast horror's new frights. *Palgrave Communications, 3*, 17075. https://doi.org/10.1057/palcomms.2017.75

Hannan, M. (1988). Social change, organizational diversity, and individual careers. In M.W. Riley's (Ed.), *Social change and the life course* (pp. 48–89). Sage.

Hannan, M., & Freeman, J. (1977). The population ecology of organizations. *American Journal of Sociology, 82*(5), 929–964.

Hannan, M., & Freeman, J. (1989). *Organizational ecology.* Harvard University Press.

Hardstark, G., & Kilgariff, K. (2016). *My favorite murder* [Audio podcast]. https:// www.myfavoritemurder.com/

Hawley, A. (1968). Human ecology. In D. Sills's (Ed.), *International Encyclopedia of the Social Sciences* (pp. 328–337). Macmillan.

Hirsch, P.M., & Andrews, J.A.Y. (1984). Administrators' responses to performance and value challenges: Stance, symbols, and behavior. In T.J. Sergiovanni & J.E. Corbally's (Eds.), *Leadership and organizational culture* (pp. 170–185). University of Illinois Press.

Hsu, G., & Hannan, M. (2005). Identities, genres, and organizational forms. *Organization Science, 16*(5), 474–490. https://doi.org/10.1287/orsc.1050.0151

Huddy, L. (2002). From social identity to political identity: A critical examination of social identity theory. *Political Psychology, 22*(1), 127–156. https://doi.org/10 .1111/0162-895X.00230

Hutchins, B., & Hutchins, S. (2018, Feb. 8). *West Cork, Audible's true crime podcast explores Ireland's longest-standing murder investigation.* Discoverpods. https:// discoverpods.com/west-cork-audible-true-crime-podcast-ireland-murder/

Ingram, P., & Rao, H. (2004). Store wars: The enactment and repeal of anti–chain store legislation in America. *American Journal of Sociology, 110*, 446–487.

Inside Radio. (2019, June 21). *Supreme court overturns conviction of man featured in the 'In The Dark' podcast.* https://www.insideradio.com/podcastnewsdaily/ supreme-court-overturns-conviction-of-man-featured-in-the-in-the-dark-podcast/ article_8627e7e4-9442-11e9-af9e-8b638119e719.html

Inside Radio. (2021, February 25). 'Son of a Hitman' creators hit by lawsuit by one of show's interviewees. https://www.insideradio.com/podcastnewsdaily/son-of-a -hitman-creators-hit-by-lawsuit-by-one-of-show-s-interviewees/article_d3a3e1ca -7790-11eb-a86b-3f63cb0b4e85.html

Iskold, A. (2007, Aug. 28). *Will podcasting survive?* ReadWriteWeb. http:// readw rite.com/2007/08/28/will_podcasting_survive

Islam, G., Zyphur, M., & Boje, D. (2008). Carnival and spectacle in *Krewe de Vieux* and the *Mystic Krewe of Spermes*: The mingling of organization and celebration. *Organization Studies, 29*(12), 1565–1589.

iTunes Chart. (2017, December 6). U.S. top 100. http://www.itunescharts.net /us/ charts/podcasts/2017/12/06

iTunes Chart. (2019, March 7). U.S. top 100. http://www.itunescharts.net/us/charts/ podcasts/2019/03/08

Jacobs, G., Christe-Zeyse, J., Keegan, A., & Polos, L. (2008). Reactions to organizational identity threats in times of change: Illustrations from the German police. *Corporate Reputation Review, 11*(3), 245–261.

Jenkins, J.C. (1983). Resource mobilization theory and the study of social movements. *Annual Review of Sociology, 9,* 527–553.

Jenkins, J.C., & Perrow, C. (1977). Insurgency of the powerless: Farm worker movements (1946-1972). *American Sociological Review, 42*(2), 249–268.

Johnson, P. (2015). Editor's remarks: The golden years, then and now. *Journal of Radio & Audio Media, 22*(2), 143–147.

Johnston, H. (2014). *What is a social movement?* Polity Press.

Katz, E., Blumler, J.G., & Gurevitch, M. (1973). Uses and gratifications research. *The Public Opinion Quarterly, 37*(4), 509–523.

Katz, J., & Gartner, W.B. (1988). Properties of emerging organizations. *Academy of Management Review, 13,* 429–441.

Kennedy, M.T. (2008). Getting counted: Markets, media, and reality. *American Sociological Review, 73*(2), 270–295.

Klandermans, B. (1984). Mobilization and participation: Social psychological expansions of resource mobilization theory. *American Sociological Review, 49,* 583–600.

Koenig, S., Snyder, J., & Chivas, D. (Producers). (2014). *Serial* [Audio podcast]. Retrieved https://serialpodcast.org/

Koopmans, R. (2004). Movements and media: Selection process and evolutionary dynamics in the public sphere. *Theory and Society, 33,* 367–391.

Kurzman, C. (1996). Structural opportunity and perceived opportunity in social movement theory: The Iranian revolution of 1979. *American Sociological Review, 61*(1), 153–170.

Kvale, S. (2007). *Doing interviews.* Sage Publications.

LancasterOnline. (2007. Jan. 24). New era 'Lost Angels' series booklet now for sale. *Lancaster New Era.* https://lancasteronline.com/news/new-era-lost-angels-series -booklet-now-for-sale/article_c67bace1-fcfe-512e-a899-b98755a6180c.html

Lavoie, R. [Facebook post]. (2019, March 10). The official *Crime Writers On...* podcast discussion group [Closed Facebook group]. https://www.facebook.com/ groups/crimewritersonpodcastdiscussion/

Lawson, M. (2015, Dec. 12). *Serial thrillers: Why true crime is popular culture's most wanted.* The Guardian. https://www.theguardian.com/culture/ 2015/dec/12/ serial-thrillers-why-true-is-popular-cultures-most-wanted

LeBon, G. (1895, trans. 1947). *The crowd: A study of the popular mind.* Ernest Benn.

Lee, A. (2022, June 20). *How Ashley Flowers achieved a net worth of $5 million.* Money Inc. https://moneyinc.com/ashley-flowers-net-worth/

Lee, H. (1999 [1960]). *To kill a mockingbird, 40th anniversary edition.* Harper Collins.

Levenson, M. (2022, Sept. 14). *Prosecutors move to overturn murder conviction in 'Serial' case.* The New York Times. https://www.nytimes.com/2022/09/14/us/adnan-syed-serial-murder-hae-min-lee.html

Levenson, M. (2022, Sept. 19). *Judge vacates murder conviction of Adnan Syed of 'Serial.'* The New York Times. https://www.nytimes.com/2022/09/19/us/adnan-syed-murder-conviction-overturned.html

Levine, M. (2021, July 1). *As police reform talks sputter, bipartisan criminal justice bills advance.* Politico. https://www.politico.com/news/2021/07/01/democrats-eager-replicate-trump-achievement-497276

Lincoln, Y.S., & Guba, E.G. (1985). *Naturalistic inquiry,* Sage Publications, Inc.

Liptak, A. (2019, February 18). *When does kicking Black people off juries cross a constitutional line?* The New York Times. https://www.nytimes.com/2019/02/18/us/ politics /black-jurors-constitution-curtis-flowers.html

Listen Notes, Inc. (2022). *Podcast discovery.* https://www.listennotes.com/podcast-discovery/

Locker, M. (2018, April 25). *Apple's podcasts just topped 50 billion all-time downloads and streams.* Fast Company. https://www.fastcompany.com/40563318/apples-podcasts-just-topped-50-billion-all-time-downloads-and-streams

Lounsbury, M. (2001). Institutional sources of practice variation: Staffing college and university recycling programs. *Administrative Science Quarterly, 46,* 29–56.

Lowrey, W. (2011). Institutions, news, organizations and innovation. *Journalism Studies, 12*(1), 64–79. https://doi.org/10.1080/1461670X.2010.511954

Lowrey, W. (2012). Journalism innovation and the ecology of new production: Institutional tendencies. *Journalism & Communication Monographs, 14*(4), 214–287. https://doi.org/10.1177/1522637912463207

Lowrey, W. (2017). The emergence and development of news fact-checking sites. *Journalism Studies, 18*(3), 376–394. https://doi.org/10.1080/1461670X.2015 .1052537

Lowrey, W., Sherrill, L.A., & Broussard, R. (2019). Field and ecological explanations of data journalism innovation: A focus on the role of ancillary organizations. *Journalism Studies, 20*(15), 2131–2149. https://doi.org/10.1080/1461670X.2019 .1568904

MacDougall, R. (2011). Podcasting and political life. *American Behavioral Scientist, 55*(6), 714–732.

Magellan, A.I. (2019, July 30). *New categories in Apple podcasts: True crime listeners love Madison Reed.* Magellan Blog. https://magellanblog.medium .com/new-categories-in-apple-podcasts-true-crime-listeners-love-madison-reed -d863070cb824#:~:text=A%20week%20ago%2C%20Apple%20started,as%20of %20July%2029%2C%202019

Manas, S. (2018, May 11). *Candidates for Baltimore State's Attorney hammer absent incumbent.* Maryland Matters. https://www.marylandmatters.org/single-post/2018 /05/11/Candidates-for-Baltimore-State%E2%80%99s-Attorney-Hammer-Absent -Incumbent

Mattoni, A. (2017). A situated understanding of digital technologies in social movements: Media ecology and media practice approaches. *Social Movement Studies, 16*(4), 1–12.

McAdam, D. (1999). *Political Process and the Development of Black Insurgency, 1930-1970* (2nd ed.). University of Chicago Press.

McAdam, D. (2017). Social movement theory and the prospects for climate change activism in the United States. *Annual Review of Political Science, 20*(1), 189–208.

McAdam, D., McCarthy, J., & Zald, M. (1988). Social movements. In N.J. Smelser (Ed.), *Handbook of sociology* (pp. 695–737). Sage Publications, Inc.

McAdam, D., McCarthy, J., & Zald, M. (1996). Introduction: Opportunities, mobilizing structures and framing processes: Toward a synthetic, comparative perspective on social movements. In *Comparative Perspectives on Social Movements* (pp. 1–20). Cambridge University Press.

McAdam, D., Tarrow, S., & Tilly, C. (2003). Dynamics of contention. *Social Movement Studies, 2*(1), 99–102.

McCarthy, J., & Zald, M. (1977). Resource mobilization and social movements: A partial theory. *American Journal of Sociology, 82*(6), 1212–1241.

McCarthy, J., & Zald, M. (2002). The enduring vitality of the resource mobilization theory of social movements. In J. Turner's (Ed.), *Handbook of Sociological Theory* (pp. 533–565). Kluwer Academic/Plenum Publishers.

McClung, S., and Johnson, K. (2010). Examining the motives of podcast users. *Journal of Radio & Audio Media, 17*(1), 82–95.

McCracken, G. (1988). *The long interview.* Sage Publications, Inc.

McHugh, S. (2016). How podcasting is changing the audio storytelling genre. *Radio Journal: International Studies in Broadcast & Audio Media, 14*(1). https://doi.org /10.1386 /rjao.14.1.65_1

McHugh, S. (2017, Aug. 31). *Truth to power: how podcasts are getting political.* The Conversation. http://theconversation.com/truth-to-power-how-podcasts-are-getting -political-81185

McNamara, M. (2018). *I'll be gone in the dark.* Harper Collins.

Meho, L. (2006). E-mail interviewing in qualitative research: A methodological discussion. *Journal of the American Society for Information Science and Technology, 57*(10), 1284–1295.

Melucci, A. (1985). The symbolic challenge of contemporary movements. *Social Research, 52*(4), 789–816.

Melucci, A. (1995). The process of collective identity. In H. Johnston & B. Klandermans (Eds.), *Social Movements and Culture: Social Movements, Protest, and Contention, vol. 4* (pp. 42–63). University of Minnesota Press.

Merry, S. (2014, November 13). *'Serial': An investigative journalism podcast becomes a cultural obsession.* The Washington Post. https://www.washingtonpost .com /news/arts-and-entertainment/wp/2014/11/13/serial-an-investigative-journali sm-podcast-becomes-a-culturalobsession/?tid=a_inl&utm _term=.d041737acd4e

Meserko, V. (2015). Standing upright: Podcasting, performance, and alternative comedy. *Studies in American Humor, 1*(1), 20–40. https://doi.org/10.5325/studamerhumor.1.1.0020

Meyer, D., & Staggenborg, S. (1996). Movements, countermovements, and the structure of political opportunity. *American Journal of Sociology, 101*(6), 1628–1660.

Mezias, J., & Mezias, S. (2000). Resource partitioning, the founding specialist forms, and innovation: the American film industry, 1912-1929. *Organization Science, 11*(3), 306–322.

Minkoff, D.C. (1999). Bending with the wind: strategic change and adaptation by women's and racial minority organizations. *American Journal of Sociology, 104*(6), 1666–1703.

Monge, P., Lee, A., Fulk, J., Weber, M.S., Schultz, C., Margolin, D., Gould, J., & Frank, L. (2011). Research methods for studying evolutionary and ecological processes in organizational communication. *Management Communication Quarterly, 25*(2), 211–251.

Moody, M., Dorries, B., & Blackwell, H. (2014). How national media framed coverage of missing Black and white women. *Media Report to Women, 37*(4), 12–18.

Moran, M. (2022, April 4). *12 podcasting statistics, facts, and trends (2022).* StartupBonsai. https://startupbonsai.com/podcasting-statistics/

Morris, A. (2000). Reflections on social movement theory: Criticisms and proposals. *Contemporary Sociology, 29*(3), 445–454.

Morris, J.W., & Patterson, E. (2015). Podcasting and its apps: Software, sound and the interfaces of digital audio. *Journal of Radio & Audio Media, 22*(2), 220–230.

Murder Accountability Project. (2018). *Victim characteristics 1976-2016.* Retrieved from http://www.murderdata.org/p/victims.html

Nelson, H. (2018, July 30). *52 great true crime podcasts.* Vulture. https://www.vulture.com/article/52-best-true-crime-podcasts.html

Nesterak, M. (2022, July 6). *American Public Media cancels award-winning 'In the Dark' podcast.* Minnesota Reformer. https://minnesotareformer.com/briefs/american-public-media-cancels-award-winning-in-the-dark-podcast/

New Beginning, Inc. (Producer). (2015). *Truth & Justice* [Audio podcast]. https://www.truthandjusticepod.com/

NYU Journalism. (2019). *Audio reportage.* https://journalism.nyu.edu/graduate/programs/literary-reportage/audio-reportage/

Oberschall, A. (1973). *Social Conflict and Social Movements.* Prentice Hall.

Obst, P.L., Zinkiewicz, L., & Smith, S.G. (2002). Sense of community in science fiction fandom, part 1: Understanding sense of community in an international community of interest. *Journal of Community Psychology, 30*(1), 87–103.

O'Connell, M. (2015). *The 'Serial' effect: Programmers ramping up on podcasts.* The Hollywood Reporter. https://www.hollywoodreporter.com/lifestyle/lifestyle-news/serial-effect-programmers-ramping-up-786688/

Olson, M. (1968). *The logic of collective action.* Schocken.

Paquet, L. (2020). Seeking justice elsewhere: Informal and formal justice in the true crime podcasts *Trace* and *The Teacher's Pet. Crime, Media, and Culture: An International Journal, 17*(3). https://doi.org/10.1177/1741659020954260

Parker, T. (Director & Writer). Stone, M., & Graden, B. (Writers). (2013, Oct. 2). Informative murder porn (season 17, episode 2) [TV series episode]. In F.C.

Agnone II (executive producer). *South Park*. Comedy Central, Braniff, and Comedy Partners.

Patel, K. (2018, September 24). *A brief history of podcasting*. Ustudio. https://ustudio.com/blog/podcasting/a-brief-history-of-podcasting/

Patterson, A. (2021, Dec. 10). *Spotify's Joe Rogan baselessly suggests white nationalist Patriot Front rally in DC was 'fake' and put on by 'the feds.'* Media Matters. https://www.mediamatters.org/joe-rogan-experience/spotifys-joe-rogan-baselessly-suggests-white-nationalist-patriot-front-rally

Perks, L.G., Turner, J.S., & Tollison, A.C. (2019). Podcast uses and gratifications scale development. *Journal of Broadcasting & Electronic Media, 63*(4), 617–634. https://doi.org/10.1080/08838151.2019.1688817

Perse, E.M., & Courtright, J.A. (1993). Normative images of communication media mass: Mass and interpersonal channels in the new media environment. *Human Communication Research, 19*(4), 485–503. https://doi.org/10.1111/j.1468-2958.1993.tb00310.x

Piper, M. (2015). Little big dog pill explanations: Humour, honesty, and the comedian podcast. *Philament, 20*, 41–60.

Plano Clark, V.L., & Creswell, J. (2008). *The mixed methods reader*. Sage Publications.

Plimpton, G. (1966, Jan. 16). *The story behind a nonfiction novel*. New York Times. https://archive.nytimes.com/www.nytimes.com/books/97/12/28/home/capote-interview.html?r=1

Pluskota, J. (2015). The perfect technology: Radio and mobility. *Journal of Radio & Audio Media, 22*(2), 325–336.

Polkinghorne, D.E. (1989). Narrative configuration in qualitative analysis. *Qualitative Studies in Education, 8*, 5–23.

Polos, L., Hannan, M., & Carroll, G. (2002). Foundations of a theory of social forms. *Industrial and Corporate Change, 11*(1), 85–115.

Pulitzer. (2019, May 14). *Finalist: Andrew Beck Grace, Chip Brantley, Graham Smith, Nicole Beemsterboer and Robert Little of NPR*. The Pulitzer Prize. https://www.pulitzer.org/finalists/andrew-beck-grace-chip-brantley-graham-smith-nicole-beemsterboer-and-robert-little-npr

Punnett, I.C. (2018). *Toward a theory of true crime narratives: A textual analysis*. Routledge.

Quirk, V. (2016). *Guide to podcasting*. https://www.gitbook.com/book /towcenter/guide-to-podcasting/details

Raff, D. (2000). Superstores and the evolution of firm capabilities in American bookselling. *Strategic Management Journal, 21*(10/11), 1043–1059.

Reddit. (2015). *Serial podcast*. Retrieved from https://www.reddit.com/r/Serialpodcast/

Resler, S. (2018, Feb. 2). *Here's why most podcast listening happens on Apple devices*. Jacobs Media. https://jacobsmedia.com/heres-podcast-listening-happens-apple-devices/

Roberts, A. (2014, December 23). *The "Serial" podcast: By the numbers*. CNN. http://www.cnn.com/2014/12/18/showbiz/feat-serial-podcast-btn/col

Romano, A. (2017, April 1). *S-town is a stunning podcast. It probably shouldn't have been made.* Vox. https://www.vox.com/culture/2017/3/30/15084224/s-town -review-controversial-podcast-privacy

Romano, A. (2022, Feb. 23). *How do you solve a problem like Joe Rogan?* Vox. https://www.vox.com/culture/22945864/joe-rogan-politics-spotify-controversy

Rosman, K., Sisario, B., Isaac, M., & Satariano, A. (2022, Feb. 17). *Spotify bet big on Joe Rogan. It got more than it counted on.* The New York Times. https://www .nytimes.com/2022/02/17/arts/music/spotify-joe-rogan-misinformation.html

Rubin, A.M., & Step, M.M. (2000). Impact of motivation, attraction, and parasocial interaction on talk radio listening. *Journal of Broadcasting & Electronic Media, 44*(4), 635–654.

Rule, J., & Tilly, C. (Eds.) (1975). Political process in revolutionary France. In J. Merriman's (Ed.), *1830 in France* (pp. 41–85). New Viewpoints.

Salvati, A. (2015). Podcasting the past: *Hardcore History*, fandom, and DIY histories. *Journal of Radio & Audio Media, 22*(2), 231–239.

Sandell, R. (2001). Organizational growth and ecological constraints: The growth of social movements in Sweden, 1881 to 1940. *American Sociological Review, 66* (5), 672–693.

Sarat, A. (2022, April 5). *Shedding light on our scandalous false convictions record.* The Hill. https://thehill.com/opinion/judiciary/3260040-shedding-light-on-our -scandalous-false-convictions-record/

Scott, W.R. (2013). *Institutions and organizations: Ideas, interests, and identities.* Sage Publications.

Shaw, G. (2020, March 2). *The longest running TV dramas of all time.* Insider. https:// www.insider.com/longest-tv-dramas-2018-10

Sherrill, L.A. (2020). The '*Serial* effect' and the true crime podcast ecosystem. *Journalism Practice.* https://doi.org/10.1080/17512786.2020.1852884

Sherrill, L.A., Zhang, J., Deavours, D., Towery, N., Lyu, Y., Singleton, W., Kuang, K., & Lowrey, W. (2022). Journalism's backstage players: The development of journalism professional associations and their roles in a troubled field. *Journal of Media Business Studies, 19*(1). https://doi.org/10.1080/16522354.2021.1899742

Shetty, S. (2014, Dec. 21). *Watch SNL's brilliant, Christmas themed parody of* Serial. Slate. https://slate.com/culture/2014/12/snl-does-serial-cecily-strong-is-sarah-koe-nig-plus-mike-myers-returns-as-dr-evil-video.html

Shorter, E., & Tilly, C. (1974). *Strikes in France 1830-1968.* Cambridge University Press.

Simpson, S. (2017, Oct. 14). *The unlikely role of true crime podcasts in criminal justice reform.* Quartz. https://qz.com/1101889/the-unlikely-role-of-true-crime -podcasts-in-criminal-justice-reform

Singh, J., & Lumsden, C. (1990). Theory and research in organizational ecology. *Annual Review of Sociology, 16*(1), 161–195.

Skiba, D.J. (2006). The 2005 word of the year: podcast. *Nursing Education Perspectives, 27*(1), 54–55.

Slakoff, D. (2021). The mediated portrayal of intimate partner violence in true crime podcasts: Strangulation, isolation, threats of violence, and coercive control. *Violence Against Women, 28*(6–7). https://doi.org/10.1177/10778012211019055

Slate (producer). (2022, Sept. 24). *ICYMI* [Audio podcast]. https://slate.com/podcasts/icymi/2022/09/adnan-syed-release-serial-journalistic-failures

Slotkin, J. (2020, Sept. 5). *After 6 trials, prosecutors drop charges against Curtis Flowers*. National Public Radio. https://www.npr.org/2020/09/05/910061573/after-6-trials-prosecutors-drop-charges-against-curtis-flowers

Smelser, N. (1962). *The theory of collective behavior*. Free Press.

Snow, D., & Benford, R. (1988). Ideology, frame resonance, and participant mobilization. *International Social Movement Research, 1*, 197–218.

Sommer, W. (2022, June 8). *True crime fans livid their fave hosts are MAGA loyalists*. Daily Beast. https://www.thedailybeast.com/true-crime-fans-livid-their-fave-podcast-hosts-are-maga-loyalists

Sommers, Z. (2016). Missing white woman syndrome: An empirical analysis of race and gender disparities in online coverage of missing persons. *The Journal of Criminal Law and Criminology, 106*(2), 275–314.

Sprangler, T. (2019, Aug. 15). *'Crime Junkie' podcast host Ashley Flowers responds to plagiarism allegations*. Variety. https://variety.com/2019/digital/news/crime-junkie-podcast-ashley-flowers-plagiarism-1203302072/

Staff. (2009, February 1). *Authorities search gravel pit for missing woman's body*. North Escambia.com. http://www.northescambia.com/2009/02/authorities-search-gravel-pit-for-missing-womans-body

Staff. (2021, March 24). *After 18 years, the search continues for Melinda Wall McGhee*. North Escambia.com. http://www.northescambia.com/2021/03/after-18-years-the-search-continues-for-melinda-wall-mcghee

Staff Reports. (2004, Oct. 4). *Arrest draws Sheriff's attention on McGhee case*. The Atmore Advance. https://www.atmoreadvance.com/2004/10/04/arrest-draws-sherrifs-attention-on-mcghee-case/

Staff and Wire Reports. (2007, March 5). New Era reporter wins top national writing award. *Lancaster New Era*. Retrieved from https://lancasteronline.com/opinion/new-era-reporter-wins-top-national-writing-award/article_3efeabb2-e936-502e-bb3b-9db571823a36.html

Stinchcombe, A. (1965). Organizations and social structure. In J. March's (Ed.), *Handbook of Organizations* (pp. 153–193). Rand McNally.

Suchman, M.C. (1995). Managing legitimacy: Strategic and institutional approaches. *Academy of Management Review, 20*, 571–610.

Swanson, D. (2012). Tuning in and hanging out: A preliminary study of college students' use of podcasts for information, entertainment, and socializing. *The Social Science Journal, 49*, 183–190.

Tech News. (2018, June 30). *Android now finally has its own native podcast app from Google*. The Star Online. https://www.thestar.com.my/tech/tech-news/2018/06/30/android-now-finally-has-its-own-native-podcast-app-from-google/

Tenderfoot TV. (2022). *Up and Vanished* [Audio podcast]. https://upandvanished.com/about/

The Center for Investigative Reporting. (2013). *Reveal* [Audio podcast]. https://revealnews.org/podcast/

The Society for the re-education of Sword and Scale fans. (2018). [Closed Facebook group]. https://www.facebook.com/groups/reedswordandscale/

Tiffe, R., & Hoffmann, M. (2017). Taking up sonic space: feminized vocality and podcasting as resistance. *Feminist Media Studies, 17* (1), 115–118, https://doi.org/10.1080/14680777.2017.1261464

Tilly, C. (1978). *From mobilization to revolution.* Addison Wesley.

Tilly, C. (1986). *The contentious French.* Harvard University Press.

Traugott, M. (1978). Reconceiving social movements. *Social Problems, 26*(1), 38–49.

Trist, E. (1977). A Concept of Organizational Ecology. *Australian Journal of Management, 2*(2), 161–175.

True Crime Database. (2019, Aug. 19). *Welcome to the True Crime Database.* Retrieved April 15, 2022 from https://docs.google.com/spreadsheets/d/1PmnKPj-coHtX7VuKHJ9 2fWihQ0PDCtABPfA8RXgxeyIM/edit#gid=2071093220

True Crime Guy [blog]. (n.d.). http://truecrimeguy.com/

True Crime podcasts (2016). https://www.reddit.com/r/podcasts/comments/ 53v2hp/the_big_list_of_true_crime_podcasts/

Undisclosed LLC v. The State. (2017, Oct. 30). Supreme Court of Georgia, S17A1061.

Van Zomeren, M., Postmes, T., & Spears, R. (2008). Toward an integrative social identity model of collective action: A quantitative research synthesis of three socio-psychological perspectives. *American Psychological Association, 134*(4), 504–535.

Verdier, H. (2018, Feb. 20). Could *A Very Fatal Murder* kill off the true-crime podcast? The Guardian US. https://www.theguardian.com/tv-and-radio/2018/feb/20/could-a-very-fatal-kill-off-the-true-crime-podcast

Vogt, N. (2016, June 15). *Podcasting: Fact sheet.* Pew Research Center. http://www.journalism.org/2016/06/15/podcasting-fact-sheet/

Vulture Editors. (2018, November 18). *This week in true-crime podcasts:* Thunder Bay, Believed, *and more.* https://www.vulture.com/2018/11/best-new-true-crime-podcasts-nov-1.html

Wales, Katie (1989): *A Dictionary of Stylistics.* Longman.

Weber, M. (1946 [1922]). Class, status, party. In H. Gerth and C. Wright (Eds.), *From Max Weber Essays in Sociology* (pp. 180–195). Oxford University Press.

Weber, M. ([1924] 1947). *The theory of social and economic organization.* A.H. Henderson & T. Parsons (Ed.). Free Press.

Weber, M.S. (2017). Unseen disruptions and the emergence of new organizations. *Communication Theory, 27,* 92–113.

Weber, M.S., Faulk, J., & Monge, P. (2016). The emergence and evolution of social networking sites as an organizational form. *Management Communication Quarterly, 30*(3), 305–332.

Weiss, R.S. (1995). *Learning from Strangers: The Art and Method of Qualitative Interview Studies.* Simon & Schuster.

Wheeler, B. (2019, Sept. 13). *'Undisclosed' podcast covering 1998 Putnam County double homicide.* Herald-Citizen. http://herald-citizen.com/stories/undisclosed -podcast-covering-1998-putnam-county-double-homicide,37250

Wilkinson, A. (2019, May 3). *The Ted Bundy movie starring Zac Efron sure does love Ted Bundy.* Vox. https://www.vox.com/culture/2019/2/5/18210945/ted-bundy -extremely-wicked-shockingly-evil-vile-review-netflix

Williams, S. (2020, June 30). *She set out to change the world, not entertain it.* Timber. https://timber.fm/stories/undisclosed-podcast-feature/

Winn, R. (2021, Dec. 28). *2021 Podcast stats & facts.* Podcast Insights. https://www .podcastinsights.com/podcast-statistics/

Wolf, B. (2016, Nov. 23). *Georgia criminal case reversals focus on need for reform.* Southern Political Report. https://www.southernpoliticalreport.com/2016/ 11/23/ georgia-criminal-case-reversals-focus-on-need-for-reform

Wolf, D., Yellen, B., Martin, J. (Writers), & Campanella, J.J. (Director) (2021, Oct. 21). The five hundredth episode (season 23, episode 6) [Television series episode]. In D. Wolf's [Executive producer], *Law & order: SVU.* Wolf Entertainment; Universal Television.

WonderyMedia. (2019, March 9). We have decided to part ways with Mike Boudet and Sword and Scale [Twitter post]. https://twitter.com/WonderyMedia/status /1104459334430339072

Woods, B. (2018, March 31). *Adnan Syed prosecutor on what the Serial case means for his State's Attorney bid.* The Real News Network. https://therealnews.com/sto ries/adnan-syed-prosecutor-on-what-the-serial-case-means-for-his-states-attorney -bid

Yardley, E., Wilson, D., & Kennedy, M. (2015). "To me its [sic] real life": Secondary victims of homicide in new media. *Victims & Offenders, 12*(3), 467–496. https:// doi.org/10.1080/15564886.2015.1105896

Young, D. (2013). Political satire and Occupy Wall Street: How comics co-opted strategies of protest paradigm to legitimize a movement. *International Journal of Communication, 73*, 71–393.

Zimbardo, P.G. (1969). The human choice: Individuation, reason, and order versus deindividuation, impulse and chaos. In W.J. Arnold & D. Levine's (Eds.), *Nebraska Symposium on Motivation* (Vol. 16, pp. 237–307). University of Nebraska Press.

Appendix

True Crime Podcasts 2005–2022

Note: Misspellings and other grammatical errors in podcast titles are copied verbatim from the podcasts' descriptions.

12/26/1975
Beyond Your Nightmares (formerly The Doe Files)
¡No Manches!
¡Que Spooky! Podcast
#fsck 'em all!
#SiblingsToo
(Sometimes) Dead is Better
. . . But What Do We Know?
. . . These Are Their Stories: The Law and Order Podcast
10 Minute Murder
10 Things That Scare Me
10 to Life
100: 1 the crack legacy
10-0: True Crime and Paranormal Stories from Behind the Headset
1000 True Crimes
1001 Heroes, Legends, Histories & Mysteries Podcast

107 degrees Maura Murray
109 Ocean Avenue
10-96 Crime Chicks
11 to 7
12 Years That Shook the World
13 Alibis
13 O'Clock
13: The search for leigh occhi
15 Minutes With . . . Drew Peterson
16 Shots
18 Days
2 Dimes & True Crime
2 Drunk Girls
2 Friends 2 Murders Podcast
2 Girls, 1 Scaredy Cat
2 Guys 1 Crime Podcast
2 Truths and a Crime
21st Century Crime
22 Hours: An American Nightmare
27 Club

2k Away
2WeiRd MoMs
3 Men and a Mystery
3 Sisters 1 Murder
3 Spooked Girls
3 Spoopy 5 Me
30 for 30 podcasts
30 Minutes With CheetahLion
30 Morbid Minutes
31 Nights of Scary Shit
32 Degrees
36 Times - Canadian True Crime
3AM
3C Podcast - True Crime in the Circle City
420 Unsolved
48 Hours
5 Live Investigates
5 Minute Conspiracies
5 Roses
50 Days of Crime
50 States of Crime
51 Days of Terror

163

60 Minutes True Crime
Podcast
70 Million
74 seconds
88 Days: The Jayme
Closs Story
90 Minute Escape
90s True Crime
911 Calls Podcast with
The Operator
911 Florida Raw Audio
911 Moms Pod
99% Chance of Wine and
Murder
A Beer A Crime A Tale
A Bloody Mess
A Brief Case
A Case of Conspiracy
A Correctional View
A Crime Crisis
A Crime Most Queer
A Crime That
A Dark and Bloody
Ground
A Dark Masquerade
A Dark Tale True Crime
Podcast
A Darker Matter
A Date with Dateline
A Day with Crime
A Funny Feeling
A History of Evil Men
A Killing in the Cape
A Little Bit Culty
A Little Bit Grim
A Little Mystery
A Little Thing Called
Murder
A Little Wicked
A Matter of Crime
A Mother of a Murder
A Mug of Morbid
A Murder of Crows
A Murder On Orchard
Street

A Murder on the Space
Coast
A Murder To Remember
A Murderess Affair
A Murderous Design
A Paranormal Chicks
A Paranormal Chicks
A Perfect Storm: The
True Story of The
Chamberlains
A Pine for True Crime
A Podcast About Murder
A Podcast on Elm St.
A Senseless Death
A Shot of Crime
A Shout from the Long
Grass
A Slice of True Crime
A Southern Sleuth
A Sprinkle of Murder
A Sprinkle of Sugar, A
Dash of Murder
A Story of Innocence
A Tale Most Foul
A True Crime Pod by
Sarah
A True Crime Podcast
A True Crime Tragedy
A Trump Show - with
Dennis Trainor Jr
Aaahh!!! Reel Horror
Stories
Aaron Mahnke's Cabinet
of Curiosities
ABC 2020
ABNRML JAPAN
About Crime
Above The Legal Limit
Absolutely True True
Crime: A Deadly Seri-
ous Podcast
Accused
Active Shooter: The
Podcast
Actual Events Podcast

Actual Innocence
Addicted to Murder
Adventures in Murderland
Podcast
Affirmative Murder
Africa Investigates
After Dark
After Dark Coast to Coast
Aftereffect
AFTERMATH
Aftermath of a Kansas
City necktie Party
Afternoonified
Against the Rules with
Michael Lewis
AHC Podcast
Aider and Abettor podcast
Ain't It Rich
Alabama Grist Mill
Alan Stoob's True Crime
Casebook
Alarmed
Alaska Unsolved
Alexandria's thoughts
Algorithm
Alibi
Alive Girl and the Big
Salamanders
All Aussie Mystery Hour
Podcast
All Bad Things - A Disas-
ter Podcast
All But Forgotten by As
the Key Turns
All Cats Are Grey In the
Dark
All Crime No Cattle
All Killa No Filla
All Rather Mysterious
All Rise Podcast
All Rise-The Gonzaga
Law Podcast
All the Rage
All Things Awful
All Things Conspiracy

Back of the Class
Backwoods Barcast
Bad Acts: A True Crime Podcast
Bad Batch
Bad Bitchez
Bad Blood: The Final Chapter
Bad Detective
bad guys & good beer
Bad In The Boondocks
Bad to the Bone
Bad Women: Ripper Retold
Bad: All About Crime
Badger Bizarre
Badlands
Bag Man
Bailstreet
Baking a Murderer
Ballarat's Children
Bang, Bang . . . Cult
Bangkok Strange
Bardstown
Barely Legal Comedy podcast (formerly Mondeo Law)
Based on a True Crime
Based on a True Scary
Based on a True Story
Bay Area Mystery club
Bayou Crimes
BC is Creepy
Be Creepy With Me
Be Gay, True Crime
Be Grave
Beanbag Talk
Bear Brook
Bearing Witness: Columbine and the News Media
Beautiful Vibes & True Crimes
Bed Crime Stories
Bedtime Stories
Beenham Valley Road

Beer Freaks
Beer, Blood, and the Bayou
Beer, Cheese & Murder
Beheaded
Behind Bars
Behind Gray Walls
Behind the Bastards
Behind The Mask with Ryan & Tony
Behind the Sugar Cane
Behind the Tape
Behind the Walls
Behind the Yellow Tape
Behind true crime
Believe Her
Believed
Benson's Bitches
Bent and Twisted
Best Case Worst Case
Best Served Cold
Best True Crime Stories Podcast 2022 Police Interrogations, 911 Calls and True Crime Investigations
Bestie Banter with Tali + Ash
Betrayal with Daryn Carp
Beyond Bizarre True Crime
Beyond Bizarre True Crime [By AbJack]
Beyond Contempt True Crime
Beyond Prisons
Beyond Reasonable Doubt by Mail+
Beyond Reasonable Doubt by Semon Hodhod
Beyond Reasonable Doubt: The Troy Davis Project
Beyond Reasonable Doubt?

Beyond Reproach
Beyond the Badge
Beyond the Badge by Jackie & Scott Campbell
Beyond the Badge by KSL
Beyond the Badge by Vincent Hill
Beyond the Beards
Beyond the Blood
Beyond the Legal Limit with Jeffrey Lichtman
Beyond The Looking Glass
Beyond the Rainbow
Beyond Unsolved
Bicoastal Crime
Big Angry Law Radio
Big Brother: North Korea's Forgotten Prince
Big Crime, Small Potatoes
Big Feelings
Big Hits Radio Call of the Weird
Big Mad True Crime
Big Savage: The Death Of Alexander Stevens
Big Trouble in Little Quartzsite
Big, If True
Bigfoot for Breakfast
Bigfoot Gumbo
Billionaire Boys Club
Binge Watch With Us
Biographics: History One Life at a Time
Bird Podcast | Stories from prison
Bitches and Murders
Bitches Be Like
Bitter Endings Podcast
Bizarre

Bizarre & Facinating Details

Bizarre States

Bizarre Tales

Bizarro Aficionado

Black Box Down

Black Girl Gone

Black Hands

Black Law and Legal Lies

Black Museum

Black True Crime

Black Widow and The Banshee Tales of True Crime and the Paranormal

Blackguard

Blackspots

Blame

Blankenship on Trial

Blanket Fort Mysteries (In Sight Jr)

Bleeped

Bless This Mess

Blondes, Booze, and Bullsh*te

Blood & Barrels

Blood & Black Lace Podcast

Blood & Firewater

Blood & Wine

Blood and Dust: Wild West True Crime

Blood and Popcorn

Blood and Truth

Blood n Blush

Blood of a Buckeye

Blood On the Rocks

Blood Sausage

Blood Sisters

Blood Ties

Blood Town

Blood, Sweat, and Fear: The Story of Inspector Vance

Bloodbath

Bloodthirsty Times

Bloody Betrayal & Works of Darkness

Bloody Murder

Bloody Pasta

Bloody Podcast

Blunt History

Blurry Photos

Bodies

Bodies in the Bayous

Body on the Moor

Bohemian Dolls Unsolved Mysteries

Bomber

Bombfire: Making a Murderer

Bonaparte

Bondi Badlands

Bonding Over Murder- True Crime Discussions

Bone and Sickle

Bone Palace Ballet

Boo Bois Podcast

Boo!Gotcha

Boo, Y'all

Boobs and Boos

Boo'd Up

Booked Bagged and Tagged

Boomtown

Boos with Booze

Booze & Bloodshed's Podcast

Booze and Ghouls

Booze With the Hound

Booze, Bullsh*t, & True Crime

BooZing Podcast

Boozy

Border City

Borderline

Borderline by Voyage Media

Bored & Unemployed

Boseak Conundrum

Boston confidential Beantown's True Crime Podcast

Boston Venue: The Channel Story

Bothered AF

Bourbon and Bloodshed

Bourbon Legends

Boushie

Bow to Fate

Bowraville

Brad is a Bad Person

Brain Bitez

Brainless Offenders

Branch Davideans: Followers of the Lamb of God

Brave Girls Club Podcast

Break in the Case

Break Stuff [Luminary]

Break The Chains of Human Trafficking - FWCAT

Breakdown

Breakfast Lunch and Danner

Breaking Hezbollah's Golden Rule

Breathless: the death of David Dungay Jr

Brew Crime

Brewing Crime

Brews and Oddities

Brian Shaffer Dead or Alive

Briana's True Crime Reviews

Bribe, Swindle, or Steal

British Murders

British Scandal

Broadcast Mysteries

Broke Busted & Disgusted

Broken Doors

Broken Harts
Broken Justice
Broken Pledge
BROKEN: Jeffrey
  Epstein
Broomsticks & Bullsh!t
Brothers Grimm Podcast
Bruh Issa Murder
Brutal Ends
Bruthas N Law
BSP: Believer Skeptic
  Podcast
Bud Trials
Building Utopia: Bhag-
  wan Shree Rajneesh
Bumblebutt Podcast
Bump in the Night
Bundyville
Buried
Buried Alive
Buried Motives
Buried Truths
Burner Phone
Business Wars
Busted Business Bureau
By All Means Necessary
Bye, go home, no one
  loves you
C.E.S. POOL
CA True Crime Podcast
Cabernet & True Crime
Caffeine & Crime
Caffeine, Crime and
  Canines
Caffiendz's podcast
Caitlin Can't Remember
Cake and Death
California Innocence
  Project
California PC 187: The
  Podcast
California True Crime
Caliphate
Camp Nightmare
Campaign '68

Campfire Conversations
Campus Crime Chronicles
Can We be Horrible for a
  Second?
Can We Cult
Can You Believe This
  Sh*t?
Canada Obscura
Canadian History Ehx
Canadian True Crime
Cancrime
CanDance and My Friend
  Jenny
Canonical: True Crime
Can't Make This Sh*t
  Up: A True Crime
  Podcast
Can't Relate
Capable: A True Crime
  Podcast
Cape Fear Unearthed
Caper
Capital Insurrection
  Report
Carolina True Crime
Carousel Sniper Victim
Carruth
Cartels, Conspiracies, and
  Camarena
Case Acquaint
Case Closed
Case Closed, Beers Open
Case Files with Kat and
  Ashley
Case Identity
Case Notes
Case of Conspiracy
Case Remains
Case Unsolved
Case X Case
Casefile True Crime
Casewatch
Cash Cow Radio
Caskets & Cocktails

Casting Lots: A Survival
  Cannibalism Podcast
Castles & Cryptids
Catch My Killer
Catching Killers
CatchingKillers
Catlick
Caught
Caustic Soda
Cautionary Tales
Center for Media at Risk
Central Crime Texas
Cereal Conversations
Cereal Killer
Cesspool Podcast
Chalk Murder To Me
Chalk Talk
Chameleon
Chaos Merchants
Chapo
charcuterie & crime
Charleston Time Machine
Charlie Crimebuster's
  Crime Talk
Charm City
Chasing Ghosts
Chasing Ghosts: Murder
  In The Sounds
Chasing Justice
Chasing True Crime
Cheap Chills Show
Cheap Wine and True
  Crime
Check the Locks: A True
  Crime Podcast
Cheers From The Grave
Cherry Avenue
Chicago Real Crime
  Podcast
Chilled with Stat
Chillin N Spillin
Chilling Truth: A True
  Crime Podcast
Chilling with Beaw
Chillingworth

Chilluminati

Chime In

Christian Underhistory

Christina Grimmie: The Murder of a Rising Star

Chronically Iconic Mistakes

Chronicles of a Medium with Psychic Medium Maryne Hachey

Chronicles of Evil

Chunky Koolaid

CimeLapse True Crime

Cimes and Consequences

Cipher: Cracking The Case Of The Zodiac Killer

Citation Needed

Cities of Blood

Citizen's Guide To The Supernormal

CiTR Documentaries

City of Sunsets

Civilly Speaking

CK's Killing It

Clandestine Podcast

Claremont Serial Killings

Class A Felons, B-Films, C-Cups

Classic City Crime

Clear and Present Danger - A history of free speech

Clemency: A True Crime Podcast

Cliché True Crime Podcast

Click for Murder

Closeted Murders with Ryan & Orion

Closing In On Justice

Clueston: True Crime in Houston, Texas

Clunes Cluedo

Coast to Ghost

Cocaine & Rhinestones

Cocktails and Conspiracies

Cocktails, Mocktails, and Crime

Code Severe

Codorus Murders

Coffee and a True Crime Dumpster Fire

Coffee and Crime

Coffee and Cults

Coffee and the Macabre

Coffee Table Fables

Coffee, Crime, and Conspiracies

Coffee, Murder, & Mystery

Coffincast

Coir: An Irish True Crime Podcast

Cola City Crime

Cold

Cold Blooded Podcast

Cold Brew: True Crime Podcast

Cold Brewed Killers

Cold Case Canada

cold case chronicles

Cold Case Files the podcast

Cold Case Murder Mysteries

Cold Case Notes from the Goober State Queen

Cold Cases

Cold Girls

Cold Ohio

Cold Traces

Coldest Cases

Color Me Dead podcast

Colorado Cold Case

Colored

Colored Red

Colors of The Wind

Come Inside

Come Play with us

Come Sail Away

ComeBack

Comfort in Death and Darkness

COMMONS

Con Artists

Confessional Podcast

CONFLICTED

Confronting

Confused and Homicidal: A True Crime Podcast

Connecting the Docs: True Stories from the Old North State

Considering the Scam

Conspeared

Conspiracies & Cryptids

conspiracies fear and mysteries

Conspiracies Over Coffee

Conspiracy Asylum

Conspiracy Cafe

Conspiracy Café

Conspiracy Club

Conspiracy Theories

Conspiracy Therapy

Conspiracy! The Show

Conspiracyland

Conspiranalysis Podcast

ConspiraTea Podcast

Conspirinormal Podcast

Constitutional Defenders

Consuming Crime

Conversations with a Killer

Conversations with Criminals

Convicted

Convicted Conversations

Conviction

Cooking and Crime

Cool & Unusual Punishment

Copland

Copulators Die First
Copycat Killers
Core Cases
Corgi Shakedown
Corky Crime Sisters
Corn on the Macabre
Coroner talk
Coronial
Corporate Crime Reporter Morning Minute
Corpus Delicti
Corrupted Beings Podcast
Cosby Unraveled
Cosmic Closet Podcast
Cosmically Cozy
Count Your Days Podcast
Countdown to Capture
Counter Intelligence
Counterclock
Counterclock by Audiochuck
Counting Worms: Murder, True Crime and Death
Country Fried Southern Crimes
County Morgue Puppet Theatre
Court Appointed
Court Junkie
Court TV Podcast
COURTROOM ANECDOTES
Courtroom Confidential
Cousins By Blood
Cover Story
Covert
Cover-up
Cozening Killers
Crack House Chronicles
Crack This Case
Cracking Open a Cold Case
Crackpot Cocktail Hour
Crafts Drafts and Crime

Crawlspace
Crazy in Love
Creep it Real KC
Creep Me Out: A Podcast of True Crime, Urban Legends, & the Weird
Creep: A True Crime Podcast
Creeped Out!
CreepGeeks Podcast
Creepiest Places in America
Creepin' It Real
Creeping It Real
Creepology
Creeps and Crime Storytime- A Paranormal and True Crime Podcast
Creeps over Coffee
Creeps, Creaks, and Coffee
Creepshow Horror Club by Creepshow Horror Club
Creepsilog
Creeptastic: A True Crime Podcast
Creepy & Crime with cait
Creepy Americana
Creepy Bus
Creepy Caffeine
Creepy California
Creepy Cases. Spooky Spaces
Creepy Chisme
Creepy Club
Creepy Conversations
Creepy Conversations by Kalai and Nikki
Creepy Friends
Creepy Hour
Creepy Kentucky
Creepy Reddit Stories
Creepy Tech

Criiime
Crime & Co.
Crime & Cocktails
Crime & Company
Crime & Conspiracies with Coffee
Crime & Dine
Crime & Entertainment
Crime & Forensics
Crime & Justice with Ashleigh Banfield
Crime & Precedents
Crime & Stuff
Crime + Investigation podcast
Crime After Crime
Crime and Cocktails
Crime and Coffee Couple
Crime and Curiosities
Crime and Hustle
Crime and Justice News
Crime and Justice with Dan Schorr
Crime and Mystery Canada
Crime and Punishment
Crime and punishment of medieval europe
crime and punishment true crime podcast
Crime and Scandal
Crime and Time on the Rocks
Crime and Wine
Crime Bar
Crime Beat [by CuriousCast]
Crime Beat [by Southern California News Group]
Crime Behind the Pine Curtain
Crime Binge
Crime Biscuit: A True Crime Podcast

Crime Bites
Crime Blotter
Crime Bot Canada
Crime by the Bar
Crime Castle
Crime Castle by
crimecastle
Crime Catalyst
Crime Chats
Crime Chats by
CrimeChats
Crime Club with Jack
Beaumont
Crime Coast
Crime Confidential
Crime Connect - Case
Discussions
Crime Connections
Crime Core
Crime Corner
Crime Countdown
Crime Couple
Crime Crack
Crime Crazy
Crime Crew
Crime Culture
Crime Diaries
Crime Diner
Crime Dolls
Crime Files
Crime Files: The Justin
Rey Letters
Crime Girl Gang
Crime Grinds Podcast
Crime Happens
Crime Historian
Crime In A Dime
Crime in Color
Crime in Movies
Crime in Music
Crime in Sports
Crime In The Coconut
Crime Inc.
Crime Junkie
Crime Lab Podcast

CRIME MACHINE
Crime n Dumplins
Crime News Insider by
the San Diego Deputy
District Attorneys
Association
Crime Night Podcast
Crime Noir the Podcast
Crime Nor Reason
Crime on Caffeine
Crime On My Mind
Crime on Tap
Crime on the Mind
Crime or Reason
Crime Over Cocktails
Crime Over Coffee by
Crime Over Coffee
Crime Over Coffee: A
True Crime Podcast
Crime Over Wine
Crime Pursuit Podcast
Crime Quad
Crime Queen
Crime Queen Podcast
Crime Redefined
Crime Roulette
Crime Salad
Crime Scene Time
Machine
Crime Scene Today with
Dan Zientek
Crime Scene: True
crime Stories and
Investigations
Crime Scholar
Crime Screen Podcast
Crime Secrets W/ Mandy
and Rosa
Crime Sesh
Crime Shark
Crime Shots
Crime Smith
Crime Spree
Crime Stoppers –
Quicksie 98.3

Crime Stories with Nancy
Grace
Crime Tales
Crime Talk BK
Crime Talk with Scott
Reisch
Crime Talk with T & Z
Podcast
Crime Tapes
Crime Tea (formerly
Crimeficionados)
Crime Theories Podcast
Crime Time
Crime Time Café
Crime Time FM
Crime Time Nerds
Crime Time Talk
Crime Time with Vito
Colucci
Crime Time: Real Fay-
etteville Stories
Crime to the core
Crime Valley Podcast
Crime Viking
Crime Weekly
Crime with Joy.
Crime Wives Podcast
Crime Writers On. . .True
Crime Review
Crime, Creeps and Coffee
Crime, Cults, & Coffee
Crime, Mystery and
Conspiracy
Crimeaholics
Crimeapolis
Crimebae
CrimeCasters Network
CrimeCore: A True Crime
Podcast
Crimehub
Crimelines True Crime
Crimeopedia
CrimeQuest
Crime-ridden
Crimeroom

Crimes & Cocktail
Crimes Against Her
Crimes and Consequences
Crimes in History
Crimes Like These
Crimes of a Decade, A
  Texas True Crime
  Podcast
Crimes of Passion
Crimes of the Centuries
Crimes of the Century
  Radio
Crimes, Curiosities, and
  Cocktails
Crimesphere
CrimeTime
Crimetown
Crimeversation
CrimeWinz
Criminal
Criminal (in)justice
Criminal Behaviorology
Criminal Broads
Criminal Canvas Podcast
Criminal Chaos
Criminal Conduct
Criminal Court Insider
Criminal Curiosity
Criminal Genius
Criminal Justice
  Evolution
Criminal Justice Office
  Hours
Criminal Justice Research
  Podcast-NIJ
Criminal Mind
Criminal Musings
Criminal Perspective
Criminal Prints
Criminal Record
Criminal Records Podcast
Criminal zodiac
Criminal/Cryptid
Criminality by Criminal-
  ity Show

CriminaliTy True Crime
  Chats
Criminality: A True
  Crime podcast
Criminally Clueless
Criminally Drunk
Criminally Speaking
Criminals Who Care
Criminology
Criminology4U
Criminworks
Crimnal Records Podcast
Crimonomicon
Critical Darkness
Critical Onions
Crochet & Crime
CrockettForReal
Crooked Cousins
Crow & Bone
Crude Acts: Murder in an
  Oil Town
Cruel & Unusual
Cruel and Unusual
Cruel Tea, True Crime
  Podcast
Cryptic Chronicles
Cryptic Compositions
Cryptic Portal
CSI Atlanta
CSI: Reality Check
Cul De Sac insomniac
Culpable by Sky Pranpare
Culpable by Tenderfoot
  TV
Cult Faves Podcast
Cult Life with Robin
  Jackson
Cult Liter
Cult or Just Weird
Cult Podcast
Cult Talk with Erin
  Martin
Cultish
Cultish with Tina Dupuy
Cults

Cults & Theories
Cults and Crime
Cults of our Lives
Cults, Coffee, &
  Conversation
Cults, Conspiracies, and
  Other Creepies
Cults, Crimes & Cabernet
Cults, Cryptids, and
  Conspiracies
Cuppa Crime
Curiosity Kills
Curious Avocado Podcast
Current Waves Podcast
Cursed Earth
Cursewords and Crayons
Curtain
Cut Short: Crime Stories
Cut-Throat:
  a true crime podcast
Cutting Class
CYBER
Cybercrime Investigations
Cybercrimeology
Cyberspeak's podcast
Dad and Daughter Do
  Death
Dad Does Drugs
Daily Kaylee
Daily Mystery Pod
Daiquiris And Death
Dakota Datebook
Dakota Spotlight Podcast
Dam Internet, You Scary!
Damsels On Elm Street
Dancing Oligarchs:
  Trump, Florida and the
  Russians
Dark & Deadly
Dark Alignment
Dark And Deadly
Dark and Dire
Dark Arts Podcast
Dark Chatter by Dark
  Chatter

Dark Chatter by Meg Jess Nicole

Dark Dangerous and Deadly

Dark Dark World

Dark Deeds by Dark Deeds Podcast

Dark Fringe Radio

Dark Heartlands

Dark Histories

Dark History by Googoomomo2007

Dark History Time with Brian

Dark History with Bailey Sarian

Dark La Crosse Stories

Dark Media Effects

Dark N Creepy Things - An Alrighty Podcast

Dark Poutine

Dark Stories

Dark Stuff: With Christian & Suann

Dark Topic

Dark Truths Podcast

Dark Water Podcast

Dark Windows

Dark Winter Nights

Dark, Dark World Podcast

Darker Minds

Darkest Corners Podcast

Darkness by The Drag Audio Production House

Darknet Diaries

Darkside Downunder

Dateline NBC

Dateline: Missing in America

Davednconfuzed

David Studdard's Podcast: Things My Granddaddy Said.

Dawn of Mantis

Day-by-day: The Nick Hillary Trial

Daytona 911

Dead & Gone in Wyoming

Dead America

Dead and Buried

Dead and Gone

Dead Bodies

Dead Cat on the Line

Dead Curious

Dead Drunk

Dead Kids Club

Dead Man Talking

Dead Pixels Podcast

Dead Rabbit Radio

Dead Souls Social Club

Dead Talk Podcast

Dead Things Podcast

Dead Wrong by The Courier-Mail

Deadly Chaotic Energy

Deadly Disabilities

Deadtime Stories

Deadtime Storiez

Dear Franklin Jones

Dear Murder Street

Dearly Departed Podcast

Death Actually

Death and D*cks

Death and Hollywood

Death Becomes Us

Death by Champagne

Death by Misadvaneture: True Paranormal Mystery

Death by Monsters

Death by Music Podcast

Death Dames Podcast

Death Do Us Part

Death Do Us Part by Laura & Jeremy

Death in Denmark

Death in Ice Valley

Death in the Afternoon

Death in the Desert

Death in the Desert by Alexis Edwards

Death in the West

Death Metal Dicks

Death of a Starlet

Death Penalty Information Center Podcast

Deathcast

Deathcast by Corpse Creek Publishing

Death's Door

Debi Marshall Investigates Frozen Lies

Debunking Cops

Decarcerated

Decarceration Nation (with Josh and Joel)

De-Classy-Fied

Decrypted

Deep Cover: Mob Land

Deep Cuts & Sensational Stories

Deep Nerder

Deeper than Most

Deeply Disturbing Things

Defense Diaries

Defrauded

Deliberations

Deliver Us From Evil

Delve & Dagger

Delving into the cold

Demented And Unusal

Demiworld Podcast

Demon Podcasts

Dennis Mahon's Podcast

Depth of Darkness

Derek's Heretics

Desperately Seeking Shelly

Destination Crime

Detective

Detective Crows true Crime

Detective Society Podcast
Detective Trapp
Detroit Strange
Devilish Deeds
Devil's Advocate: A Safe
  Space for Skeptics
Devil's Teeth
Devilution
Devious Destinations
Diagnosing A Killer
Dial Femme for Murder
Dial M for Mueller
Dial U for Unexplained
Dial-A-Crime
Dialogues on Law and
  Justice
Diamond State: Murder
  Board
Did Some Digging
Did You Hear?
DIE-ALOGUE: a true
  crime conversation
Diggin' Oak Island
Digital Forensics in Real
  Life
Dig-Sirens Are Coming
Dillightful Crime
Direct Appeal
Dirty John
Dirty Money Moves:
  Women in White Col-
  lar crime
Dirty Rats
Disappeared
Disappeared by Caitlyn
  Karl
Disaster Area
Disaster Tales
Disasters from History
Discussions With a His-
  tory Buff
Disgraceland
Disorganized Crime:
  Smuggler's Daughter
Disquietude

Dissected
Disturbed Minds
Disturbed State
Disturbed: True Horror
  Stories
Disturbing Interests
Disturbingly Pragmatic
Divulgence
Do Go On
Do Justice
Do No Harm
DO NOT CROSS
Do Not Cross
Do You Know Who Mur-
  dered Me?
Doc to Me Podcast
Docs That Rock Podcast
Documentary of the Week
Documentary WOW
Documenteers: The Docu-
  mentary Podcast
Doe
Does This Make Me A
  Bad Person
Dogma: a Podcast about
  Cults
Doin' Crime
Doll Heads
Dolls and Doom The
  Podcast
Domino Effect of Murder
Don't Be Suspicious
Don't Fall Asleep
Don't Go In There
Don't Kill Your Darlings
Don't Look Behind You:
  Tales of Lore, Legends
  and the Paranormal
Don't Look Now
Don't Look Under The
  Bed!
Don't Talk To Strangers
Don't Talk To Strangers
  Podcast
Don't Trust The Rats

Double Date with Death
Double Dismembered
Double Loop Podcast
Down & Away
Down A Rabbit Hole
Down Home Fear
Down Home Murder
Down in Mississippi
Down Murder Lane
Down the Hill: The Del-
  phi Murders
Down the Path
Down the Rabbit Hole
Down the Rabbit Hole by
  TCFV
Down the Rabbit Hole
  Pod
Down The Rabbit Holes
Dr. Death
Dr. History's Tales of the
  Old West
Dreamin' Demon Pulpit
  of DOOM
Drift & Ramble Podcast
Drilled by Critical
  Frequency
Drink Wine and True
  Crime
Drinking With the Dead
Drop Dead Gorgeous
Drop Dead Podcast
Drop Dead Sisters!
Drugs & Stuff
Drunk Bill Explains
Drunk in Crime
Drunk Mysteries
Drunk Mysteries by
  Ben Potesky & John
  Naffziger
Drunk on True Crime
Drunk Women Solving
  Crime
Dubious
Dude, It's a Cult Podcast
Dude, That's F****d Up

Family Secrets
Famous Fates
Famous Last Meals
Fancounters Podcast
Far Side Chats
Far Side Chats
Fascinating Nouns
Fast Facts
Fastpass to the Past: The Theme Park History Podcast
Fat, French and Fabulous
Fatal
Fatal Females
Fatal True Crime Stories
Fatal Voyage: The Mysterious Death of Natalie Wood
Fatalities
Fatwa
Fault Lines by Al Jazeera
Favorite Daughters Podcast
FBI Confidential
FBI Retired Case File Review With Jerri Williams
FBI This Week
FBI Untold
F'd Up
Fear and Fame Podcast
Fear Cage - True Crime and Paranormal
Fear of the Unknown
Fearless, Adversarial Journalism – Spoken Edition
Fears and Beers Podcast
Feature Felony
Feeling Murdery
Felon True Crime podcast
Felonious Florida
Female Criminals
Female Killers Podcast
Femicide

Femme Fatale: A True Crime Podcast
Femme Fatales
Fiasco
Field of Screams
Fiercely Altered Perspectives
File on 4
Final Argument: The Disappearance of Ray Gricar, District Attorney
Final Minutes
Financial Crime Matters
Finding Hoffa
Finding Tammy Jo
Finding The Lost Podcast
FindJodi
Fine Wine and Evil Spirits
Finish Line WBUR
First and Felony
First Day Back
First Question
Firsthand
Flagged Podcast
Flatrock
Flawed Justice: The Kimberly Long Story Podcast
Flawed Laws
Flesh Lemon
Flipbook Podcast
Florida Men
Fool Me Twice
Foot Off the Bed
Footbridge Forum's Podcast
Footnotes of History
FOR DUMMIES: The Podcast
For Richer or Horror
For The Defense With Brad Koffel
Force of Law
Forensic Archives

Forensic Files
Forensic Files II
Forensic Fools
Forensic Geek
Forensic InService
Forensic Psychology
Forensic Transmissions
Forgotten Australia
Forgotten Darkness
Forgotten Friday's
Forgotten History
FORGOTTEN NEWS PODCAST
Forgotten Prison
Forgotten True Crime
Forked
Formidable: A True Crime Podcast
Fort Weird
Foul Play
Foul Play UK
Four Corners Crime Cast
Fox Cities Murder & Mayhem
Fox Hollow
Fox Hunter
Fox4 Crime Files
Framed: An Investigative Story
Frank Turner's Tales From No Man's Land
Frankensquad Podcast
Fraudcast
Freak Me Out
Freak Nation Podcast
Freaks and Treats
Freaky Geeks' Podcast
Fred Jeffs: The Sweetshop Murder
Free John Giuca
Fresh Hell
Fresh Hell Podcast
Freud and Fava Beans
Fried Crime and Biscuits
Friends And Felonies

Frightday Podcast
Fringe Drinking
From Crime to Crime
From Hell They Came
From the Files
From the Vault
Frozen In Time: Cold Cases
Frozen Truth
Fruit Loops: Serial Killers
FT Investigation
Full Rigor: Florida True Crimes
Funeral Stories
Futility Closet
Future Hindsight
Future is Bright?
Future State
Gangland Wire
Gangster Capitalism
Gangster House
Garnet and Gore
Gatecrash
Generation Cult
Generation Why
Gertie's Law
Geshcast
Getting High on True Crime
Getting Off
Getting Scarried Away
Ghastly
Ghost Hoes
Ghost Stories for the End of the World
Ghost Stories in the Sunlight
Ghost Town
Ghostly
Ghosts and Cornbread
Ghosts in the Attic Bodies in the Basement
Ghosts-n-Heaux
Ghoul Chat
Ghoul Friends Podcast

Ghoul Girls
Ghoul Intentions
Ghoul on Ghoul
Ghoulish Tendencies
Gills & Thrills
GIMG.tv
Gimme Some Murder
Gimme the Creeps
Gin & Terror
Girl, You Haven't Heard?? True Crime & Black History
Girlfriends Happy Hour
Girls Talk Crime
Give Me Murder or Give Me Death
Gladiator: Aaron Hernandez & Football Inc
Gloom & Bloom
Go For Charles' Podcast
God Trip
Going Mad
Going West: True Crime
Gone
Gone at 21
Gone Cold
Gone Cold: Philadelphia Unsolved Murders
Gone Fishing
Gone Medieval
Gone South
Gone, But Never Forgotten
Good Company in the Car: The Bigfoot and Murder Podcast
Good Law | Bad Law
Good Luck Sleeping
Good Morning Jonestown
Good Nightmare
Good Nurse Bad Nurse
Goodnight Marylin Radio: The Investigation. The Life. The Movie.

Goose Chase Podcast
Gore Lore & More
Gossip Girls
Gotcha Podcast
Goth and Bougie Podcast
Grand Ramblings
Graphic Detail
Grave Girls Podcast
Grave Tales Australia: the series
Gravely Gossip
Graves & Shay
GraveYard Tales
Great Disasters
Great Lakes True Crime
Great Trials in History
Greybeard's Tales
Grinding True Crime
Grisly Grapes
Grits With a Side of Murder
Grove Road
Grovers Mill
Growing Up Gone Wrong
Gruesome Gossip
Gruesome: Horrific True Crime
GSMC Classics: Crime Classics
GSMC Weird News Podcast
Guilty
Gumshoe Weekly
Guys Who Law
Habeas Corpses
Habeas Humor
Hackable Me
Hacked
Hacking Humans
Hag & Sleuth
Haint Blues
Half Sisters, Whole Crime
HalfAsked
Halfway to Thundertown
Halloran Road Mysteries

Halloween Unmasked
Hammerson Peters
Hamptons Uncovered
Handcuffed Podcast
Hanging
Hanzai: True Crime from Japan
Happy Face
Happy Hour Gets Weird
Hard to Handle
Harleyverse
Hashtag History
Haunt Jaunts
Haunted
Haunted Canada: True Crime Stories
Haunted Family Podcast
Haunted Hills
Haunted Hometowns
Haunted Places
Haunted Road
Haunted Talks - The Official Podcast of The Haunted Walk
Haunted Tourism
Haunted with History Podcast
Hauntedology
Haunting Cases
Haunting Crimes
Haunting History
Hauntings and Homicide
Have You Seen Kamiyah?
Have You Seen This Man?
Head Trauma
Headlong: Running from COPS
Headlong: Surviving Y2K
Hear Me Roar
Heaven's Gate
HeidiWorld: The Heidi Fleiss Story

Heinous Hotels
Heist Club
Heist podcast
Hekyll n Shyde
Hell and Gone
Hell and High Horror
Hellbound
Hello My Name Is: TRUE CRIME
Hello, Creeps!
Help Solve the Case
Henry - The life and legacy of Wheeling's most notorious brewer
Her Name Podcast
Here Be Monsters
Here's A Crazy Story
Heritage Road
Heroes & Zeros- A True Crime Podcast
Heroes Hustlers and Horsemen
Hey, Have You Heard About . . .
Hidden
Hidden Among Us
Hidden Histories
Hidden Staircase
Hidden Truth
Hide and Seek
High Crime
High Crimes
High Crimes and History
High Mystery
High Quality Nonsense
Highly Paranoid
High-Tech Crime Investigations
Hillbilly Horror Stories
Historical Blindness
Historical Controversies
Historical Figures
Historical Horrors
historicly
Histories & Mysteries

Histories, Mysteries & Conspiracies
Historium Unearthia: Unearthing History's Lost and Untold Stories
History by Hollywood
History Creeps Podcast
History Dweebs
History Impossible
History in Technicolor
History Lessons for Misanthropes
History of 1995
History of a Haunting
History of Organized crime
History of the 90s
History Snippets
History Told by Idiots
History Uncensored Podcast
History, Drinks, and Yes!
Hit Man
Hit Me Baby One More Crime
Hoax
Hogtown Empire: The Disappearance of Ambrose Small
Holiday Horrors
Hollow9ine's American Crime Story Podcast
Hollyshook: A Celebrity Scandal Podcast
Hollyweird Paranormal
Hollyweird Podcast
Hollywood and Crime
Hollywood Crime Scene
Hollywood Profiles of Yesteryear
Hollywood Using Criminals
Hollywoodland: unsolved
Home on The Strange

Home Sweet Homicide:
The Murders of Jalen
Merriweather and
Donovan Cowart
Homebrew Murder Crew
Homestead Horrors: A
True Crime Podcast
Hometown Homicide
Hometown Horrors
Hometown Murder Tour
Podcast
Hometown Tales Podcast
Homicidal
Homicidal Tendencies
Homicide Homegirls
Homicide Worldwide
Podcast
Homiecide
Homocidal Hangout
Honestly? Hell Yeah
Hooked on Crime Pod
Hooked on Weird Stuff
Hooligan Radio
Hoosier Homicide
Hops & Homicides
Horrible Sanity
Horrible Things
Horrific History Podcast
Horror Cave & Friends
Podcast
Horror Happy Hour
Horror House: True
Crime and the Macabre
Horror on the Brain
Horror Talk with the Toys
Horror VS Reality
Horse Mysteries
Horseman Five
Hostage
Hot Crimes Cold Drinks:
A Space City True
Crime Podcast
Hot Cup Cold Case
Hot for Justice: Cold Case
Stories

Hot Tea and Cold Cases
Hot Tub Crime Machine
HotmessHeroes Podcast
House of Mystery Radio
on NBC
House of Snark
Housewives of True
Crime
How Am I Still Alive?!
How Bizarre
How Do I Rob This?
How I met My Murder
How I Survived
How Not to Die
How to Avoid Murder
and Other Awkward
Situations
How to survive a murder
HUB History - Our
Favorite Stories from
Boston History
Hudson Valley Legends
Human Delicatessen
Human Monsters
Human Trafficking and
Modern Slavery
Human Trafficking True
Crime
Humans Are Evil - His-
tory Podcast
Humans For Sale
Hundred Proof History
Hungry For Crime
Hunted: Inside Ted Bun-
dy's Trail of Terror
Hunting Warhead
Hysteria 51
I Ain't A Killa Podcast
I am a Killer
I Barely Got Here Podcast
I Can Has True Crime
I Can Steal That!
I Catch Killers with Gary
Jubelin
I Got the Hell Out

I Lived Through This
I Met My Murderer
Online
I Said God Damn
I Should Totally Be Dead
Right Now
I Spy
I Survived . . . the Podcast
I Swear I Never
I Was a Teenage
Murderer
I Was There When
Podcast
I would do anthing for
my daughter
I would Never Murder
You
I, Survivor
I, Witness
I'm Sorry . . . What?! The
Podcast
Icelandic True Crime
ICTJ Podcast
If I'm Being Honest with
Katie Crenshaw
If the Magnolias Could
Speak
If These Walls Could
Talk Podcast
If You Go Out in the
Woods Today
Ignorance was Bliss
I'll Be Gone in the Dark
I'll Drink to Fact
Illegal Tender
Ill-Natured
I'm a Survivor
I'm Dead Serious
I'm Horrified!
I'm Not In An Abusive
Relationship
I'm sorry . . . What?! The
Podcast
I'm Tellin' You What . . .
Imaginary Histories

It's the Mystery for Me (A True Crime Podcast)
Jack Ruby - The Trial of the Century
Jacob Hawley: On Drugs
Jim Harold's Crime Scene
Jimmy Akin's Mysterious World
Jitter Joint
Joey's Social Club
John Alite - The Mob, The Mafia, and The Man
Jolted
Jon Jeremy's Daily momwnt.
Jon Ronson's Escape and Control
Jonathan Pramana
Joseph Morris
Journalism Land
Judge and Jeremy
Judgey & Juryish
Judgy Crime Girls
Juicing the People
Juror Number 8
Just a Couple of Horrors
Just a Story
Just Another Murder
Just another true crime podcast
Just Asking Questions Podcast
Just Cases
Just in Crime
Just Killin' Time
Just Lawful
Just Peachy
Just Released Podcast
Just Science
Just the Tip-sters
Justice by Elizabeth Musser

Justice for Jennifer: Missing in Nashville
Justice in America
Justice Interupted
Justice is Served
Justice Journal
JUSTICE with prison philanthropist Edwina Grosvenor
Justice with Rutledge
Justice . . . Delayed
Juvie
Kaden's True Crime and Conspiracy Theories
Karas on Crime
KarTier Krimes
KayMo's Review Podcast
Keep It Weird
Keiser Report
Kentucky Colonels of Truth
Kentucky Gone Cold
KickBack - The Global Anticorruption Podcast
Kid Cryptid
Kids Court pocast
Kill one Purl two
Killafornia dreaming
Killer
Killer Babes
Killer Bee
Killer Cases
Killer Cocktails
Killer Country
Killer Crossroads
Killer Fun
Killer Fun Crime and Entertainment
Killer Instinct
Killer Jobs
Killer Pillow Talk
Killer Psyche with Candice DeLong
Killer Queens
Killer Reactions

Killer Role
Killer Spirits
Killer Stories
Killer Vibes
Killerology
Killer's Crawlspace
Killers, Cults, and Nutjobs
Killin' It: The Crimecast
Killing Lorenzen: Love •Basketball•Murder
Killinois With Bird and Cam
Kills and Chills
Kim Knows Nothing
Kinda Murdery
Kingpins
King's Last March
Kitchen Table Cult
Kit's Myths and Mysteries (formerly True Mysteries of the Pacific Northwest)
Kiwi Crimes
Knife to Meet You
Knock Knock
Knocked South: A Creepy Podcast
Know Your Disaster with Miss Alex
Knowhere in the Middle
Knowledge Fight
Known Unknowns
KOIN Vault
Korean True Crime
Koryo True Crime: True Crime in Korea
KPBS Investigates
KXAN Catalyst
L.A. Not so Confidential
Lady Justice True Crime
Lady of the Dunes podcast
Lady Teal's Curios
Ladykillers

LAGIM: A Filipino True Crime Podcast
Larger Than Life
Las Brujas and Friends Podcast
Las Chicas del Crime
Last Call for Bullsh**
Last Day
Last Man Standing Podcast
Last Podcast on the Left
Last Seen
Late Night Crimecast
Late Night Murder Podcast
Late Nights With Lila
Law & Crime's Daily Debrief
Law and Disorder
Law Focus
Law Sisters
Lawless
Lawyer Talk Off The Record
Lawyers on the Rocks podcast
Leap in the Dark
Learn Me Something
Leave the Lights On
Leeds True Crime Podcast, The
Left Behind
Legal lingo
Legal Wars
Legally Insane
Legally Unfiltered
Legally, Dirty, Blonde.
Legends in the Dark
Legends of the Old West
Less Than Dead - Marginalized and Murdered
Let Me Tell You a story
Let Them Fight: A Comedy History Podcast
Let's Freak Out.

Let's Taco 'Bout True Crime
Lethal Dose
Lethal Lonestar
Let's Be Realistic
Let's Freak Out
Let's Get Real With Ashley
Let's Get Weird with Tim and Zach
Let's Go to Court
Let's Never Meet
Let's Not Meet: A True Horror Podcast
Lets Overthink This
Let's Take a Look
Let's Talk About Sects
Let's Talk Forensics
Let's Talk Murder
Liar City
Liar Liar
Lie, Cheat, & Steal
Lies and Alibis
Life After Dark
Life After Linc
Life After Midnight: Strange History, Salem Style
Life and Crimes with Andrew Rule
Life and Death Row
Life Bytes
Life's Hauntings Podcast
Lifetime Sentence
Light the Fright
Lights Out by Mile Higher Media
Lights Out/After Dark
Lights, Luminol, Action!
Like Crazy Thinks Podcast
Lil Ghost Gurls' Podcast
Lil Stinkers
Limetown by Ethan Tarnowski

Liquor and Luminol
Little Boy Lost
Little Girl Lost
Little Missteries QLD
Live Laugh Murder Podcast
Living Dead Girls
Living Viscariously
Lizard People: Comedy & Conspiracy Theories
Locating Leah
Locating the Lost
Locations Unknown
Lock Your Doors
Locked Inside
Locked Up Abroad
Logan & Gabby
Lohrs Lore
Lone Star Law & Disorder
Long Lost: An Investigative History Series
LongBall Presents. . .
Longform
Longreads
Look What's Kooking
Loose Units
Loose Units: The Podcast
Lords of Death
Lore
LORE20 Podcast
Lori Vallow and Chad Daybell-The Real Story
Losing Paul
Lost and Found Podcast
Lost Angels: The Untold Stories of the Amish School Shootings
Lost Boys of Hannibal
Lost Chalk Lines
Lost Hills
Lost in Larrimah
Lost in Sydney
Love and Murder
Love is Amazing

Love Murder
Love or Obsession
Love Thy Neighbor
LRC presents: All the
  President's Lawyers
Luminol
Luminol Cocktail
Lure
Lurk
Lustmordia
LVM Podcast
Lying in State: The Life
  Esidimeni Tragedy
Lynching in America
Lyss and Lex Get Spooky
M&M True Crime
  Conspiracies
M3: Murder, Mystery and
  Mayhem
Macabre London
Macabre Masters
Mad About Crime
Mad As A Hatter
Mad or Bad
Maddie
Made in Sweden
Madlogic Mysteries
Mafia
Mafia Cops Conspiracy
Mafia Tapes
Mafia Wife Life
Magic & Mystery
Magnum B.I.
Mainland
Majored in Sike
Make It Modern
Makeup, Masking &
  Murder
Making a Mania
Making a Murderer by
  Justin
Making a Murderer by
  Netflix
Making Marsy's Law
MAKTAC

Malice & Mocktails
Malice: A True Crime
  Podcast
Malicious Life
Mama Mystery - A True
  Crime Podcast
Man in the Window: The
  Golden State Killer
Mania
Maniacly Midwest
Manson's Lost Girls
Maple Moose Mysteries
Marble Forest Podcast
Marble Orchard
Marcia Clark Investigates
  the First 48
Mared & Karen-the WVU
  Coed Murders
Margs + Mystery
Margs and Mayhem
Mark Buck
Markus Rooney's Podcast
Marmalade Mysteries
Marriage, Hauntings, and
  Murder
Married to Murder
  Podcast
Martinis & Murder
Martinis & the Macabre
Marvelously Morbid
Mary Buck
Mason Jar Chronicles
Mason Road Podcast
Mass Exoneration
Matricide Podcast
Mature Audiences Only
Mayhem with Michele
  McPhee
Me Time & Murder
Medical Error Interviews
  Podcast
Medical Mysteries
Medieval Podcast Crime
  And Punishment

MediMess: A True Crime
  Podcast
Meet Me in the Basement
Melanin Macabre
Memories of Murder
Memos of Mind
Memphis Murder
Mens Rea Podcast
Mercado Airwaves
Merchants of Menace
Merlot and the Mob
MetalsHorrorHouse
Method and Madness
MI Crime Time
Michigan and Other May-
  hem by Ali & Jenn
Michigan and other May-
  hem by Michigan and
  other Mayhem
Michigan Crime Stories
Michigan Murders &
  Music
Mid-day Musings
Middle-Aged and
  Mediocre
Midnight Balloon
Midnight Facts for
  Insomniacs
Midnight Hollow
Midnight Scario
Midnight Thoughts
Midwest Mayhem
Midwest Monsters
Midwest Murder Corner
Midwest Mysteries
Midwest Mystery Files
Midwest Not So Nice
Midwretched
MilCrimes
Mile High Murder
  Podcast
Mile Higher podcast
Mile Marker 181
Mile13
Military Justice

Military Murder
milk & serial
Milk and Murder
Milk Break
Millennial History
Millennials Killed True
Crime
Millionaire Murder
Mind Bogglers: True
Crime Stories
Mind of a Monster
Mind on Crime
Mind Over Murder
Mindhunter Companion
Minds of Madness
Minds of Murderers
MINDSHOCK
Minnesota Mysteries
Minnesota's Notorious
Crimes
Minnesota's Most
Notorious
Minor Murderers: Chil-
dren Who Kill
Minute Murders Podcast
Minute Mysteries
Misconduct
Misdeeds & Intrigue:
Scandals, Royals &
Crimes
Misery Loves Garlic
Bread Podcast
Misery Murder
Misfortune
Misfortunes
Miss Murder
Missing (formerly Miss-
ing Maura Murray)
Missing 411
Missing Alissa
Missing and Murdered
Missing and Murdered in
Georgia, USA
Missing and Murdered in
the Midwest

Missing In Canada
Missing in Ohio
Missing In The Desert -
Missing Persons Cases
Explored
Missing in the Metro
Missing Molly
Missing on 9/11
Missing Person Cases
with Chloe
Missing Pieces Fox 5
Missing Pieces KHOU
Missing the Missing
Mistory
Misty Mysteries
Mitchum
Mixed Babble
Mixed Drinks and
Mysteries
Mixology and
Misdemeanors
MJP Radio
Mob Queens
Mobcast
MobShot
Mode of Horror
Modem Mischief
Mogul
Mom & Merder
Mommy Doomsday
Moms and Murder-
Melissa and Mandy
Moms Who Talk Crime
Monday Morning
Macabre
Money, Romance and
Greed
Monograph
Monster Presents:
Insomniac
Monster Stories Podcast -
Living with Evil
Monster: DC Sniper
Monsters Among Us
Monsters and Mixers

Monsters and Mothers
Monsters N Friends
Monsters Walk with Us
Monsters Who Mur-
der: Serial Killer
Confessions
Monstruo
Montana Murder
Mysteries
Monti's Mysteries
Moonrise
Morbid Academy: A
Podcast
Morbid and Mundane
Morbid and the Mystical
Morbid Curiosity
Morbid Instinct
Morbid Moment
Morbid: A True Crime
Podcast
Morbidly Insane
Morbidly Intoxicated
Morbidology
More Content Talk
More or Less: Behind the
Stats
More Perfect
More Than Murder
More to the Story
Morgan & Morgan Whis-
tleblower Attorneys
Morning Cup of Murder
Most Fashionable Crime
Most Hexcellent
Most Notorious
Most wanted 360 Podcast
Mostly Murder
Motel Hell
Mothers Who Kill
Motive
Motive to Murder
Motrue Crime
Mountain Murders
MountainLore
Mouthfuls of Madness

Moving Past Murder with Collier Landry
Moxie & Mayhem
Mr. And Mrs. Drama
Mr. Ballen Podcast: Strange, Dark, and Mysterious Stories
Mr. Bunker's Conspiracy Time Podcast
Ms. Demeanor & Ms. Conduct: The Podcast
Muderella
Mueller, She Wrote
Muenster Mash Podcast
Mugshot
Mugshots and Miracles
Mums Mysteries & Murder
Murd Up
Murdah Ink
Murdaugh Murders
Murder & Coffee
Murder & Margs
Murder & Mediumship
Murder & Movies Podcast
Murder & Mysteries
Murder & Myths
Murder Alphabet Soup
Murder and Ghosts
Murder and Malfeasance
Murder and Mayhem: South African True Crime
Murder and Misery
Murder and More
Murder and Mysteries with Massnick
Murder and Mystery in the Last Frontier
Murder and Such
Murder Archives
Murder at Bedtime with Lyndom

Murder At Land Between The Lakes
Murder at Ryan's Run
Murder Avenue
Murder Between Friends
Murder Blows
Murder Book
Murder Book Podcast
Murder Brides
Murder Bucket
Murder Burrito
Murder Cases 101
Murder Ciru
Murder City
Murder Con Sazon
Murder Dictionary
Murder Down South
Murder Down Under
Murder Garage
Murder in 20
Murder in Alliance
Murder in America
Murder in Illinois
Murder in Oregon
Murder in Retrograde
Murder in the Arts Degree
Murder in the Black
Murder in the Hudson Valley
Murder in the Kitchen
Murder in the Land of Oz
Murder in the Mountains
Murder in the North
Murder In The Rain
Murder in the Rain
Murder Incorporated
Murder is My Sign
Murder Made me Famous
Murder Man
Murder May I
Murder Me on Monday
Murder Metal Mayhem
Murder Mile UK True Crime

Murder Minute
Murder Monday Podcast
Murder Most Foul
Murder Most Irish
Murder Murder News
Murder Mystery & Makeup with Bailey Sarian
Murder Mystery Cases Solved by Paper Work Party
Murder Obsessed
Murder on My Street
Murder on our Minds
Murder on Tap
Murder on the 420 Express
Murder on the Map
Murder on the Millennial Express (MOTME)
Murder On The Space Coast
Murder Phone
Murder Pod
Murder Road
Murder Road Trip
Murder Roadtrip: A True Crime Podcast
Murder Sandwich: A True Crime & Mystery Podcast
Murder Savvy Podcast
Murder She Joked
Murder She Read
Murder She Sang
Murder She Spoke
Murder She Spoke by Joannagh & Emma Taylor
Murder She Told
Murder Shelf Book Club
Murder Shows and Comfy Clothes Podcast
Murder Sisters
Murder Speaks

Murder Squared
Murder Starts with J
Murder Under the Midnight Sun
Murder Was the Case
Murder We Wrote
MURDER WITH FRIENDS
Murder with Mannina
Murder with My Husband
Murder With My Mother
Murder, Alaska
Murder, Eh!
Murder, etc.
Murder, Madness and Movies
Murder, Maya and Me
Murder, Mayhem and More
Murder, Mayhem, And the Military
Murder, Mirth & Monsters Podcast
Murder, Monsters, and Mayhem
Murder, My Dude
Murder, Mystery & Mayhem Laced with Morality
Murder, mystery and mayhem
Murder, Mystery, & Mayhem
Murder, Mystery, and Mac 'n Cheese
Murder, Mystery, and Mac 'n' Cheese
Murder, Myth, & Mystery
Murder, Not Murdering
Murder, She Read
Murder, She Sang
Murder, She Watched
Murder, Supernatural & Chill
Murder, They Spoke

Murder? I Hardly Know Her
MurderCast
Murdered Missing Unsolved
Murderers and Their Mothers
Murderess Podcast
Murderific True Crime
Murderino & a Tech in ATX
Murderish
Murderlaide
Murderotica
Murderous lunatics
Murderous Minors
murderous podcast
Murderous Roots with Denise & Zelda
Murder's a Drag
Murders In
Murders in Paradise
Murders with Mum: A True Crime Podcast
Murders, Ghosts and Beyond. What's in your bowl?
Murders, Missing, Misconduct: A True Crime Podcast for the Natural State
Murders, Mysteries, and Mimosa's
Murdertown by Gary Pascal and Shannon Noll
Murderverse: True Crime Hub
Murderville
MurderX Podcast
Muriel's Murders
Museum of Lost Objects
Music & Murder
Music of Mind Control
Must Watch: Scandals!
My Aryan Princess

My Father the Murderer
My Father's Crimes
My Favorite Detective Stories
My Favorite Murder
My first Podcast
My Funeral Home Stories
My Grandma: Wanted by the FBI
My Life of Crime with Erin Moriarty
My Mother The Lizard Person
My Name is Cleo
My Three Shrinks
My True Crime Obsession
myfavoritemystery
Mysteries & Thrillers
Mysteries Abound
Mysteries and Urban Legends
Mysteries of History Podcast
Mysteries of the Un-Gnome
Mysteries on the Bayou
Mysteries Within The Mountains' podcast
Mysteries, murders, and conspiracies oh my!
Mysteries, Murders, Monsters, and Your Mom
Mysterioulsy Listed
Mysterious AF
Mysterious Brews
Mysterious Circumstances
Mysterious Disappearances
Mysterious Midwest
Mysterious Radio
Mysterious Universe
Mysterious(ish)
Mysteriously Listed True Crime

Mysteriously Missing
Mysteriously Morbid
Mysterium
MysteriYes
Mystery a la Carte
Mystery and Murder:
 Analysis with Dr. Phil
Mystery Canucks
Mystery In Our History
 Podcast
Mystery Moms
Mystery Murder &
 Magick
Mystery Murdery Thingy
Mystery No. VI
Mystery of the Week
Mystery on the Rocks
Mystery Show
Mystery Team Inc.
Mystifyingly Missing,
 True Crime & Though-
 provoking Events
Mythical Monsters
Mythical True Crime
Mythology
Myths and Misfortunes
Myths and Mysteries
Myths, Magic and Murder
Myths, Mysteries, &
 Monsters
Mythunderstood : A
 Greek (& other)
 Mythology Podcast
Naively Optimistic
 Podcast
Naked Mormonism
 Podcast
NameUs/Unsolved
Naomi Goodwin Talks
Nap Time Investigations
Naptime Nancy True
 Crime Podcast
Narcissist Apocalypse
Narcotica Podcast
Nashville Demystified

Nat-igating Through True
 Crime
National Park After Dark
Native America Calling -
 The Electronic Talking
 Circle
Natural Disasters
Nature vs. Narcissism
Necronomicast
Necronomipod
Needles, Hooks, and
 Crooks: A Podcast
 about Fiber Felonies
Nefarious New York
 Podcast
Neosouled Radio
Nerdy Bones
Never Found
New England Legends
 Podcast
New England's Unsolved
New Idea Investigates
New Thinking
New York City Crime
 Report
Newseum Podcast
Nice Try!
Night Parade
Night Swims Podcast
Night Talk
Nightgeist
Nightline
Nightmare Nation
Nightmare Next Door
 by ID
Nightmare Society
Nightmare365 Podcast
Nightmares Before
 Bedtime
Nightmares Come True
 Podcast
NightmareTown
Nighttime
No Better Death
No Comment

NO HOME FOR
 HEROES
No Man Knows My
 Herstory
No Man's Land
No One Likes Us
No One Told Us
No Podcast for Old Men
No Remorse
No Thank You, Next
No Thanks, I'm Full
Noble Blood
Noir Factory
NOIR True Crime Files
 Podcast
Nolan True Crime
Nomadic North
None Dare Call It
 Ordinary!
None of What You Hear
Nope. I'm Scared
Nopeville
Nordic True Crime
Not a Monster, Not a
 Boogeyman
Not Another Horror
 Podcast
Not Another True Crime
 Podcast by Betches
 Media
Not Another True Crime
 Podcast by Dannie
 Speaks
Not Another True Crime
 Podcast by Tahir Ali
Not for the Dinner Table
Not Forgotten
Not Guilty
Not in My County
Not Perfect or Functional
Not Your Century
Not Your Mama's True
 Crime
Not Your Mom's Podcast

Pretty Much Experts
Pretty Scary
Prime Time Crime
Prime Time True Crime
Principled Uncertainty: A
  True Crime Podcast
Prison City Murders
  Podcast
Prison Counts
Prison Life
Prison Professors
Private Zoo
Problem Child - The story
  of Keli Lane and the
  murder of baby Tegan
Profession Confession
Professionally Silly
Professor Birdsong's
  Dumb Criminals
  Podcast
PROFILER
Profiles In Eccentricity
Profiling Payne
Project Cold Case
Project Mmmk Gotcha
Project Random
Proof: A True Crime
  Podcast
Proper Villains
Protect Kids Online
Protected
Psych Your Crime
Psyched Podcast
Psycho Killer: Shocking
  True Crime Stories
Psychodocs
Psychologia Podcast
Psychology After Dark by
  Dr. Jessica Micono and
  Dr. David Morelos
Psychopath in Your Life
Pub Dread
Public Official A
Pubtime Podcast
Punt PI

Pure Nonfiction: Inside
  Documentary Film
Pursuit of Justice
Pursuit of the Paranormal
Putting Racism on the
  Table
Q6 Cold Case Files
QAnon Anonymous
Queen City Creeps
Queen of the Con
Queens of Crime
Quid Pro Quo
Quiet Town
Quite Honestly
Quite Unusual
R U Serial
Rabbit Holes Podcast
Rackets Podcast
Radio Espial
Radio Free Mormon
Radio Rental
RadioFace Stories
Rambling is a Crime
Rants & Rambles
Raven 23: Presumption
  of Guilt
RD Talks
Ready Set Horror
Ready Set Horror Podcast
Real Crime Café
Real Crime Profile
Real Crime with Danny
  lopez
Real Crime: Feature
Real Crime: Interview
Real Crime: The REELZ
  Files
Real Life Real Crime by
  Cloud10
Real Monsters
Real Mysteries.US
  Podcast
Real Narcos
Real Strange
Realm of Unknown

Reanimated
Reasonable Doubt
Rebutting a Murderer
Red Ball
Red Collar
Red String Society
Red Wine and Mystery
  Stories
Red, Blue, and Brady
RedHanded
Redrum & Rosé
Redrum Blonde
REDRUM true crime
Redrum, Redrum: Girls
  on Murder
Reducing Crime
Reel Murders: A True
  Crime Podcast
Re-Enacted: An Unsolved
  Mysteries Podcast
Reentry Radio
Relic: The Lost Treasure
  Podcast
Remains to be Seen
Repeat
Reply All
Reporter
Reporting Live From My
  Sofa
Resting Witch Face By
  Resting Witch Face
Resting Witch Face By
  Resting Witch Face
  (Grant & Bailey)
Reveal
Revolution Rosies
Riddle Me That! True
  Crime
RidicuLiz Podcast
Ridiculous Crime
Right the Wrong
Riki Rachtman's Cat-
  house Hollywood
  Podcast

Ripley's Believe It or Notcast
Rippercast
Riri's Story Time
Rise and Crime
Ritualistic Podcast
River City Charlie - The Military True Crime Podcast
RN Presents
RNZ: Black Sheep
RNZ: Eyewitness
RNZ: Killjoy
RNZ: Pants on Fire
RNZ: The Lost
RNZ: The Podcast Hour
Roadside Horror Show
Roasting the Rich
Roberta Glass True Crime Podcast
Robots For Eyes Podcast
Rock and Roll Heaven
Rom Crime
Ron Iddles: The Good Cop
Room 20
Root Access
Root of Evil
Rotten Mango
Route 29 Stalker
RoySchreiber41's podcast
Rt 66 Fear Fix
Ruined Heroes
Run, Bambi, Run
Russia Rising
Russia, if you're listening . . .
Rusty Hinges
Ruthless: A True Crime Podcast
S is for Serial
S&T Mysteries
S.P.I.C.E
Sacred Scandal

Sad Tales from Underground
Salem 1692 Podcast – I Hate Stuff
Sam Sheppard: Case Closed
Sanctioned: The Arrest of a Telecom Giant
Santa Fe Crime and Punishment
Santa Fe: Life After the Shooting
Sara's Century
Sasquatch Ate My Baby
Saturday Morning Mysteries
Saturday Morning Serial
Saucy Southwest
Sawbones: A Marital Tour of Misguided Medicine
Say What, SheShe?!
SBS True Stories
Scam Goddess
Scam Kings
Scamfluencers
Scammer Stories
Scamming the Scammer
ScamWow
Scandal 101
Scandal Sheets
Scandalous Behavior
ScapeGoats a Comedy Conspiracy Theory Podcast
Scared A Latte
Scared A Paranormal True Crime Podcast
Scared of the Dark
Scared Sheetless
Scary and Creepy Stuff
Scary Encounters with HazyChaos
Scary Instinct
Scary Mysteries

Scary Savannah and Beyond
Scary Social Club
scary(ish) podcast
Scarytales
Scene of the Crime
Scene of the Crime by AbJack Entertainment
Scientology: Fair Game
Scorched Justice
Scoundrel: History's Forgotten Villians
Scream Kings
Screamish
Screen of the Crime
Screwed-Up Stories Podcast
Sea Witch on the Prairie
Search for Closure
Searching for Ghosts
Searching for Rachel Antonio
Searching: A True Crime Podcast
Secret Transmission Podcast
Secrets and Lies
Secrets from the Crime Lab
Secrets in a Small Town
Secrets in the cornfield: Iowa's Unsolved
Secrets of the Fifth Estate
Secrets True Crime
Sects Ed
Security Matters
Seduced By Satan
See No, Hear No, Speak No
Seeing Red
Selena: A Start Dies in Texas
Sentence(s) Podcast
Seoul Suspect
Septic Podcast

Serial
Serial Access
Serial Chillers
Serial Killer Brain
Serial Killer Countdown
Serial Killer Documentary
Serial Killers
Serial Killers & Seltzer
Serial Killing: A Podcast
Serial Napper
Serial Sistaaas
Serial Sisters
Serial Spirits
Serial Spoon
Serially Disturbed
Serially Obsessed
Serially Speaking
Seriously, This Time!
Seriously, What the
    Frick?
Service Roads
Sesh Sessions
Sex Appeal: Women on
    Trial Podcast
Sex Crimes
Sex Love & Murder
Sex, Drugs, & Spirituality
Sgt Dorsey Speaks
Sh!t Happens
Shadocides
Shadow of a Doubt
Shadow of the Zodiac
Shadowproof Presents
Shadows of the Mitten
Shady
Shady History
Shady Sands Adventures
Shanni Horror and Vibez
Shattered
Shaun Attwood's True
    Crime Podcast
She Says
She Sleuths Podcast
She Survives
Shear Crime

SHEattle on Tap
Shed The Light
Shedunnit
Shh, Look Behind You
Shiny Things Podcast
Ship Hits the Fan
Shitz Grim
Shiv's Murder Temple
Shockingly Wicked: A
    True Crime Podcast
Shoes Boos and Tattoos
Shotgun Road Podcast
Shots Fired by Police
    Magazine
Shots in the Dark
Should We Be Talking
    About This?
Show Me The State
Shreds: Murder in the
    dock
shunned
Sick
Sick & Wrong
Sick Sad Podcast
Sick Sad World
Sideline Sleuths
Silence on Set
Silent Waves
Simply Strange
Sin and Juice
Since Columbine
Sinful Sisters
Sinister America
Sinister Sanctuary
Sinister Sissies
Sinister Sisters
Sinister Stream
Sinister Sunrise
Sinisterhood
Sinners VS Saints
Sins of Detroit
Sip and Shine Podcast
Sip Happens Podcast
Sip. Survive. Repeat.

Sirens A True Crime
    Podcast
SISPICION
Sistas Who Kill
Sista'z Thru Crime
Sisteresque Podcast
Sisterly History Mysteries
Sisters in Crime
Sisters Spooked
Sisters Talk Crime
Sitting Crooked Podcast
Six Impossible Things
    Before Breakfast
Skeletons in the Closet
Skeptical Skeptics
Skeptical: A True Crime
    Podcast
SKRIM
Skullduggery
Slate Presents Standoff
Slaughter SoulSisters
S'laughter: True crime
    podcast
Slay or Survive
Slay Queens Podcast
Sleuth
Sleuth Be Told
Slice Of Death
Slim Turkey
Slits & Giggles
Slow Burn
Slumtown
Smack Dab in the Middle
Small Town Big Crime
Small Town Dicks
Small Town Murder
Small Town Secrets
Smashing Security
Smitten Mi-tten
Smoke After Dark
Smoke Filled Rooms:
    Political True Crime
Smoke Til It's Gone Or
    Die
Smoked

SNAFUD Podcast
Snapped The Podcast
Snow Files
So Dead
So I Heard This Interesting Podcast
SO Scared
So-Called Satanism: True Crime
Sofa King
Sold In America
SOLD!
Solvable by Audiochuck
Solved! D.B. Cooper The Real Story
Solve'em When You Get'em
Solving Cold Cases with Dr. Jim
Some Place Underneith
Somebody Knows More
Somebody Somewhere
Someone Knows
Someone Knows Something
Someone knows something . . .
Someone You Know: Facing the Opioid Crisis Together
Something In the Night
Something in the Shadows
Something Scary
Something Sick
Something Was Wrong
Something's Not Right
Sometimes Dead is Better
Song Crimes
Sorry, Dad!
SOTW: True Crime, Ghost Stories, and Urban Legends
Sound Africa
Sounds Like a Cult

Sounds like MLM but ok
Sour Path
Sour Sweet & Spooky
South Carolina Spookshow
Southern Belles and Chilling Tales
Southern Discomfort
Southern Disgrace
Southern Fried True Crime
Southern Gone
Southern Gothic
Southern Grimoire
Southern Macabre
Southern Mysteries Podcast
Southern Nightmare: The hunt for the south side strangler
Southern Onion
Southern Spirits Podcast
Southwest Louisiana Unsolved
Speaker for the Living 'Human Trafficking' Podcast
Speaking Secrets
Spear Creek
Special Criminals
Spectacle: True Crime
Spine Chillers and Serial killers
Spirits
Spirits and Demons
Spirits, Oddities & Mysteries
Splice and Slice
Split Second Podcast
Spoiler They Die
Spook Show
spooked- the (s)podcast
Spooks and Crooks
Spooky Boo's Creepypasta, True

Scary Stories, Paranormal, and True Crime
Spooky Boys
Spooky In-Laws
Spooky Ish Podcast
Spooky Mama
Spooky Nerds Podcast
Spooky Psychology
Spooky Scary Podcast
Spooky Scary Show
Spooky Sh*t
Spooky Sisters
Spooky Spouses
Spooky Tea
Spooky Times with Eric D
Spooky U
Spooky!
Spoop Hour
Sports Criminals
Spotlight in Darkness
Spread the Dread Podcast
Spree Podcast
Spy Affair
Spy Stories
Spycast
Square Mile of Murder
Squaring the Strange
SSI True Crime
SSI True Crime
Stab in the Back
Standup, Speakup
Stat!
State of Crime
State's Exhibit
States of Crime by States of Crime
Status: Pending
Stay Away with Matthew MaGill
Stealing Hope Podcast
Steve McNair: Fall of a Titan
Steve Warner's Dark City

Stiff Crowd with The Boner Sisters
Still at Large
Still Missing
Still . . .
Stolen Lives True Crime
Stop and Search
Stop! Horror Time!
Storical
Stories From The Bunker
Stories from the Closet
Stories of the Shadows
Stories, A History of Appalachia
Story Crime
Story Hunter Podcast
STORYCAST
Storytelling with Lu
S-Town
Straight-Up Enigmas
Strange & Unexplained: Utah
Strange & Unusual
Strange and Unexplained
Strange Brew Podcast!
Strange Country
Strange Exchange
Strange Ireland
Strange Little Worlds
Strange Matters
Strange People Weird World
Strange Stories UK
Strange Talk
Strange Things with Chris James
Strange uncles podcast
Strangeful Things
Stranger Still
Stranger Than Fiction by Adam Davila
Stranger Than podcast
Strangers to Fiction
Strangeworld
Stranglehold

Stranglers
Stressed and Crime Obsessed
Strict Scrutiny
Strictly Confidential
Strictly Crime
Strictly Homicide
Strictly Stalking
Studying Scarlet
Stuff They Don't Want you to Know
Stuff You Should Know
Sublime True Crime
Subliminal Deception: A Conspiracy Theory Podcast
Suffer the Little Children
Sugar Coated Murder
Suicide by Cop
Suicide Pact
Sun Crime State
Sunshine and Murder
Sup Doc: A Documentary Podcast
Super natural with the unnatural
Super natural with the unnatural by Bridget and Sarah
Superduperstitious
Supernatural with Ashley Flowers
Surreal Talk
Survival
Survival Talk Radio
Surviving Justice: Realities of Reporting Rape
Surviving Scientology
Surviving the Badge. True Crime Podcast
Surviving The Impossible
Surviving The System
Surviving This
Survivors

Survivor's Tales of Famous Crimes
Suspect
Suspect Convictions
Suspect Zero
Suspect Zero by Dawn Washburn and Michael Arntfield
Suspicion
Suspicious Circumstances
Suspicious Transaction Report
Suspiria
Sweet Bitters
Sweet Bobby
Sweet Nightmare Podcast
Sweet Tea & Mystery
Swimming in True Crime
Swindled
Swindle's Search for Truth
Sword and Scale
Sword and Scale Daily
Sword and Scale Rewind
Sworn
Sworn Statement
Sympathy Pains
Tabloid [Luminary]
Taboo and Murder
Tail Waggin' True Crime
Take a Peek
TAKEN: The Murder of Mary Jo Templeton
Tale of Two Dead Girls
Tale of Two Dead Girls
Tale Wagging
Tales From A Cult Insider
Tales from Rat City
Tales From The Darkness
Tales from the Midnight Society
Tales From The Rabbit Hole
Tales of the Old Burying Ground

Tales of the Wicked

Tales of Two Cities
Podcast

Talk Crooked

Talk Deadly To Me

Talk Forensics

Talk More About That

Talk Murder to Me

Talk Salad . . . With Reya
& Kiki

Talk Spooky To Me

Talk Stranger

Talking Crime

Talking Feds

Talking Feds: Women At
The Table

Talking Hart Island

Talking Justice

Talking Murder With My
Mother Podcast

Talking Shit-with Fraser
Youbastard

Talking Terror by John F.
Morrison

Talking Till Dawn

Tangent

Tantamount - True
Crime - The Freeway
Phantom

Tapes Unwound

Targeted True Crime
Domestic Violence

Task & Purpose Radio

TayesTrueTalks

TCFM's Armchair
Detectives

Tea and Tarts Podcast

Tea Time Crimes

Tea Time Horrors

Teachers Talk Crime

Teen Girls Investigate
Crime

Telephone Stories
[Luminary]

Tell me More About That

Tell Me Something
Creepy

Tell Me Something Weird

Tell Tale Science

Telling Crime

Telltale Podcast

Ten Days in a Madhouse
by Nellie Bly

Tenfold More Wicked

Tequila and Terror

Tequila, She Wrote

Teresa Rodriguez Stories
beyond the headlines

Terminus: The Stories of
Atlanta

Terrible

Terrified and Inebriated

TERRIfying

Terrifying & Twisted

Terrifying Texas Podcast

Terror in Old Town

Terror is a Mood

Terror Por La Noche

Terror Talk

Terror Talk - Horror and
True Crime Psychology

Terrorism 360

Testify

Testimony-A True Crime
Podcast

Testimony-A True Crime
Podcast by Laudable

Texas 10-31

Texas Chicks Who Talk
Murder

Texas Crime Files

Texas CrimeCast

Texas Matters

Texas True Terrors

Texla True Crime

Textbook Atypical

That Crime Couple

That Dead Body Show -
True Crime Podcast

That Got Dark

That Guy's Dead

That Murder & Mystery
Show

That Was Genius

That's Weird

That's a Crime

That's a Cult?

That's Ancient History

That's KC

That's Messed Up

That's Not a Bag of Trash
. . . etc. etc.

That's Ridic Podcast

That's So Taboo

That's Spooky

That's Sus

That's Suspicious

That's Whack!

That's What People Do

The (Not S0) Great
Outdoors

The (Not so) Perfect
Crime

The 50 Year Secret

The 666 podcast

The 8th Sin

The 9/11 Commission
Report by The 9/11
Commission

The Abandoned Carousel

The After Midnight
Podcast

The Age of
Enfrightenment

The Alarmist

The Alibi

The American Crime
Story Podcast

The Apex and the Abyss

The Apology Line

The Appeal

The Arcanum Project

The Armchair Detective

The Art of Murder

The Art Of The Exit

The Darkness Inside Podcast
The Dating Game Killer
The Day Helen Disappeared
The Dead History Podcast
The Deadball Podcast
The Death Box
The Death of Dr. John Parker
The Deck
The Deep Dark Truth
The Delusional Sleepy Podcast
The Deprived Podcast
The Derby City Betrayal
The Derek Izzi Show
The Desi Crime Podcast
The Devil Came Knocking
The Devil Within
The Devil, the Witch, and My wardrobe
The Dig
The Dirty Bits of History
The Disappearance of Amanda Jones
The Disappearance of Des
The Disappearance of Genette Tate
The Disappearance of Natasha Lynn Starr
The Disappearance of Olivia Perry
The DisBeer and Distress's Podcast
The District
The District of Crime
The Divorce Alternative
The Docket
The Documentary Podcast
The Dollop
The Dollop - England & UK

The Domestic Abuse Project Podcast
The Doorstep Murder
The Double Loop
The Dreadful Archives
The Dream
The Dropout
The Drunk Detectives
The Drunk Files
The Dweller Archives
The Ectoplasm Show
The Eerie Americas
The Eldritch Estate by The Eldritch Estate
The End Of The World with Josh Clark
The Enemy At Home
The Enforcer
The Event Horizon
The Extreme
The Fairyland Murders - True Crime in Edwardian London
The Fall Line
The Fallout Files
The Family Crime Cast
The Fantastic Story Society
The fascination with crime - Audio
The Fault Line: Dying for a Fight
The First Degree Podcast by Alexis Linkletter, Jac vanek, Billy Jensen
The Five Shems Podcast
The Florida Files
The Florida Justice association
The Frightmare Collective
The Frontline Dispatch
The Gainsville Ripper
The Gallows
The Gangster Chronicles
The Gateway: Teal Swan

The Ghost Museum
The Ghoul Gang
The Good Wives Guide to True Crime
The Good wives Guide to True Crime by Fancy Macelli
The Goth Librarian
The Grave Truth podcast
The Gravy Train
The Great Crime
The Great Trials Podcast
The Great Unsolved
The Grenfell Tower Inquiry with Eddie Mair
The Grey Mask
The Grift
The Grim Curriculum
The Grimdark Diaries
The Grimm Mystics
The Guardian's Audio Long Reads
The Hate Crime Files
The Haunted Heart
The Haunted Heart Podcast
The Hayloft Hour
The Heebie Jeebie Babes
The Heidi Allen Case
The Hidden Staircase
The High Cost Podcast
The High Street Abduction
The Hindsight Podcast
The Historical AF Podcast
The Historical Paranormal
The History Hour
The History of Organized Crime
The History of Witchcraft
The Home Babies
The HOMOcide

The Hot Zone with Chuck Holton
The House on Valencia Street
The Hurricane Tapes
The Husband Did It!
The I Am The Night Podcast
The Illuminati Social Club
The Inspectagators
The Investigation
The Investigation Continues
The Investigation Guru
The Invisibles Podcast
The Irish Crimes
The Jane Doe
The Jeffrey Epstein I Knew
The Jinx Podcast
The Jonah Show
The Jury Room by Kevin Cook
The Jury Room Podcast by CBS Reality
The Killer Kind Podcast
The Killer Podcast & Sh . . .
The Killing of
The Kitchen Table Historian
The Kitchen Table Historian
The Ladies of Strange
The Ladies of Strange
The Lady Dicks Podcast
The Lady Killers Podcast
The Lady of Crime
The Lady of Crime Podcast
The Lady Vanishes
The Land of the Unsolved
The Last Days of August

The Last Voyage of the Pong Su
The Last Word: A True Crime Podcast
The Law & Murder Podcast
The Leeds True Crime Podcast
The Left Hand Path
The Legal Brief
The Les and Mo Show
The Less Dead
The Lets Read Podcast
The Lexington Podcast
The Lighthouse
The Line Begins to Blur
The Line Begins to Blur by Christopher Guerrero
The Lineup
The Little Podcast of Horrors
The Live Drop
The Lizzie Bordern Podcast
The Lone Gunman
The Lonestar187's Podcast
The Long Dance
The Lost Crimes Library
The Lost Ones
The Macabre Millenial
The MacAleese Files
The Mafia's Web
The Mainstream Paranomal Podcast
The Making of a Massa-cre [Audible]
The Making of Crimecon
The Man With A Thou-sand Faces
The Mannina Files
The Marcabe
The Martyrmade Podcast

The Mass Hysteria Podcast
The McCarthy Report
The Mckimmey Files
The Mend
The Midnight Bells
The Midwest Crime Files
The Mind of a Murderer
The Minds of Madness
The Missing and the Unsolved
The Missing Cryptoqueen
The Missing Minority Project
The Missing Star Podcast
The Mist
The Mistresses of Murder
The MLK Tapes
The Monster Goes On
The Morbid Anatomy Transmission
The Morbid Curiosity Podcast
The Mortuary
The Most Dangerous Town on The Internet
The Most Haunted Boys in School
THE MOST WONDER-FUL WONDER
The Mountain Mysteries
The Muddled Exploits
The Murdaugh Family Murders
The Murdaugh Murders, Money & Mystery
The Murder and Wine Club
The Murder Club Podcast
The Murder Diaries
The Murder Games Podcast
The Murder In My Family
The Murder Mamas

The Murder Mitten
The Murder Pawcast
The Murder Police
The Murder Project
The Murder Shed
The Murder Sheet
The Murder Squad
The Murderandmystery's
  Podcast
The Murdertown
  Chronicles
The Mysterious Mr.
  Epstein
The Mysterious, Missing
  & Murdered
The Mystery Files
The Mystery Theory
The Naked Ladies
  Podcast
The New York Crime
  Chronicles
The Next Call
The Next Chapter | True
  Crime
The Night Stalker
The Nightmare Hour
The Noir and Bizarre
  Podcast
The Nonsense Podcast
The Nowhere dispatch
The Object
The ODDentity Podcast
  [formerly Haunt Heads
  Podcast]
The Oddities of Life
The offi-
  cial true crime podcast
The One True Way
The Online Fraudcast
The Opperman Report
The Opportunist
The Ouija Broads: Tales
  from the Pacific
  Northweird
The Our Boys Podcast

The Outlines Podcast
The Outlines Podcast: UK
  True Crime
The PA Prisons and
  Parole Podcast
  (formerly Lockup
  Lowdown)
The Panduh Monium!
  Podcast
The Paranoid Strain
The Path Went Chilly
The Payless Murders
The Perfect Scam
The Peripheral
The Permanent Record
The Philosophy of Crime
The Piketon Massacre
The Pink Moon Murders
The Pinks Podcast
The Pit
The Plain People's
  Podcast
The Podcast from the
  Crypt's Podcast
The Podcast From The
  Crypt's Podcast
The Podcaster's Guide to
  the Conspiracy
The PodGOATs
The Podiac Killer
The Pop List
The Pope's Long Con
The Prairie Files: A True
  Crime Podcast
The Pros & Cons
The Pros & Cons Podcast
The Prosecutors
The Question
The Radium Girls Podcast
ThE RaGe RoOm
The Real Crime Podcast
The REal Crime POdcast
The Real Killer
The Real Prime Suspect
  Podcast

The Reckoning
The Redemption
The Redemption Podcast
The Redhead Report
The Reform Podcast
The Report
The Response
The revenant Podcast
The Revisionists
The RFK Tapes
The Right Podcast
The Right Wrong Turn
The Rise and Fall of
  Lularoe
The Rise and Fall of Mars
  Hill
The Rock Star & The
  Nanny Podcast
The Room Above the
  Attic
The Royal Mile Podcast
The Salad Bowl Podcast
The Salty Canadian True
  Crime Podcast
The Scales of Justice
The Scarecast
The Scofflaws: A History
  of Law and Disorder
The Score: Bank Robber
  Diaries
The Score: Behind the
  Headlines
The Secret Room | True
  Stories
The Security Brief with
  Paul Viollis
The Serial Killer Docu-
  mentary Show
The Serial Killer Podcast
The Serial Serial
The Serialholic
The Sesh
The Shadow Girls
The Shot
The Shrink Next Door

The Sicario Effect
The Sick Sad Podcast
The Silent Evidence's
  Podcast
The Silent Truth
The Sisters Grimm
The Sisters Skelton
  Podcast
The Sit Down: A Mafia
  History Podcast
The Sitdown with Mike
  Recine
The Sleepaway Podcast
The Smoking Gun
  Podcast
The Sneak
The Snuff Box Podcast
The Society of the
  Strange
The SoJo Files
The Sonic Hubbub
The Sound of Crime
The Spaghetti Bandit
The Spectator: Who
  Killed Molly Zelko
The Spookies
The Stack Pack
The Standoff
The Starved Rock
  Murders
The State of Perfect Bal-
  ance: A True Crime
  Podcast
The State We're In:
  Captured
The Story of Sandra
  Marie
The Storyteller: Murder
  Most Foul
The Strange and Unusual
  Podcast
The Strange Death of
  Innes Ewart
The Strange Doctors
The Strange Land Podcast

The Strange Sessions
The Strange South
  Podcast
The Stranger You Know
The Stranger You Know
  by TSYK Podcast
The Superhero Complex
The Synful Show
The Tape Room Podcast
The Tea True Crime
The Teacher's Pet
The Thing About Helen
  & Olga
The Thing About Pam
The Thread
The Tip of the Iceberg
  Show
The Tip Off
The Tipsy Archives
The TM Podcast
The Toliver Cast
The Toll
The Torn Page
The Totally Wong
  Podcast
The Trail Went Cold
The Triad
The Trials of Frank
  Carson
The Trials of the Vampire
The Trojan Horse Affair
The True Crime Academy
The True Crime Club
The True Crime
  Enthusiast
The True Crime Files
The True Crime Files
The True Crime Witch
  Podcast
The truecrimescoldcase-
  files's Podcast
The Truest Crime Podcast
The Truth About True
  Crime with Amanda
  Knox

The Truth Is Somewhere:
  A Conspiracy Theory
  Podcast
The Truth Sharing Pod-
  casts (Partage des véri-
  tés) [bilingual]
The TX Files
The Uh Oh Feeling
The Undercovers
The United States of
  Horror
The Unnamed Murder
  Podcast
The Unresolved
The Unsealed Podcast
The Unseen Podcast
The Unsolved
The Utterly Unrelated
  Podcast
The Valley of the
  Shadows
The Vanished
The Verdict Podcast
The Very True True
  Crime Podcast
The Vibe
The VICE Guide to Right
  Now
The Vocal Minority
  Report
The Way it Was: A
  podpast
The Week in Scary
The Weekly Watch
The Weird History Eerie
  Tales Podcast
The Weird History
  Podcast
The What Cast
The What If? Podcast
The Where is Podcast
The Wicked Weird
  Podcast
The Wild and Vile Case-
  File Files

The Witching
The Women of Death Row
The Wonderland Murders
The Worst People in Earth
The X Podcast
The XIII Club
The Bazaar: A Podcast For Everything Bizzare
the cloaked
The CrimeVine Podcast
Theories on Toast
Theories, Crimes and all the Vines
Theory and Crime
Theory: True Crime Podcast
There Might Be Cupcakes Podcast
These Dark Mountains
They Called Her Georgia Lee . . .
They Walk Among America
They Walk Among Us-UK True Crime
Thin Air podcast
Things Get Dark
Things Police See: First Hand Accounts
Things That Keep Me Up at Night
Think Funny
Thinking Sideways
Third Strike
This Could Be My Last Podcast
This is Actually Happening
This is Awful
This is California: The Battle of 187
This IS Genocide Podcast

This is Gonna Sound Weird
This Is How We Die
This Is Murder Podcast
This is Not a Dream: A True Crime Podcast
This Is Real
This is the Place
This Is Why We Don't Have Friends
This Land
This Might Sound Crazy
This Place Scares Us - A Podcast
This Podcast is Haunted
This Podcast Sounds Exhausting
This Podcast Sounds Exhausting
This Spooky Show
This Strange Life
This Strange Planet
This Week in Crime
This Week In Scary
This Week in True Crime History
Those Conspiracy Guys
Those Murder Girls Podcast
Those Two Chicks
Those Weirdos From Michigan Podcast
Thought Abduction
Thought Spirals
THREAD OF EVIDENCE
Thrice Cursed: A true Crime and Paranormal Podcast
Thrill & Chill
Through the Abyss
Throughline
Thunder Bay
Thurdyish

Til Death Do Us Part by Natalia and Stephanie
Tim Dillon is Going to Hell
Time of Death Podcast
TIME the Podcast by Friends and Ladders
Timeline: The Disappearance of Cassie Compton
TIME's Top Stories
Timesuck with Dan Cummins
Timothy Jones Trial
Tipsy Sisters
Tipsy Tales
Tis Odd
TKC Unsolved
To Be Blunt
To Die For
To Have and to Homicide
To Live and Die In LA
To Love & To Perish
Today in True Crime
Today in True Crime
Toil and Trouble: A Podcast Of The Macabre
Token Skeptic Podcast
Tom Brown's Body
Tombstone Shadows
Tony Lavorgne's Legends & Lore Podcast
Tony Talks Charles County Crime
Too Close to Home
Too Macabre Ladies
Too Many Podcasts!
Too Scared To Sleep
Toronto True Crime
Totally Sourdough
Totally Weird and Twisted
Totally Weird Los Angeles

Toxix Endeavours
  Podcast
Trace
Trace Evidence
Trailer Trashy Podcast
Trans Panic the Podcast
Transmissions from
  Jonestown
Trashy Divorces
Trauma and Laughs
Trauma Queen
Travel with a Chance of
  Murder
Traveling Transgressions
Trial by Error | The
  Aarushi Files
Trial Lawyer Confidential
Triple F'd Podcast
Tripping on legends
Trish Wood is Critical
truck stop murder and
  true crime's podcast
True Blue True Crime
True Cold Case Files with
  Jason and Daisy
True Consequences
True Creeps
True Crime & Chill
True Crime & Chill
True Crime & Knit
True Crime & Red Wine
True Crime Addict
True Crime After Dark
True Crime All the Time
True Crime All the Time
  Unsolved
True Crime and a Glass
  of Wine
True Crime and Chill
True Crime and Coke
True Crime and Mysteries
True Crime and Story
  Times
True Crime and Urban
  Legends

True Crime and Wine
  Time
True Crime and Wine
  Time by Teri Dusold,
  JT Hosack
True Crime Asia
True Crime Astrology
  with Shawn Engel
True Crime Auction
  House Podcast
True Crime Australia:
  Pushed
True Crime Banter
True Crime Beyond Bad
True Crime Binge
True Crime BnB
True Crime Book Club
True Crime Boulevard
True Crime Brewery
True Crime Bullshit
True Crime by Jenna
  Julian
True Crime Café: A Caf-
  feinated True Crime
  Podcast
True Crime Cam
True Crime Campfire
True Crime Canon
True Crime Cascadia
True Crime Cases with
  Lanie (formerly True
  Crime Fan Club)
True Crime Chronicles
True Crime Chronicles:
  South Africa
True Crime Clique
True Crime Conversations
True Crime Corner
True Crime Couple
True Crime- Couple Talk
True Crime Crossroads
True Crime Daily by
  Audio Garage
True Crime Daily by True
  Crime Daily

True Crime Date Podcast
True Crime Deadline
True Crime Denmark
True Crime Diary
True Crime Diary by True
  Crime Diary
True Crime Down Under
True Crime Dumpster
True Crime Eden
True Crime Ends Well
True Crime False
  Memory
True Crime Family:
  Chronicles of Crime
True Crime Fan Club
True Crime Finland
True Crime Fix
True Crime Flint
True Crime Garage
True Crime Girl Time
True Crime Girls
True Crime Grapple
True Crime Guys
True Crime Happy Hour
True Crime Historian
True Crime Horror Story
True Crime Horror Story
  Podcast
True Crime in the 50
True Crime Intensified
  with Dailaesse
True Crime Investigators
  UK
True Crime Island
True Crime Japan
True Crime Journal
True Crime Lab
True Crime Mamas
  Podcast
True Crime MC
True Crime Medieval
True Crime Medieval
True Crime Melting Pot
  with Jess
True Crime Nerds

True Crime Never Sleeps
True Crime New England
True Crime New Zealand
True Crime Obsessed
True Crime on Our Minds
Podcast
True Crime P.I.
True Crime Podcast by
Emily Larkey
True Crime Psychology
and Personality: Nar-
cissism, Psychopathy,
and the Minds of Dan-
gerous Criminals
True Crime Queen
True Crime Real Time
True Crime Recaps
True Crime Recliner
True Crime Replay
True Crime Reporter
True Crime Research
Podcast
True Crime review
True Crime Rhymes With
Vodka
True Crime Salad
True Crime Salt & Lime
True Crime Salt and Lime
True Crime San Antonio
True Crime San Antonio
by Just Another San
Antonia Native
True Crime Scotland
True Crime Scotland
True Crime Sisters
True Crime Snacktime
Podcast
True Crime Society
True Crime South Africa
True Crime Space
True Crime Squad (for-
merly True Crime
Paranormal)
True Crime Stories With
Stephanie

True Crime Storytime
True Crime Sweden
True Crime Talks
True Crime Talks
True Crime Taurus
True Crime Tea
True Crime Tea Time
True Crime Teachers
True Crime Teachers by
True Crime Teachers
True Crime Tell-Alls:
Charles Manson
True Crime This Week
True Crime Time
True Crime Trucker
True Crime Twin Logic
True Crime Twins
True Crime Uncensored
True Crime Uncorked
True Crime University
True Crime Updates
True Crime With a Twist.
Make it Arkansas
True Crime With
Annabelle
True Crime With Bel and
Dee
True Crime with
Dickerson
True Crime with Elle
True Crime with Hailey
True Crime with Kendall
Rae
True Crime with Mari
True Crime with me
True Crime With
Millennials
True Crime with Nancy
True Crime with
Savannah
True Crime with Tab
True Crime Works
True Crime Worldwide
True crime
True Crime: By The Book

True Crime: Predators
with Cathy Cassidy
True Crime: Ruthless
True Crimecast
True Crimes with Marty
True Grim
True Murder
True Nightmares-A True
Crime Podcast
True North Crime
True North Strange &
Weird
True North True Crime
True Spies: Espioinage
Investigation Crime
Murder Detective
Politics
True Stories Of
Tinseltown
True Whispers: A True
Crime Podcast
TrueCrimeIRL
Trueish Crime
Truer Crime by Joe Wilde
Truly Criminal
Trump, Inc.
Trust Issues
Trust Me: Cults, Extreme
Belief, and the Abuse
of Power
Trusting Evil
Truth & Justice (formerly
Serial Dynasty)
Truth About True Crime
with Amanda Knox,
The
Truth and Reconciliation
Truth Be Told
Truth if you Dare
Truth is Justice
Truth Seeker
Truth, Lies & Alibis
Trying Our Best
TSF Entertainment
Podcast

Twelve Past Three
Twin Flames
Twin Talk
Twisted
Twisted Britian
Twisted History 101 Podcast
Twisted Listers
Twisted Philly
Twisted Sisters Podcast
Twisted Tangents
Twisted Travel and True Crime
TwistedTales True Crime Podcast
Two Creepy B's
Two Ghouls One Grave
Two Girls + a Podcast
Two Girls and a Theory
Two Girls True Crime
Two Girls, One Murder
Two Gurls One Murder
Two Gurls One Murder by Blair & Eleni
Two Jane Does
Two Jane Does
Two Jane Does by Kayla and Emmalea
Two Scared Siblings
Two Spooky Broads
UK Confidential
UK True Crime podcast
Ultimate Betrayal
Unacquainted
Unbelievable True Crime
Unbelievable True Crime
Uncanny Dispatch
Uncertain Terms
Unconcluded
Uncorking the Truth
Uncover
Uncovered: The Lovers' Lane Murders
Uncovering Unexplained Mysteries

Uncuffed
Under Oath With Rick Lomurro
Under the Gavel
Under the Influence of True Crime
Undercover Coven
Undercurrent: Bear 148
UnderState
Underworld
Undisclosed
UNDISCOVERED
Undiscussable
Unearthly Upstate
Unequal
UnErased
Unexplained
Unexplained Encounters (formerly Darkness Prevails)
Unexplained Evil
Unexplained Mysteries
Unfinished
Unforgotten
Unfound
Unheard: The Fred and Rose West Tapes
Unknowable
Unlikely Murder
Unmasking a Killer
Unobscured
Unpleasant Dreams
Unpopular Culture
Unpopular True Crimes
Unprisoned: Stories from the system
Unqualified Gays
Unravel True Crime
Unraveled
Unraveled by Discovery+
Unremembered Hollywood
Unreserved
Unrest
Unsavory

Unsettled: Mapping #MeToo
Unsolved and Solved: True Crime Mysteries
Unsolved and Uncharted
Unsolved as Told By the Unqualified
Unsolved As Told By The Unqualified
Unsolved by Milwalkee Journal Sentinel
Unsolved Death Murder Crimes
Unsolved Murders: True Crime Stories
Unsolved Mysteries
Unsolved Mysteries of the World
Unsolved of Delaware
Unsolved podcast
Unspeakable
Unspeakable Crime: The Killing of Jessica Chambers
Unspookable
Untold History Revealed
Untold: The Daniel Morgan Murder
Untrue Crime
Unusual Universe
Unwholesome Content
Up and Vanished
Up At Night
Up North Cold Case
Upper Balcony
Upstate Unsolved
Urban Creeps
Urge to Kill
Useless Information Podcast
V is for Vamp
Vacant Frames
Valley of the Lost Podcast
Vancouver True Crime

Vanished

Vanished: The Tara Cal-
ico Investigation

Veritas True crime

Versus Trump

Very Scary People

Victimology

Victims

Vile

Vile Podcast

Vile Virginia

Villains

Villains of History

Villians Among Us

Vines' Crimes, and Try-
ing Times

Vintage Homicide

Violent Delights

Violent Times

Viva America

Viva America by Viva
America

Voice For The Voiceless

Voice of the Victim

Voices for Justice

Voices From Gilgo

Voices of Youth Justice

Voir Dire

Volsteadland

Voodoo City

Voodoo Medics

Vulture City - How our
bankers got rich on
swindles

Wait! Don't kill Me

Wait, Where?

Wait,Whaaat?

Walk With The Weird

Walking Through Fire by
Brian Hoops

Wander the Podcast

Wanted

Wanted by the FBI

Warden's Watch

Warm Red Earth

Was I in a Cult?

Watching ID

We are Resilient: A
MMIW True Crime
Podcast

We are Starting a Cult

We Are the Missing

We Are the Worst

We Don't Sleep

We Drink And We Know
Things

We Hate Cops

We Like Coffee and
about 4 People

We Love Dead Things

We Love Dead Things

We Saw the Devil

We Saw the Devil: A
True Crime Podcast

We Shouldn't Talk About
This

We Wanna Know Podcast

We Would Be Dead

We Would Have Burned

Web Crawlers

Websleuths Radio

Weed, Wine, and True
Crime

Weekend Weird

Weekly Infusion

Weird + Wayward: A
Drunken Podcast
of Weird Tales and
Legends

Weird AF News

Weird and Feared

Weird Brunch

Weird Crap in Australia

Weird Darkness

Weird History and
Mysteries

Weird Island

Weird On the Rocks

Weird Religion

Weird Tales and the
Unexplainable

Weird World

Weird World Weekly

Weird!

Weird: A Podcast of
Curiosities

Weirder Hings Podcast

Weirdington

weirdobscureworld's
podcast

Weirdos & Wine

Welcome...to DIE

We're (Kinda) Sorry

We're all Wicked

We're Here For The Boos

We're Just Sayin

We're Not Sure Yet

We're Starting a Cult!

West Cork

Wetwork

What a Creep

What A Way To Go

What A Wonderful World

What Did You Do?

What Do Ya Got?

What Had Happened: A
True Crime Podcast

What Happened to Baby
Doe?

What Happened to Holly
Bartlett

What Happened to Jodi?

What Happened to Sandy
Beal

What Happened to Vishal

What Have You Done

What in the Actual
Podcast

What Lies Behind the
Shadows

What Lurks in the
Shadows

What Lurks On Channel X - Mass Grave Pictures
What Makes a Killer
What Rhymes With Murder
What the Actual Hell
What the Con
What the Crime
What the Doc?!
What the F Podcast
What the F*ck Happened?
What the Fact?!
What the Psychology?!
What They Want You To Think - a conspiracy podcast with Benn James
What Was That Like?
What Went Wrong
What Were You Thinking
What Will You Do?
What You Didn't Know with Tess and Matt Stevens
Whatever Remains Podcast
What's Blood Got to Do With It?
What's In Your Hometown?
What's The Damage
What's Under the Bed?
What's Up, Doc(umentaries)?
What's Wrong With Them
What's Yer Weird Story?
Wheel of Crime Podcast
When it Goes Wrong
Where Have All the Children Gone?
Where is Joleen?
Where is Kerry Jones?
Where is She?

Where is the Line?
Where Murder Meets Mystery
Where the Monsters Are
Where the Vile Things Are
Where the Weird Things Are
Where's William Tyrrell?
Which Murderer?
Whine about History.
Whiskey and Crime
Whiskey Dicks and Jane
Whiskey, Wine and True Crime
Whispered True Stories
White Eagle
White Lies
White Silence
White Wine True Crime
Who Are These Podcasts?
Who Did What Now?
Who F**ken Knows
Who Killed Elsie Frost
Who Killed Jennifer Short?
Who Killed Theresa
Who Killed Tommy?
Who Killed Whitney?
Who Killed...?
Who Stalks You at Night
Who the (Bleep) Did I Marry?
Who the Hell is Hamish?
Who You Let In Podcast
Whoever Writes Monsters Podcast
Whores Talk Horror
Whose crime is it Anyway
Whose Crime Is It Anyway?
Why do Women Love True Crime
Why I'm Afraid Of

Why So Cold?
Why the Supernatural is Natural and You'e Life is a Lie
Why Women Kill: Truth, Lies, and Labels
Wicked and Grim: A True Crime Podcast
Wicked and Witchy (formerly Dead Academy)
Wicked Buzz
Wicked Crimes South Africa
Wicked Garden Podcast
Wicked Gay
Wicked Minds
Wicked Sisters
Wicked: A True Crime Podcast
Wicked: A Washington True Crime Podcast
Wickedly Macabre
Wide Atlantic Weird
Wiehl of Justice
Wife of Crime
Wild Cat Crime
Wild Wasteland
Wild West Extravaganza (Bloody Beaver)
Wild West Podcast
Wildcat Crime
Wildfire
Will Be Wild
William Ramsey Investigates
William Ramsey Investigates
Win at All Costs
Wine & Crime
Wine & Punishment
Wine and Crime: A True Crime Podcast
Wine Not Talk About It?
Witch Hunt

Index

About the Author

Lindsey A. Sherrill (PhD, the University of Alabama; MBA, the University of Montevallo) is assistant professor of business communication at the University of North Alabama. Before a decade-long career in wholesale management, Lindsey spent several years writing for small-town newspapers, where her fascination with unsolved and missing persons cases began. Her dissertation, "'Suddenly, the Podcast Was Sexy': An Ecological and Social Movement Theory Approach to True Crime Podcast Phenomena," won the 2020 University of Alabama College of Communication & Information Sciences Outstanding Dissertation Award. Lindsey's research has been published in numerous outlets, including *Journal of Communication*, *Journal of Broadcast & Electronic Media*, *Communication Research*, *Telematics & Informatics*, *Mass Communication and Society*, and *Journalism Studies*. She splits her time between Florence, Alabama, and New Orleans, Louisiana, with her constant travel companion, Freddie Mercury, a 13-year-old Portuguese pointer.

www.ingramcontent.com/pod-product-compliance
Lightning Source LLC
Chambersburg PA
CBHW062022270326
41929CB00014B/2286